MW00610935

BUILDING
BETTER
ORGANIZATIONS

BUILDING
BETTER
ORGANIZATIONS

How to Fuel Growth and Lead in a Digital Era

Claudy Jules

BK

Berrett–Koehler Publishers, Inc.
a BK Business book

Copyright © 2022 by Claudy Jules

All rights reserved. No part of this publication may be reproduced, distributed, or transmit-
ted in any form or by any means, including photocopying, recording, or other electronic or
mechanical methods, without the prior written permission of the publisher, except in the case
of brief quotations embodied in critical reviews and certain other noncommercial uses
permitted by copyright law. For permission requests, write to the publisher, addressed
"Attention: Permissions Coordinator," at the address below.

Berrett-Koehler Publishers, Inc.
1333 Broadway, Suite 1000
Oakland, CA 94612-1921
Tel: (510) 817-2277
Fax: (510) 817-2278
www.bkconnection.com

ORDERING INFORMATION
Quantity sales. Special discounts are available on quantity purchases by corporations,
associations, and others. For details, contact the "Special Sales Department" at the
Berrett-Koehler address above.
Individual sales. Berrett-Koehler publications are available through most bookstores. They
can also be ordered directly from Berrett-Koehler: Tel: (800) 929-2929; Fax: (802) 864-7626;
www.bkconnection.com.
Orders for college textbook / course adoption use.
Please contact Berrett-Koehler: Tel: (800) 929-2929; Fax: (802) 864-7626.

Distributed to the U.S. trade and internationally by Penguin Random House Publisher Services.

Berrett-Koehler and the BK logo are registered trademarks of Berrett-Koehler Publishers, Inc.

Printed in the United States of America

Berrett-Koehler books are printed on long-lasting acid-free paper. When it is available, we
choose paper that has been manufactured by environmentally responsible processes. These
may include using trees grown in sustainable forests, incorporating recycled paper, minimiz-
ing chlorine in bleaching, or recycling the energy produced at the paper mill.

Library of Congress Cataloging-in-Publication Data

Names: Jules, Claudy, author.
Title: Building better organizations : how to fuel growth and lead
    in a digital era / Claudy Jules.
Description: First Edition. | Oakland, California : Berrett-Koehler
    Publishers, [2022] | Includes bibliographical references and index.
Identifiers: LCCN 2021059176 (print) | LCCN 2021059177 (ebook) | ISBN 9781523000449
    (hardcover) | ISBN 9781523000456 (pdf) | ISBN 9781523000463 (epub)
Subjects: LCSH: Organizational change. | Personnel Management—
    Technological innovations. | Artificial intelligence. | Work environment.
Classification: LCC HD58.8 .J854 2022 (print) | LCC HD58.8 (ebook) |
    DDC 658.4/06—dc23/eng/20211203
LC record available at https://lccn.loc.gov/2021059176
LC ebook record available at https://lccn.loc.gov/2021059177

First Edition

30 29 28 27 26 25 24 23 22   10 9 8 7 6 5 4 3 2 1

Book production: Westchester Publishing Services
Cover design: Adrian Morgan

For Cecile, Marie, and Adrienne and the love of learning

Contents

**PART III. Lead a Better Organization: Top Priorities for Leaders
Seeking Investment Optimization ■ 257**

There are no CEOs alive who don't want their organization to operate more effectively. Nor is there an investor alive who doesn't worry about scaling the organizations they invest in to drive profitable growth. This book offers a playbook for doing both of those things and more: building better organizations in the digital era.

Without question, the pandemic has pulled the digital world front and center. However, what's surprising is how advances such as artificial intelligence (AI) have highlighted—not diminished—the importance of familiar organizational topics such as talent, leadership, and culture. Property and equipment are no longer a company's most valuable assets; people are.

Nowhere is this truer than in tech companies. Among the S&P 500, the value of intangible assets such as human capital and culture have risen since 1975 from 17 percent of total assets to a stunning 90 percent in 2020.[1] As founders, investors, and board directors alike catch their breath after the fallout from COVID-19, they will do well to examine the organizational practices that may no longer serve them.

To begin with, leaders must rethink their value-creation strategies and overcome the organizational challenges of scaling. The way forward is to hone their digital edge to enhance their organizational edge by adopting the tenets of an organization's health in seven vital areas that are a focus of this book: strategic direction, culture, leadership, talent, organizational design, EID (equity, inclusion, and diversity), and well-being. No matter what type or size of business, those essential conditions can be leveraged for increased value and growth.

AI is what will get us there. Advances in technology such as machine learning and quantum computing, which can help companies monitor and measure improvements as well as extrapolate next steps, enable leaders to build organizations that can compete and win in the future.

Finally, an investor mindset will enable leaders to invest wisely in the technology (and leveraging that tech) that sets their organizations apart. By investing in the health of an organization and by investing equally in digitally enabled strategies and business models for the AI era, companies win. In this book, I chose to draw examples from companies in the portfolios of private equity (PE) and venture capital (VC) firms. Why? Because while PE and VC are not historically known for their focus on "warm and fuzzy" organizational aspects like culture, design, or employee well-being, in recent years such investment firms have demonstrated a deep understanding of today's business imperative: to scale and grow, companies must get the organizational elements right. That begins with having the right strategy, the right CEO to drive it, and the right top talent, culture, and org design to realize a company's potential. More recently, investment firms have recognized, too, the critical importance of other org topics such as EID and employee well-being.

My point of view about organizational effectiveness developed over more than 20 years of shaping, testing, and evolving the ideas in my work as a consultant, advisor, practice builder, and researcher. I cut my teeth in organization development by way of instrumentation, where I first understood the powerful impact of leadership assessments on organizational change. While I completed my graduate training in the behavioral sciences (including interpersonal, group, and organizational dynamics), I was introduced to strategy consulting—focused on the management sciences, including competitive and industry analysis, forecasting, and business case development.

During those formative years as a consultant, I began to integrate both content and process consulting and developed the belief that both had merit. Why? Because I observed again and again how the strategic and economic plan of a business—its business strategy—is only as effective as the corresponding behavioral agenda of that business—the organizational strategy. Today I think of my work as an animated synthesis of the "tech stuff" and the "org stuff." I focus on organizational elements for companies seeking to scale and pivot quickly in the age of AI. I do this by drawing on observations, professional experiences, and insights gained from advising fast-growing startups, government agencies, nonprofits, and businesses.

Despite their differences, I observed all these organizations share one consistent characteristic: when they invest in the essentials that make up organizational health, they improve the odds of delivering a step-change in performance. As these essentials align and function better, organizations overcome inertia and improve their odds to scale and grow.

Those new insights compelled me to write this book, which I believe fills a vital gap in the literature—namely, how organizational health, digital, and an investment mindset can work in tandem to build better organizations. Moreover, by exploring organizational health, I hope to spur dialogue around a different way to boost the performance of companies—and perhaps to deepen how organization development gets taught to students in graduate and MBA programs.

Intellectual Themes and Sources of Inspiration

As I undertook the research for my book, I drew on the work of management and organizational thinkers like Warren Bennis, Ed Schein, John Kotter, Jennifer Chatham, David Nadler, Carol Dweck, Christopher Worley, Robert Thomas, Rob Cross, and Amy Edmondson. I also found helpful the work of authors who view themselves not as organizational theorists but as organizational strategists. These included Jon Katzenbach, Colin Price, Scott Keller, Bill Schaninger, and Patrick Lencioni.

I then turned to recent articles and books written by thinkers who are focused on organizational issues, their impact on growth and scaling across tech and nontech companies and a variety of asset classes, including private equity funds and venture capital firms, and the lessons publicly traded companies can learn from private equity. These writers included Sandy Ogg, David Ulrich, Geoffrey Moore, Huggy Rao, Robert Sutton, Roger Martin, and the work of Benoit Leleux, Hans van Swaay, and Esmeralda Megally.

Later, I turned to more recent materials by writers pondering how to build a better and healthier organization in the age of artificial intelligence. These included the works of Marco Iansiti and Karim Lakhani, Shoshana Zuboff, Kai-Fu Lee, Sue Cantrell, Kevin Kelly, Thomas Malone, Joseph Allen, and John Macomber.

While I have relied on a variety of sources to ground and push my thinking, I also draw heavily from publicly available cases featured in *Harvard Business Review, MIT Sloan Management Review, Private Equity International, Fortune*, and several other key journals; interviews I conducted with leaders across the business, tech, and investor landscapes; and direct experiences with leaders and organizations with whom I'd had the privilege of counseling and advising. I also gained insights from audience interactions during talks and workshops I conducted on the book's themes. Throughout this process, I sought to mine these sources for insight and examples as to how leaders and investors fuel growth, lead, and build better organizations in a digital era.

Finally, I want to emphasize that the ideas in the book represent my opinions and do not necessarily reflect the views of my partners at McKinsey & Company or of the firm's organization and private equity practices. My use of the term "organizational health" in the book has its origins in literature I was introduced to as a graduate student and in my own work developing an organizational health framework at Google. More recently, I've focused on digital technologies to scale organizations and serve investors on organizational matters across the private equity and venture capital landscape, utilizing the science of org health as measured and practiced by the growing discipline of people and organizational analytics.

Introduction

Start with a Better Foundation

Every organization produces exactly the results it is designed to produce. The simplicity of that truism belies just how difficult it is to get the design right in the first place. Most organizations can't do it.

The problem doesn't lie with the design of the product or service that a business offers—not usually, anyway. Instead, in a study of nearly 300 startup failures, the decline most often had to do with "people issues," matters to do with the organization itself—often the company's culture or how it treated its customers. Only 2 of the top 20 reasons that startups failed was due to money or lack thereof.[1] Every account of a failed attempt to turn around a decrepit business model, to capture the benefits of a blockbuster merger and acquisition, or to scale a tantalizing startup inevitably points to fundamental missteps in handling some aspect of the people, culture, and organization. Consider the dissolution of blood-testing company Theranos, and its massive, years-long fraud to deceive investors. Or how Blockbuster's debt and leadership challenges led to a fragile infrastructure that couldn't pivot quickly enough to successfully move into streaming.

Organizations perform poorly because their leaders have overlooked organizational matters, in particular the health of the organization itself. By that I mean the effectiveness of the organization as defined by its strategic direction, culture, leadership, design, talent, employee well-being, and the workforce's EID—how equitable, inclusive, and diverse it is.

Some would call these things the "soft side" of business. But with investors citing precisely those dimensions as responsible for more than half their portfolio failures, clearly they are anything but soft. Getting the people and culture right, in fact, appears to be foundational, the stone and mortar underlying success. As such, the conditions comprising an organization's effectiveness or what is sometimes called "org health" enable the success of the business, both immediately and in the long term. Those conditions determine no less than the organization's ability to achieve its strategic goals, change with rapidly shifting market realities, grow from within, and evolve over time.

The high success rate of well-designed organizations outside of corporate America confirms that idea. I'm thinking of course of professional sports teams. When it comes to the structure and management of teams, no one on ESPN questions the value of organizational health, although they might use different terms during their off-season debates. They'll say, "They should fire the coach" or "The coach has lost the locker room—the team doesn't respect him." They'll talk about how some coaches hate the management office because it's too focused on analytics, when it's often the little things that make all the difference on the field or on the court or the diamond, things you can't necessarily measure. What those pundits understand is what analytics can't tell you—like whether a player had a fight with his significant other last night and is in no shape to play today—but a good coach can.

In other words, it's common to look at coaches, general managers, and even owners and discuss their prowess and success in terms of how well they invest, construct, and manage *human potential*. Precisely everything depends on the design of the team, on the people and their unique talents.

Today, as more and more of our corporate value comes from creating and monetizing knowledge and intellectual property, the focus on the element of *people*, whose well-being underlies the health of any organization, is sharpening. Accordingly, just as they do in sports, the rewards will accrue to managers and organizations who can build and construct a better team. This has never been truer than it is today, with the constant change and extreme uncertainty that the pandemic-laden era has engendered. Organizational health is even more critical in such times, when "the ability to quickly align, execute, and renew can be the difference between floundering and thriving."[2] Indeed, the corporate highway is littered with once-successful organizations—Digital Equipment Corporation, Blockbuster, and Sears, to name a few—that rested on their laurels and failed to change because their choices around strategy and technological advancement were not integrated into their companies' organizational health.

All of which brings us back to our opening conundrum. Clearly leaders need to get better at building better organizations, designing businesses with solid foundations that enable their people to perform to their full potential. But how? That is the question this book endeavors to answer.

In my direct experiences with leaders and organizations whom I've had the privilege to advise and work with (or work for), and based on hundreds of interviews I conducted with senior leaders, innovators, and investors in business and technology, I have identified three elements—inseparable, in my estimation—that together are crucial for building better organizations. Specifically, the types of organizations that will be needed to survive today's uncertain environment and thrive in the future will depend on the following building blocks: (1) a solidly healthy organizational foundation, combined with (2) strategic and ethical use of artificial intelligence (AI)—all while (3) working in partnership with investors, including but not limited to entities such as venture capital funds, growth equity funds, leveraged buyout funds, and special purpose acquisition companies (sometimes called SPACs or "blank check companies").

This book will explore in detail why those three elements are so crucial for building better organizations and how they work together. But here's the short explanation: When the essential conditions of an organization are aligned, the business can more effectively tackle challenges like digitization, AI adoption, speed, and agility. And because of the nature of business today, from economic malaise to the ever-tightening vise of regulation and increased global competition, it's more important than ever that the "players" in the organization—investors, founders, CEOs, board directors, and the like—understand how to approach the health of their organization in a digital context to fast-track business growth.

While a number of the ideas in this book have been put in practice by some organizations somewhere, no single company operates at the intersection of organizational health, digital advances like AI, while applying lessons from investors in the way I propose. Rather than a "best practices" book, then, this book is intended as a guide for agenda shaping around the most promising practices and directional strategies emerging today. My goal? To provoke corporate and investor leaders to think deeply about the organizational issues of their companies, or the companies they acquire and/or invest in, especially during periods of disruption, hyperscaling (the ability of an organization to scale appropriately as increased growth ensues), and growth. Accordingly, in this book I have attempted to capture what leaders intuitively know; integrate that with social, behavioral, and decision-science research (i.e., the quantitative techniques used to inform decision making at the individual and organizational levels), and research about organizational behavior; and offer a set of lessons that leaders across the investment landscape can use to set the stage for building a better organization in the digital era.

Several seminal articles and books have been written on organizational health and effectiveness, and I have learned much from them. (See the sidebar "Organizational Health: A Look Back.") But none embed that perspective in a digital and AI-first context. This book is laser-focused on the role of the organization in the digital era, rooted in a value-creation (investor/owner) perspective, and indispensable to leaders of all kinds in their management of complexity—be they startup founders, investors, CEOs, senior executives, board directors, or consultants. Ultimately, this book intends to pull back the curtain on the hows and whys of building healthy organizations that will thrive in an AI-first world that in many ways is already with us.

In the remainder of this introduction, I will touch on the three elements—organizational conditions, digital/AI, and outside investors—that, working together, are crucial for building better organizations. I also will describe how various kinds of readers (in different roles and at an array of organizational levels) might use the ideas herein, and I'll conclude with how this book will unfold.

But first, let's look at one company's efforts to craft what I consider to be the cornerstone of the three elements I've named for building better organizations: the health of the company itself.

The Case of National Grid

In the mid-2000s, the U.K.-based utility National Grid prided itself on being one of the largest investor-owned global energy companies. Moreover, it was on its way to becoming the second-largest utility in the United States, serving 3.3 million electric customers and 3.4 million natural gas customers in the Northeast.

But in 2007, when John Pettigrew became group chief executive at the company's Electric Distribution Operations (EDO) business, he faced steep challenges.

EDO struggled with an array of divergent operating models, systems, performance metrics, organizational cultures, and wide-ranging labor-management conflicts. For years, it had been paying penalties to regulators due to service outages, and its dismal record of recovery from those outages had also hurt its reputation with customers. Profitable growth was unlikely in an organization hobbled by a culture of conflict, antiquated operating models encased in a siloed structure, backward-looking leaders, and broken talent practices.

Pettigrew understood that reviving National Grid's EDO business would take nothing short of a radical transformation. He would have to marshal massive improvements in safety, reliability, and customer satisfaction. That would mean overcoming long-standing organizational obstacles blocking EDO's way. In fact, Pettigrew's analysis of the problem convinced him that the business's financial health would depend almost entirely on how much he could improve *the health of the organization itself*—its culture, operating model, leadership, and talent practices. For Pettigrew and his top lieutenants, the arduous task of leading transformation would build a better EDO business—which would ultimately benefit the larger organization, National Grid.

The most pressing need, as Pettigrew saw it, was to find a way to quickly develop new leaders throughout the business unit who could tackle the unprecedented competitive pressures EDO faced. Simply put, he wanted to shape leadership behaviors that would foster a healthy organization, not just provide new knowledge. He began, therefore, by creating an immersive program—dubbed "action labs"—based on both reflection and action and grounded in the realities of the competitive environment and EDO's need for transformation. The labs would help executives and managers learn from experience, not just from formal, classroom-based programs. Ultimately, these would give leaders a taste of what the future demanded.

Before entering the action labs, however, managers were rigorously assessed on their individual personalities and leadership styles and given extensive feedback and individual coaching. In the action labs themselves, managers learned through a series of forums and workshops supported by laboratory-like environments for action learning. Practice assignments (carried out between lab sessions) gave leaders the opportunity to integrate their learning with on-the-job action.[3]

In the end, the action labs became a permanent, ongoing feature of EDO's leadership development work. By aligning the EDO business's extended leadership team around its strategic intent and operating model, and then by practicing the unique leadership behaviors necessary to navigate a difficult change journey, the organization was able to cultivate its next generation of leaders more effectively.

As a result of this transformational work, Pettigrew could point to a number of tangible business benefits. Whereas three years prior, National Grid had been paying more than $40 million in penalties for compliance failings on acceptable standards of electricity supply, Pettigrew's transformation initiatives reversed that trend. For example, the number of "lost time" injuries was halved over a two-year period, and the utility's reliability metrics became markedly better. A year's worth of work on asset strategies and a 40 percent increase in capital investments also contributed significantly to this performance improvement. By 2010, the utility was meeting its reliability goals and had stopped paying penalties, which enabled EDO to raise and meet higher reliability targets.[4]

John Pettigrew is one of a handful of leaders in recent decades who have understood intuitively that without a healthy organization, their companies have little chance of reaching and maintaining their financial goals. Let's review some of the main features of this all-important building block for businesses today.

Building Block 1: Mind the Health of Your Organization

Because organizational change can be difficult to carry out, especially in today's volatile, uncertain, complex, and ambiguous world, many companies, especially young companies, never attempt it. Instead, they find workaround solutions and they plaster over the cracks in an attempt to avoid dealing with the organization's foundation issues.

The problem is that, as companies mature and attempt to cross the threshold from startup to pre-IPO to mature incumbent—if they even make it that far—the plaster falls away and the cracks become apparent. So even though they might have the financial backing for scaling and fueling growth, these companies lack the organizational health they would need to truly run with the opportunities that the digital era offers. Simply put, if a leader wants different results from last quarter's or last year's numbers, then a different organizational design is called for.

Business and investor leadership are increasingly realizing they must care about their or their portfolio companies' organizational health. As John Pettigrew did, these leaders are coming to understand the clear connections between healthy companies and strong performance: healthy companies generate total returns to shareholders (TRS) three times higher than those of unhealthy ones,[5] with organizational health explaining up to 50 percent of performance variation across companies.[6] Healthy companies are more agile too; a McKinsey study found companies with both speed and stability have a 70 percent chance of being ranked in the top quartile by organizational health.[7] In an era in which sustainable competitive advantage is being replaced by *"exploiting temporary competitive advantages"* and the need for a *"strategy of continuous reconfiguration"*[8]—and at a time when companies are increasingly competing on speed even more than strategy—healthier companies are far more likely to achieve the holy grail of continuous adaptivity.

That is why I believe that org health, often under the purview of HR, is expanding to the domain of executive leaders—founders, CEOs, boards, and the like—who embrace a broader agenda for their organizations. These leaders understand that unleashing performance and scale with speed and agility will, in the end, depend on the health and well-being of their people and organization. Something remarkable happens when such a mindset originates from the top, as we saw in the case of John Pettigrew at EDO. It permeates the organization, guiding decision making and the business practices that drive people's behavior. That is how leaders move from actively managing org health as a set of intangible assets to elevating those assets into tangible performance outcomes.

All of which brings us to the specific conditions—seven in total—that I believe are at the heart of building any organization's health. These are the things that failed IPOs everywhere *wish they had put in place*—specifically: (1) a clear strategic direction, (2) an adaptive culture, (3) agile leadership, (4) top talent, (5) nimble organizational design, (6) a diverse workforce supported by equitable and inclusive practices, and (7) employee well-being.

For any real change to occur, all seven conditions are required. Giving insufficient attention to any of these conditions not only puts the organization in peril but also makes the job of the organization's leaders much harder than it needs to be. With these conditions in place, organizations can find the balance between having a clear and compelling strategic direction while meeting standards that enable flawless execution. Without them, the prospects for winning become dim indeed.

For example, condition number 6—a diverse workforce and inclusive practices—has already been proven crucial when it comes to investment decisions and the way that firms function. "Diverse teams drive better performance," notes managing director and chief diversity, equity, and inclusion officer Kara Helander of the Carlyle Group, a multinational private equity, alternative asset management, and financial services corporation. "The evidence from our experience of portfolio companies and the evidence that already exists out there gives [us] a pretty powerful thesis to move forward from. . . . We believe we can drive greater impact through ensuring diverse workforce composition in our portfolio companies, and a set of practices that drive equity, diversity, and inclusion throughout them."

Yet many investment firms not only struggle to diversify their portfolio company boards and management teams, they also struggle to diversify their own firms from within. A study by the data analysis firm Preqin found that only 17.9 percent of private equity employees worldwide are women, the lowest figure of any asset class.[9] And a variety of other studies point to low racial and ethnic diversity in the private investment sector: Black and Latinx founders, for example, still receive fewer venture capital investments than their peers do.[10]

Whether we're talking about diversity and equity or any of the other six organizational conditions that foster optimal health, companies today simply cannot continue with business as usual and hope to succeed. Instead, leaders can work with these seven conditions to drive the behavior of people across all organizational circumstances—and through them, deliver results. The challenge, of course, is finding ways to help leaders understand those conditions well enough to guide action and change amid demanding and rapidly shifting market and social realities. Designing these conditions purposefully and using digital advances to scale them over time can make a constructive and meaningful difference. That is why, in the coming chapters, we will examine each of the seven conditions in detail.

Now let's look at the second of the three building blocks required for disruptive innovation today: harnessing the power of AI and the digital era.

Building Block 2: Use Digital and AI Strategically

The next wave of digital technology—artificial intelligence—is of course already with us. Generally understood as "smart" machines that can perform tasks normally requiring human intelligence, AI has revolutionized how we live, work, play, and connect. Our smart devices create our grocery lists and tell us jokes. They adjust the temperatures of our homes and direct us around traffic jams. They suggest "friends" on social media and songs for our playlists.

Meanwhile, companies such as Amazon, Google, and Meta Platforms (formerly Facebook) have long been using AI to transform their businesses, targeting ads to consumers based on things like browsing behavior and demographics. Other companies are either wholly or on the journey to be AI-driven: health services provider Anthem and digital financial services company Ally rely on AI to scale up digital solutions for customers and accelerate growth. AI is shifting mindsets and behaviors so quickly that founders and product developers are likely to embrace the latest AI trends (and platforms) before most investors and senior business leaders even know they exist. That is why Kevin Kelly calls AI the "ur-force in our future."[11] Companies that don't follow suit will almost certainly be left behind as competitors and nimble new entrants reap the benefits of AI-based platforms.

The challenge today, then, is no longer how to craft "mobile-first" or "digital-first" organizations. "AI-first" is the only option—and soon, becoming an AI-fueled organization will likely be table stakes to survive and thrive, not only for tech companies but for all companies. Consider this: AI will add an estimated $13 trillion to the global economy over the next decade.[12] According to a report from KPMG, a total of $12.4 billion has been invested in AI technologies to date, with a predicted $232 billion in deal flow by 2025.[13] From "digital born to AI-first," digital disruption is creating change across many sectors at an unprecedented pace. More and more, companies are launching or transitioning to become platform companies, where their operating models are designed and built off AI and digital assets to absorb the necessary tasks of scaling and operating with speed.

Organizationally healthy companies in a digital and AI-first context operate from the premise that digital in general and AI in particular can shape their operating models and services. As Microsoft's CEO, Satya Nadella, notes: "AI is the 'runtime' that is going to shape all that we do in terms of applications as well as the platform."[14] In their book *Competing in the Age of AI*, Marco Insanti and Karim Ikhani state that AI is becoming the new operational foundation of business—the core of a company's operating model—defining how the company drives the execution of tasks and changing the very concept of the firm.[15]

Consider how one retailer in Asia Pacific boosted its margins by 4 percent to 7 percent. By leveraging an AI tool, merchandisers and buyers were able to effectively collaborate and avoid working independently. This enabled the Asian Pacific retailer to better match inventory purchased and store space.[16] The upshot is that businesses today need to find ways to design a superior and relevant user experience, align the organization, processes, and technology to power it, and work with ever-widening ecosystems to achieve scale.

And make no mistake: AI will make organizational matters more important than ever before, not less—contrary to what some people might think. That is, AI is not going to eliminate the human factor or render it ephemeral through the massive substitution of machines for people. Instead, AI will make competition *more* dependent on leaders' human intelligence, cunning, empathy, and resourcefulness. Those who fail to grasp this irony won't just fall behind. They will miss out on one element that builds better organizations: businesses that can fast-track growth in a digital-first world. Why? Studies show that today's workforce places more weight than ever on things like purpose and meaningful work. To prevent turnover, then, leaders must be adept at facilitating meaningful interaction. They need to build trust with their teams as those employees create and manage a range of digital systems that will continue to depend on human interaction.[17] More broadly, organizational structures need to connect cross-functional and multidisciplinary teams across an ecosystem, help them better collaborate and form trusted relationships, and leverage those connections to ensure the best possible outcomes for innovation and impact—both on the business and society.

In short, today's most successful companies not only understand the value of AI, they also understand how organizational health works hand in hand with such digital systems. They commit top management and financial resources to optimize their business models and organizational practices to accommodate AI.

Paradoxically, however, it's often the leaders who champion an AI-first perspective to scale, grow, and govern their businesses who then find themselves at odds—both culturally and in terms of investment priorities—with the executives who can turn it into reality. Those are the leaders in charge of portfolio and business operations—management groups that, in turn, also have divergent priorities and perspectives from each other. The result can be a triangular discord that makes scaling, not a cakewalk in the best of times, even more perilous. Therefore, this book will examine the perspectives of each stakeholder group—investors, CEOs, and boards—to answer a vital question: What will it take to harness digital technologies and the conditions that foster an organization to reach its full potential?

For AI-centric organizations, that question won't be answered by using the playbooks of the past. Rather, they must develop and rethink the organizational conditions and principles of the company to thrive in a new era. Namely, achieving and sustaining organizational health in the time of AI will require leaders to adopt a more holistic view of their organizations. That will mean applying advances in digital to scale and grow their organizations—and balancing a healthy risk tolerance with an investor mindset at an unprecedented pace and level of resilience. That brings us to our final building block.

Building Block 3: Think Like an Investor

Investors are in a unique position to look at whole portfolio companies, compared to one company, function, or point solution at a time. They are incentivized to deliver returns and to do so with speed. In a digital-based world where speed is the next currency for high performance, the investment industry thus offers more valuable insights than traditional publicly traded companies.

Investors and boards of private equity or venture capital–backed companies play a major role in providing effective governance and oversight of the organization's health and how it achieves that health. Their approach to building a better organization and elevating the health of that organization will change depending on where exactly the organization is in terms of its growth phase. Regardless of the type of company or whether it is PE- or VC-backed, there are predictable "growing pains" specific to a business across a number of growth phases as a company matures. What goes right or wrong at each stage can affect the design of an operating model tailored to a company's growth trajectory. As companies grow in size, scope, and complexity, they often feel a strain on their organization's operating model. By taking stock of these conditions that uniquely shape the health of an organization, leaders can rely on advances in digital technology—namely, AI—to amplify human potential.

Who Should Read This Book

This book is devoted to helping CEOs and senior executives, board directors, consultants, startup founders, deal makers, and investors unleash the full potential of an organization in a digital, AI-first world. Its primary focus is on hypergrowth companies—those in a rapid expansion phase that seek to grow and scale quickly—although many of the lessons can apply equally well to large organizations seeking to continuously adapt and compete in a volatile digital economy.

I mentioned earlier that the leaders who champion the AI-first perspective to scale, grow, and govern their businesses often find themselves at odds with the executives who can turn it into reality. Consider, therefore, the varying perspectives that could be latent among a key stakeholder group. Each of these groups are also potential readers of this book.

- **Investor and CEO perspective.** Investors and dealmakers are ultimately beholden to the numbers and are often confronted with financial realities that force them to determine how to blend traditional practices with the luster and enthusiasm for costly investments in AI technologies. And they may wonder whether AI investments really yield enough value to justify the investment, as opposed to traditional cost-cutting and operational initiatives that would improve margins. No matter what the calculus, quantifying a return on AI investments, especially in today's business climate, can be a precarious exercise, and this book can offer valuable perspective.

- **Chief performance officer perspective.** Increasingly, private equity firms and venture capital firms are appointing chief performance officers—sometimes called human capital partners or portfolio talent leads—to design and execute organizational interventions, such as mining people and organizational data as part of first-look audits and pre-/post-deal due diligence for portfolio companies that are relevant, simple, and pragmatic for the portfolio company's organization effectiveness.

- **Board perspective.** For board directors, it can be daunting to see their domain intruded upon as environmental, social, and governance (ESG) issues take a starring role in board and top management agendas. And for them as well as for governance professionals, it can be a challenge to identify where to start and when to hold back in terms of driving new investments, which today can include everything from real-time analytics to 3-D printing, human-machine teaming, AI-laden operating models, and quantum computing power.

Given these perspectives, this book is for a number of key stakeholders, including general and limited partners who are interested in scaling their businesses, and investors, technologists, operators, and entrepreneurs interested in the successful investment and management of a business or portfolio of businesses (the latter includes startups from seed through IPO). More to the point, this book is for you, whether you are a wealthy business angel looking to invest your own money, a venture capital fund comprising entrepreneurs who are focused on seed/early-stage financing, a growth equity fund focused on later-stage financing, or a leveraged buyout fund affiliated with an investment management firm that uses a relatively small portion of equity and a relatively large portion of outside debt financing. To sum up, this book is for leaders who take a broader view of organizational issues versus individual point solutions or programs to determine how to transform a company to scale and grow effectively.

How This Book Unfolds

The book aims to help business leaders set an agenda for fast-tracking growth. It is divided into three sections, one for each aspect of building better organizations. It bears repeating that, although they are presented separately, in successful organizations each of the three aspects—organizational health, digital advancement, and investment—must work in tandem. Like three poles supporting a teepee, all are needed or the structure collapses.

Part 1: Design the Conditions for Effectiveness. This section sets the stage by drawing an analogy to organizational life from the field of holistic health. One of its core principles posits that human beings are greater than—and different from—the sum of their parts. Healing human malaise, the belief goes, requires a comprehensive view of mind, body, and spirit, and therefore should focus on understanding the underlying cause of the illness, not simply treating symptoms. Similarly, the sum of a company is greater than its parts, and organizational context requires consideration of all its components. Unfortunately, companies more commonly take a "Western medicine" approach and focus on isolated elements. These traditional approaches in the end rely on a machine model that, like Western medicine's inherent weakness, is less useful in healing holistic, functional disorders than in treating the symptoms of discrete diseases.

Accordingly, each chapter in this section focuses on one of the seven conditions that must work with all of the others in order for the organization to succeed in the digital era: (1) a *strategic direction* that prioritizes purpose over profit, (2) a *culture* focused on creating a shared but adaptive identity, (3) *leadership* that is agile and human-centric in the age of intelligent machines, (4) *talent* whose full potential has been unlocked, (5) *organizational design* around agility and sustainability, (6) *equity, inclusion, and diversity* (EID) built on an organizational bias for radical transparency and belonging, and (7) *employee well-being* as an organizational priority. For a company to be healthy, the seven conditions must be aligned, in sync, and functioning well in coordination. Any indication that one is out of sync suggests the need for intervention and realignment. Moreover, the chapters in this section explore why each organizational condition matters against the backdrop of today's business context in the digital era, and how each can be radically improved with new advances in digital technologies. Ultimately, investor goals too will be met as organizations align themselves with the conditions required for health.

Part II: Grow into a Better Organization. This section offers practical insights for using digital advances, AI in particular, to unleash an organization's full potential to scale and adapt. I start by discussing how to invest in digital to conduct continuous organizational-health checks. Just as the monitoring of one's physical health is critical to optimizing it, so too is monitoring the health of the organization indispensable to prioritizing management practices. I then explore the unique aspects of building a better organization in AI-first companies (by which I mean companies like Amazon, Alphabet's Google, and Microsoft) and how having the right organizational conditions is the key to unleashing the AI-first enterprise.

Part III: Lead a Better Organization. This section looks at top priorities for leaders when it comes to the role of investors and boards of private equity or venture capital–backed companies in providing effective governance and performance oversight with the aim of improving the organization's health. Because private equity sponsors and venture capitalists are relentless in their pursuits to invest in building better businesses, they focus on identifying the right value-creation levers and performance improvement initiatives to boost their returns. The promise of adopting the lessons and practices that this discipline of management offers could potentially elevate the performance of public companies. The section also includes a chapter on the critical responsibility, in VC and PE firms specifically, of the emerging role of the chief performance officer. It's a role that falls somewhere between an operating partner (i.e., former C-level executives, functional leaders, or consultants) and an executive-in-residence. As investors seek to boost investment returns, leveraging people and organizationally focused senior advisors or experts has become increasingly prevalent to internal operating groups. Often these advisors or experts are tasked with providing strategic, organizational consultation and support to their portfolio companies. This includes conducting due diligence by assessing the organization's overall effectiveness and leading initiatives to improve portfolio company value, growth, and exit support. The section ends with a chapter on how CEOs can become fluent in the language of change in order to build better organizations.

The book concludes with a few words about building agile and sustainable organizations in an AI-first era, and how this era is already so different from what came before. Research by McKinsey and the Harvard Business School, for example, reveals that organizations that launched agile transformations before the pandemic outperformed those that had not during the crisis.[18] A more dynamic, agile approach to talent helped many organizations quickly redeploy employees according to changing business needs.

The promise of this book, in short, is to take readers in a new direction: toward understanding how healthy organizations can help navigate the emergent challenges and opportunities in the digital world, turning ordinary organizations into stellar ones that grow, scale, adapt, and create sustainable outcomes for all stakeholders. My mission here is to provide actionable insights that will help organizations rise to their full potential. When the right essentials and the digital and AI capabilities to exercise them are guided by a clear purpose—a vital prerequisite for organizations that are truly agile and sustainable in an era of turbulence and change—investors, CEOs, organizational strategists, and board directors can accelerate the growth of an enterprise.

Let's begin by delving into the first requirement for a healthy organization: crafting a *strategic direction* that prioritizes purpose over profit.

Organizational Health: A Look Back

Although organizational health has long been a topic—the earliest academic reference dates to 1962 in a seminal piece published by the late Warren Bennis[19] and appears again in John Kotter's classic book *Organizational Dynamics,* published in 1978—it was another three decades before it began to enter mainstream discussions. By the mid-2000s, "organizational health" referred to a measure of culture, decision, and organization effectiveness, with advanced science and analytical rigor applied to the perceived "soft" stuff. Org health soon became a growing focus and popular theme for business books, articles, and consulting methods.[20] (See the table "Organizational Health: A Brief Review of the Literature.")

I accept, as a baseline, the definition and premise applied by Harvard Business School professor emeritus and management consultant Dr. John Kotter back in 1978: "A way to help managers and organization development specialists diagnose, understand, and improve organizational functioning." But another definition adds richness by saying more about the value and link between organizational performance and financial performance. Organizational health is "how top management makes money and how they choose to run the place," says Bill Schaninger, a McKinsey & Company senior partner and an author of the 2020 McKinsey article "Why Healthy Institutional Investors Outperform."[21]

Yet organizational health continues to be a difficult concept to pin down. It's often referred to in shorthand as the "effectiveness" of a business. It's fair to say that many business leaders, and even more so, investor leadership, still struggle to define the term, let alone say how it affects the long-term performance of their organizations. This book helps to close the gap and argue for a more holistic view.

Organizational Health: A Brief Review of the Literature

Year	Contributor	Perspective	Emphasis
1962	Bennis	Organizational behavior	• Applying principles of the scientific method and mental health for tackling and measuring the effectiveness of organizations
1978	Kotter	Organizational diagnosis	• Link between diagnostic methods and a systematic diagnostic process to improve organizational performance
2010	Blenko, Mankins, and Rogers	Decision effectiveness	• Link between 10 dimensions of organizational health/performance and decision effectiveness • Link between 4 elements of decision effectiveness and financial performance
2011; 2019	Keller and Price; Keller and Schaninger	Performance and health	• Link between 9 dimensions of organizational performance and financial performance • Science between the *what* and the *how* of organizational change
2012	Lencioni	Disciplines to teaming	• Link between effective teaming, questions leaders need to answer to spur cooperation and to effectively communicate, and the critical reinforcement systems needed for moving in a shared direction
2017	Price and Toye	Agility and complexity	• Analyzing or improving performance not only at the organizational level, but also at the individual and team levels

DESIGN THE CONDITIONS FOR EFFECTIVENESS

Seven Essentials for Successful, Healthy

Organizations in the Digital Era

PART I

DESIGN THE CONDITIONS
FOR EFFECTIVENESS

1 ■ Strategic Direction

Prioritize Purpose over Profit

Organizational matters *matter*—not only to financial performance but also to creating value for organizations, the people employed by them, and society at large. For decades, the first of our seven conditions of building a better organization—strategic direction— was designed for one purpose only: to create maximum value for shareholders. But in the digital era, that formula no longer fits. Why? Because strategy that is rooted in a deeper, social purpose ultimately enables speed and resilience. Today, successful organizations create strategies that prioritize purpose over short-term profit, creating long-term value for shareholders *and* for customers, communities, the environment, and employees.

In the summer of 2020, after the death of George Floyd while in police custody, protests erupted around the country and then the world. Floyd was by no means the first unarmed Black man killed by police. But what was unique was the *speed* with which a video taken at the scene spread worldwide, igniting a global protest—a phenomenon unimaginable in the predigital era. Equally remarkable was how quickly the public discourse broadened, from a renewed call for racial justice and police reform into a social challenge for businesses everywhere.

Almost overnight, it seemed, corporations that had long dawdled with often-ineffectual "diversity training" were suddenly tackling compelling reformation, and in some cases radical transformation, of their existing talent and organizational practices. For example, retailer Sephora unveiled new customer-service protocols aimed at reducing racial bias in stores, and both Sephora and Ulta Beauty significantly increased shelf space for Black-owned brands.[1] Meanwhile, Netflix has doubled the number of Black professionals in its organization.[2] Both Netflix and Google's YouTube have made good on their promises to feature more talent and programming from Black artists, and each of the companies has also pledged $100 million toward economic development in Black communities and racial justice initiatives.[3]

Healthy organizational practices have always mattered, of course, but today the digitization of everything has made them vital for survival. By prioritizing organizational health, businesses can find the tools they need to account for and adjust to the speed and unpredictability with which events unfold. The power and velocity of social media, which enabled the George Floyd video to quickly go viral and become a key piece of evidence resulting in the conviction of his killer, is just one example of the impact of recent technology and digital speed. Consider, too, the following:

- An increasing number of organizations are following the lead of companies such as Microsoft and FirstEnergy, which tie a percentage of CEOs' pay to meeting diversity goals.[4]
- Top-line growth is increasingly tied to how well companies harness data and analytics to shape their operating models and to inform their strategic planning, resource allocation, and decision processes.

- Consumers' changing expectations regarding speed, service, and cost are prompting companies to reshape their operating models to achieve operational excellence.
- The U.S. Securities and Exchange Commission (SEC) is pressuring companies to disclose information on their human capital initiatives, per the Human Capital Management Coalition's petition and Investor Advisory Committee's 2019 proposal to modernize required disclosures.
- Employee advocacy and stakeholder activism have increased around issues such as climate policies, racial equity, firearm sales and financing of the gun industry, and selling facial-recognition products to police forces (particularly regarding the potential for discrimination those products present against people of color). Such activism has already prompted action by regulators and investors on several fronts—for example, legislation around more consistent use of police body cams.
- The influence of investors is growing around how well businesses monitor organizational topics and environmental, social, and governance (ESG) criteria—and how well they integrate those criteria into mainstream business and investment practices.

Consider too that it isn't just digital and AI-first companies that are giving more attention to organizational matters; they are also becoming increasingly important to "old economy" companies and to investors. Historically, a focus on people-related issues was limited. But AI-first companies—and their investors—are beginning to understand that org health is the secret sauce to executing on a vision. As Stanford professor and author Jeffrey Pfeffer writes, business success "comes from successfully implementing strategy, not just from having one."[5] That implementation depends in large measure on the betterment of the enterprise itself.

Today, as businesses worldwide begin to rebound from the havoc wreaked by the COVID-19 pandemic—while simultaneously contending with continuing social, environmental, and financial uncertainty—the companies that survive and thrive will be those that purposefully develop healthy organizational conditions. In this sense, we can draw from organizational life an analogy to the field of holistic health. Unlike Western medicine, which often focuses on isolated elements of the body, a core principle of holistic health posits that human beings are greater than—and different from—the sum of their parts. Healing human malaise, the belief goes, requires a comprehensive view of mind, body, and spirit, and therefore should focus on understanding the underlying cause of the illness, not simply treating symptoms. Similarly, the sum of a company is greater than its parts, and organizational context requires consideration of all its components.

Note that not every element of organizational health will be salient to all stages across the maturity and growth of a business, or even throughout the life cycle of a deal. That is why leaders in both publicly held and private companies need to hone their ability to identify and manage the relevant aspects at any given stage. For example, in a startup, crafting a well-understood vision and purpose that guides the company's strategy and key decisions needs the most attention. In a mature, post-IPO company, on the other hand, your focus would be on evolving the company's structure, job architecture, and career paths to support product expansion and new growth areas.

No matter where your business finds itself within the growth cycle, however, its strategic direction—the first of our seven organizational conditions—will always be central to success. In this chapter, we will explore strategic direction in detail and how identifying an underlying purpose is key to creating a strategy that can harness the power of big data and artificial intelligence to benefit both organizations and society.

Purpose Wanted: Now More Than Ever

What characterizes a successful business strategy? Certainly, it needs to articulate a clear long-term vision and mission. It should account for external environments and market conditions and leverage existing assets and capabilities—or define a clear plan to develop or acquire them. But in the current hypercompetitive and hypergrowth marketplace, companies' strategies have been challenged by changes in the business environment. In short, constantly changing macro-environmental factors shorten the shelf life of many strategies. Dealing with such disruption requires a series of strategic "micro battles," discrete, time-boxed initiatives that rapidly bring strategic choices to action and formulate ways to scale the results, resolving conflicts as quickly and as close to the customer as possible.[6]

But while changes to the business environment often force companies to quickly rethink individual business strategies—that is, the set of actions needed to capitalize on growth opportunities—a company's *strategic direction* or its articulation of its ambitions, including trade-offs, risks, priorities, and main efforts, is less prone to disruption. Ideally, a clear strategic direction provides the structure to support the organization through stormy weather.

That's where purpose comes in. The driving force of an underlying purpose is the first and arguably the most important thing that an organization needs when it comes to formulating its direction. Purpose is one of three elements—along with first principles and aspirations—that require wide agreement from the board, founders, and other company leaders. Let's define these three elements in turn.

- **Purpose.** A company's reason for being that guides organizational behavior at all levels of the company and decisions about the business model and key investments— and how to leverage the operating model to execute against those decisions. An example of purpose is CVS Health's "helping people on their path to better health."
- **First principles.** The value-creation drivers that will help the company grow and clarify its value proposition to differentiate itself from its competitors. For example, Haier Group, headquartered in Qingdao, China, transformed from its traditional manufacturing model to a customer-relationship management model by focusing on giving customers what they want most. The company created a

statement, the Win-Win Value Added Approach (WWVA), that helped it to operationalize its first principles of being "user-centric, driven by a new, open Internet of Things (IoT) ecosystem linked to other companies' products and services."[7]

- **Aspirations.** The envisioned future and objectives—and the key results a company will seek to achieve in pursuit of those. For example, as it rebranded itself as a health services company, CVS decided to stop selling cigarettes— a bold aspiration and move that initially cost the company $2 billion in lost revenue.

Google offers an example of how organizations can convey purpose, first principles, and aspirations to sharpen strategic direction. The company, which grew from a garage startup in 1998 to a large, complex organization, has always aspired to embody its famous motto of "Don't be evil." The company's bedrock first principles, known as the three "respects" (respect the user, respect the opportunity, and respect each other), are words that are etched into employees from the beginning—as they were for me from my early days as a "Noogler" (or new Google employee).

Historically, the organization has "long believed that over time, companies tend to get comfortable doing the same thing, just making incremental changes," according to Google cofounder Larry Page in a blog post. "But in the technology industry, where revolutionary ideas drive the next big growth areas, you need to be a bit uncomfortable to stay relevant." Therefore, when Google's existing structure began to limit its potential to expand, it restructured to a holding company, Alphabet. This allowed Google and the portfolio of "Other Bets" to grow autonomously so that Alphabet could meet stakeholders' expectations and, indeed, outperform competitors.

The change, however, didn't relieve Google of its responsibility in the portfolio to grow and be profitable. Therefore, Google made the big pivot from being a mobile-first to an AI-first company— marking an important inflection point not only in the company's history but also in the tech industry overall.

Because I believe purpose is the most important of the three aspects of setting strategic direction, that is where I will focus for the rest of this chapter.

Purposeful Strategic Direction in the Age of AI

Why is purpose so important? The answer comes back, again, to the need for companies today to embody a clearly articulated ambition and enact it with speed. In the current age of digitization, in which artificial intelligence will soon become a default application, technology companies and investors must proactively work together to understand key organizational conditions, such as purposeful strategic direction. This is where we begin to see how our three main building blocks, as described in the introduction—the health of the organization, digital advances, and investment—come together. Dynamic, rapid, and agile investment decision making will depend on such mutual understanding and prioritization.

Here's why. Near-real-time responsiveness has become the new competitive advantage, but organizations can act only as quickly as their people are willing to do. So, the first essential way to be fast is to capture the hearts and minds of employees at all levels of the organization. A common commitment to a meaningful purpose does that. Purpose offers a strategic direction for the organization, yes, but it also provides something that employees care about. It defines right behaviors and actions to beat the competition, and it empowers people to own their decisions—thereby pulling the company's strategic purpose directly to customers.

Today's most purpose-driven organizations—CVS Health, Google, and Patagonia to name a few—place purpose at the heart of their strategic direction, serving as a kind of guiding north star for how they plan to compete. In other words, purpose goes beyond culture to strategy—defined as the long-term roadmap to realize top management's vision and meet business goals.

But what, exactly, *is* purpose? It is an organization's aspirational, human-first reason for being. By this definition, a company's purpose serves many stakeholders—shareholders and owners, yes, but also employees, customers, the environment, and society.

Once seen as a rather soft corporate issue whose value wasn't always understood by the C-suite, purpose is now becoming a central tenet of organizational life. Leaders at many levels are using the concept to anchor and guide the decisions they make in response to new situations and unforeseen events—making purpose an inescapable focus for companies grappling with the challenges of today's disruptive business environment. That is why management teams worldwide are realizing that it's time to welcome back purpose as a key focus of an organization's effectiveness.

Consider the following recent headline: "Shareholder Value Is No Longer Everything, Top C.E.O.s Say."[8] On August 19, 2019, close to 190 corporate CEOs belonging to the Business Roundtable (BRT) took a moment to pause, reflect, and reevaluate what had become clear: along with any financial investments they considered, companies must also invest in and make new commitments to employees, communities, suppliers, and, most of all, customers. In other words, these CEOs of major public companies that together have a market capitalization exceeding $13 trillion declared their commitment to a broader group of stakeholders. The BRT statement issued a forward-looking view that redefined the purpose of a corporation: to not only advance the interests of shareholders but to also equally advance the interests of employees, customers, suppliers, and the planet. That purpose places ESG criteria, and its stance behind fair and ethical engagement of multiple stakeholders, at the forefront. For most businesses operating in today's context, this statement reflects a management reset of corporate norms, which many companies are already starting to follow and adopt.

More recently, the coronavirus pandemic has led an increasing number of companies to take a purposeful, employee-first approach, sometimes referred to as "stakeholder capitalism." In a survey of Fortune 500 CEOs, nearly half said that the pandemic accelerated stakeholder capitalism as a way to address the human suffering caused by the crisis. (Only 18 percent felt the pandemic was slowing such capitalism while companies focused instead on short-term financial pressures.)[9]

With purpose increasingly on the radar of senior executives, it's no surprise that companies are spending a significant sum of time, resources, and money on purpose-driven campaigns and initiatives. These organizations are wise to place their attention on purpose—after all, a large chunk of their consumers and their own workforces are doing the same. Millennials, who make up the largest portion of the workforce today and who are worth $1 trillion in consumer spending, have become increasingly vocal over the last decade regarding their expectations about where they spend their money, the products they consume, and the companies in which they work.[10]

Specifically, this group—sometimes referred to as the "purpose-driven generation"[11]—expects their jobs to have an underlying purpose that goes beyond a paycheck and returns for shareholders, and they expect their companies to make a meaningful impact on society and the environment. Consider a recent *Fast Company* survey, which found that nearly 40 percent of millennials choose a job because of a company's focus and role in environmental sustainability as part of its mission, compared with less than a quarter of Gen X respondents and 17 percent of baby boomers.[12]

No wonder companies that have a guiding purpose are so desirable. In today's climate of uncertainty and disruption, purpose serves as an anchor for people at all organizational levels. Regardless of their job description, people instinctively seek the kind of grounding that a common and meaningful underlying purpose can provide. What's more, when you walk into a purpose-driven organization, you can feel the difference. It's in the air and in the way employees act. People are clearly engaged in what they are doing day to day, rather than resigned or just going through the motions. They are very clear about the company's strategic direction, and they believe in it, actively translating that higher ambition into the work they do and how they do it. They appreciate their company's broader societal impact and take pride in their jobs as adding value to a common core purpose.

For organizations themselves, the strategic clarity of a purpose-driven organization pays off in real business results: higher performance on measures such as total return to shareholders (TRS), improved ESG scores, and gains in market share are evident. A Harvard Business School study, for example, cited the importance of a clear sense of purpose to inspire a team to work together and achieve success. This research found that an increase in clarity of purpose can increase return on assets (ROA) by as much as 3.89 percent per year.[13] Although some might argue that this emphasis on purpose is overdone, the evidence suggests otherwise: purpose-driven companies saw 400 percent more returns on the stock market than the Standard and Poor 500.[14]

Take, for example, one leading investment bank, where Organizational Network Analysis was used to identify the instillers of purpose among the bank's top 600 leaders. The question "Who among you leaves you feeling a greater sense of purpose in your work after an interaction?" revealed that the top quartile of leaders created a sense of purpose for nearly 16 people on average as compared to the bottom quartile leaders, who gave a sense of purpose to fewer than one person, on average. Meanwhile, leaders in the top quartile also were able to attract higher performers to work for them, saw lower attrition rates, and had teams with higher engagement scores.[15] No company is immune to the impact of a clear and compelling purpose on the bottom line. In short, purpose pays.

Companies That Win by Doing Good

Evidence of the significance of purpose over profit across multiple industries is not difficult to find. In the retail sector, for instance, former REI CEO Jerry Stritzke has said, "Purpose drives everything we do at REI. Our belief that a life outdoors is a life well-lived anchors everything. It's our North Star." REI has famously closed its doors on Black Friday, encouraging customers and employees alike to instead take an "Opt Outside" day.[16] Unlike in years past, today only 7 percent of Fortune 500 CEOs believe their companies should "mainly focus on making profits and not be distracted by social goals."[17]

At the same time, institutional investors are much more assertive about purpose not only to mitigate risks but also to clarify their ethical value proposition to shareholders and stakeholders, including employees, suppliers, and consumers. At Bank of America, for example, employees are given days off to volunteer and to vote.[18] By taking this stance, institutional investors can influence how companies invest responsibly as they tackle environmental challenges like climate change or social issues such as economic inclusion.

There are many reasons why a purpose-infused strategic direction benefits companies and top management. When an organization aligns its top team around a common purpose, it takes a powerful step toward executing any organizational change, enabling speed and effective direction setting of internal initiatives while eliminating redundant investment in nonstrategic activities. For investors, purpose can guide decisions, including those that involve strategic bets and investment choices. Take the financial services industry, which must deal with fiercely competitive demands and performance expectations. Larry Fink, CEO of the world's largest institutional investor, BlackRock, puts it simply: "Without a sense of purpose, no company, either public or private, can achieve its full potential."[19] In a letter published in 2018, Fink encouraged companies to "not only deliver financial performance, but also show how their company makes a positive contribution to society." For example, through its Social Impact Challenge, BlackRock runs a skills-based hack-a-thon where employees help a local nonprofit solve an organizational challenge.

Or consider Ally Financial, which at the height of the great recession of 2008 managed to reboot itself as an online bank after being spun off from its parent company. Weathering the greatest economic headwinds in a generation, Ally's spinoff gave it the chance to form a new brand and sense of purpose that was rooted in its brand name—being a relentless ally for its customers by starting with a basic question to clarify its business proposition, most notably: What is every single thing that we hate about banking? As Ally chief marketing officer Andrea Brimmer states, "The world didn't need a new bank, but it certainly needed a better bank."[20]

Leaders like Stritzke, Fink, Brimmer, and Ally CEO Jeffrey Brown not only model the courage and conviction of a leader's commitment to purpose, but they also fundamentally believe they have a responsibility as citizens of the world to do the right thing. Such leaders are outmaneuvering their competitors by anchoring their strategic direction in a deep sense of purpose, while taking stock of their business's current trajectory and market implications.

All of which is to say that organizations must step up and demonstrate that their focus around environmental, social, and governance issues are more than just a superficial overlay. Given society's expectations and the demographic trends that lean more toward sustainability, managers need to make a more concerted push to incorporate purpose, such as ESG metrics, into *everything they do* and demonstrate the economic value that comes from a focus on these issues.

One company that has taken the rallying cry of purpose to heart is Unilever. Facing unprecedented competitive pressures during the last recession, the company doubled down on a strategy and set of initiatives that connected its leaders' personal purpose to real and evolving business problems. Unilever's approach turned the elusive concept of purpose into a permanent feature of business model innovation—and became a case study offering lessons for other companies.

Unilever's Blueprint for Purpose

In 2009, amid a fast-moving consumer marketplace characterized by volatility, uncertainty, and complexity, Paul Polman took over as CEO of Unilever, the British-Dutch multinational consumer goods company based in the U.K. As one of the world's leading suppliers of nondurable consumer goods, Unilever counts among its products such household name brands as Ben & Jerry's, Hellmann's, Lipton, Dove, and Vaseline. The company sells products used by 2 billion consumers every day in more than 190 countries.

Despite Unilever's prior success, Polman quickly found himself contending with a number of forces transforming the consumer goods market at the time: shifting consumer demographics and lifestyles, changes in health and wellness concerns, shrinking shelf space amid retailer consolidation and expansion, replacement of food with non-food SKUs, promotion pressure, and rising costs. In its developed global markets, the company struggled with a decline in consumer confidence, high inflation, and low GDP growth. Meanwhile, in its emerging markets Unilever faced a slowdown in the pace of growth, increasing competition, and a series of natural disasters and geopolitical disruptions. Yet somehow the business still needed to see volume and market share gains, continued margin improvement, and strong cash generation if it hoped to meet customer demands and counter unprecedented margin constraints.

Two key trends were impinging on the business: shifts of economic power to Asia, most notably to Southeast Asia, and Latin America; and the shift of power in general to the consumer, because of digitization and social media. Faced with a growth-triggered transformation caused by rapidly shifting market conditions and long-term priorities for growth in profits, volumes, cash flow, and market share, Polman knew he needed to employ a different strategy than what the company typically used. In the past, Unilever had transformed the business through such actions as acquisition and manufacturing rationalization, aligning the organization behind a unified strategy, leveraging global scale and simplifying operations, and growing consumer segments. But if Polman were to take the company to the next level of competitiveness, he and his team knew they had to be audacious and bold and to set ambitious, aspirational goals guided by and rooted in purpose.

A New Strategy. Under Polman's leadership, Unilever's top team crafted a new, purpose-led agenda for the company.[21] Dubbed Unilever's Compass Strategy, the proposition set out to double the size of the company's revenues while dramatically reducing its environmental impact and increasing its contribution to social well-being. At the core of Unilever's Compass Strategy was the Unilever Sustainable Living Plan (USLP), which was intended to help 1 billion people improve their health, halve the environmental footprint of the company's products, and enhance the livelihood of those in its value chain, which meant, for example, sourcing many of its agricultural raw materials from sustainable sources. The scale of the ambition required a clear link between purpose and social impact on the one hand, and business results on the other—and a new approach to engaging company leaders and the organization. Specifically, the new strategy set out to create, capture, and deliver value across four key areas:

- Ensuring its brands developed superior products and aimed at reaching more consumers
- Leveraging its global scale and local knowledge to address all consumer needs in all markets, given shifting consumer demographics and buying behaviors
- Achieving speed through a lean, simple, and agile operating model
- Attracting, developing, and retaining talent, especially in the emerging markets

To execute on Unilever's new purpose and Compass Strategy, Polman built a commitment to sustainability into every aspect of the way the company was run (i.e., how it makes money) and organized (i.e., its operating model and its culture) to leverage scale. However, he had to begin with clarifying the company's values, such as integrity and respect.

But Paul Polman didn't make these values just empty talk.[22] He put in place actions to ensure that the values, purpose, and strategy were embedded in the culture and operations of the company. (See the sidebar "From Purpose to Impact: Unilever's Approach to Business Model Innovation.") To ensure success, each leadership layer created its own personal purpose that was tied to Unilever's organizational purpose, thereby clearly laying out performance expectations and accountabilities. To achieve this, Polman started an initiative to clarify expectations for leadership behaviors with his senior team, and then went on to clarify them with his top 100 executives and then the next 500 executives.

Polman also challenged these leaders to identify the big challenges they could face in creating new businesses—putting business model innovation into action—while adjusting the performance management system to reward people leading new businesses that delivered results. He also addressed the workforce challenges in the company's emerging markets by leveraging the Unilever Compass vision and

From Purpose to Impact: Unilever's Approach to Business Model Innovation

Unilever's CEO, Paul Polman, an ardent advocate of purpose-driven leadership, launched UL2020 as an effort to grow leaders equipped for a volatile, rapidly shifting world. He emphasized purpose, based on the premise popularized by Bill George (former Medtronic CEO and Harvard Business School professor) that authentic leaders—men and women with a good self-understanding and a high regard for their followers—would prove more flexible, resilient, and open to learning and growing throughout their careers. In other words, they would be ideally suited for a world that demanded constant innovation and change, while tackling some of Unilever's biggest challenges, like accomplishing growth while simultaneously reducing environmental impact and addressing rampant social and economic inequality.

UL2020 evolved from a leadership development program into a process of business model innovation that also developed leaders. The program enlisted managers in teams of five to take on huge business challenges that not only had the potential to generate breakthrough results but that would also dare them to learn new things about themselves as leaders.[23] They were challenged to ask: "How can I use my company to make the world better? And how can I enlist my purpose and those of my teammates to achieve growth and alleviate pressing societal and ecological problems?"

Along the way, the UL2020 purpose-to-impact initiative teams were provided with tools like systemic dynamics, resilience, and mindfulness training to help leaders get equally comfortable with taking risks and recovering from failure. They also employed design thinking and digital strategy to learn from disruption and beat competitors. Thus, they tackled problems as diverse as enabling the growth of millions of

(*continued*)

microentrepreneurs in emerging markets, creating new models of city-based marketing and distribution, and combating water scarcity. Their efforts were judged by a group of senior executives and leadership advisors, both internal and external, along two dimensions: breakthrough thinking and development as leaders. Their teammates were enlisted to be one another's coaches, cheerleaders, and critics along the way.

Over a period of about five years, the results were substantial. In excess of hundreds of millions in new revenue was generated. Moreover, at least one likely "billion dollar" product was uncovered. Rural residents in Vietnam and Indonesia now have access to affordable water purifiers. Equally important, participants, their supervisors, and direct reports attested to durable changes in behavior and attitude of these leaders. As one leader put it, he learned "more about myself as a leader . . . and what it takes to enlist other people's energy . . . than I had in 20 years of grinding on the numbers alone."

Ultimately, Unilever created a cohort of entrepreneurial, purpose-driven leaders. UL2020 leaders continue to proactively seek out opportunities to solve big problems that have the potential to generate profit, improve their skills, and prepare themselves for senior leadership roles.

a newly created equity, inclusion, and diversity strategy to attract, acquire, and engage employees ahead of the growth curve.

While much of the workforce was aligned with Unilever's purpose-led strategic agenda, it wasn't without its naysayers, particularly regarding the USLP, which some skeptics thought was unattainable. As a result, some executives voluntarily decided to pursue careers elsewhere. Others who held on to outdated assumptions and mindsets were encouraged to leave the company.

A New Focus on Performance and Values. In the end, Polman's efforts paid off. During Paul Polman's tenure as CEO, Unilever outperformed its industry on both the top and bottom lines and delivered an impressive 290 percent shareholder return. In short, his focus on purpose not only delivered better business results but also better results for Unilever's people and society, based on his ambition to make an environmental impact, while nurturing the next generation of purpose-driven leaders. Despite the odds, Polman's tenacity over time enabled him to successfully steer the company it has become today by going back to its roots and making sustainability an integral part of the business model—to make it, in fact, the strategy.

Polman's success was due to his use of purpose as an enterprise compass and critical component of the strategic direction that differentiated Unilever in the market. Then he not only aligned his top teams around that purpose with clear targets and accountabilities, he also empowered employees to live and act based on Unilever's purpose. Not unlike John Pettigrew's method at National Grid (described in the introduction), Polman relied on a holistic approach. Rather than taking a siloed perspective to organizational health, he focused instead on a global view and was relentless about keeping his efforts on track. What Unilever and National Grid have in common is a focus on leaders articulating a clear strategic direction, developing new capabilities to lead differently and drive impact, building on that foundation with an operating model designed to be fit for purpose, and an adaptive culture to drive speedy execution.

Continued Impact Today. Polman retired in 2018, but his legacy of purpose lives on, and most recently it helped steer the company through the tumultuous time of the COVID-19 pandemic. Purpose has served to anchor employees in making decisions close to the customer, enabling newfound speed and adaptiveness. As Unilever's current CEO, Alan Jope, explains, "We're actually moving away from scenario planning and trying to focus on building agility and responsiveness into the company. . . . We've discovered a new responsiveness in Unilever that I wish we had unlocked years ago, but it's taken this crisis to do that."[24]

In short, a purpose-led strategy, like the one that Polman put in place at Unilever, is only gaining relevance, releasing the speed and responsiveness needed for the digital era. Whether you are a senior leader, an investor, or a board member, the Unilever story illustrates how a clear, purpose-infused strategic direction is essential for delivering profitable growth.

Not every company, of course, manages to build the success story that Unilever did. The challenges in the process are real. Leaders who are working to infuse purpose into the heart of their organizations should be aware of the pitfalls—and how to avoid them. Read on.

Three Pitfalls to Avoid on the Road to Purpose

As anyone who has ever been on the receiving end of shallow slogans or campaigns can attest, some purpose-driven initiatives have a very short shelf life. Recent research shows that often official corporate values espoused in support of an organization's purpose have no correlation to corporate culture at all.[25] Further, when the commitment to becoming a purpose-driven company and the set of initiatives to support it have little connection to employees' individual purpose or day-to-day activities, it is even less likely to matter.

All of which is to say that leaders who try to define a purpose-infused strategic direction for their organizations typically face three common challenges: (1) fuzzy priorities—or a lack of clarity about direction, (2) fuzzy accountability—or a lack of agreement and/or support from senior leadership around the shift in focus, strategy, or value proposition, and (3) culture clash—or a clash between the company's established culture and the new strategic direction.

Let's look at each of these pitfalls and how leaders might address them. Note that in each case, the solution often lies in a triage approach among the three building blocks for better organizations: boosting the health of the organization, leveraging digital tools, and ensuring that you have enough support to carry out your vision with investor resources.

Fuzzy Priorities

Strategic direction, anchored in a rock-solid purpose, is at its best when there are clarity, engagement, and action. Only then can leaders engage in productive debate, turn insight into an actionable value-creation plan against which they are willing to allocate resources, and execute a chosen course of action in a timely way. Such organizational agility depends on the interplay among three key elements—priorities, accountabilities, and capabilities. These must be carefully coordinated and tightly integrated into a company's strategic direction.

How, then, do leaders prioritize opportunities, resources, and actions to improve performance across an enterprise? The first key to achieving this is foresight. Yet the environment has grown so uncertain that leaders can't exactly plan anymore. For example, how can you develop and launch new ideas faster when new market entrants like Instacart, Pinterest, Airbnb, and countless others are digitally disrupting incumbent organizations across all industry sectors and introducing new business models? Such realities are prompting today's enterprises to shift from scenario planning to scenario *modeling*—in essence, using advanced algorithms to provide real-time data by scanning the environment. Gathering data is how leaders turn strategic insight into actionable strategies for a multitude of potential futures which are explicitly articulated and sufficiently detailed. Airbnb, for example, used scenario modeling to increase the volume of global rentals without owning any assets to do so.

Fortunately, such turbocharged, data-driven, AI-enabled approaches to strategy formulation and development are already well underway in a number of organizations. For example, companies may use advanced analytics and sophisticated algorithms to perform "sentiment analysis" against social-media feeds and news-media content, thus evaluating users' positive or negative feelings about a company's product or service. The application of advanced analytics to specific business challenges has started to deliver value not only for blue-chip companies but also for institutional investors. Today, investment managers can conduct rapid reviews of quarterly earnings of thousands of companies and pinpoint key stocks worthy of more in-depth analysis. Portfolio managers are then able to prioritize and make better, unbiased investment decisions quickly and consistently. What used to take an army of human analysts employing spreadsheets and crunching data around the clock for weeks can now be done in just a matter of hours and with far greater accuracy, driving faster insights to shape business and investment strategies.

Truly healthy organizations, however, have leaders who realize that data and insights must be supported by good judgment and decisions that can be understood and adopted by senior leaders throughout the organization. Similarly, value creation always comes back to strategy. (See the box "How Digital Advances Can Improve Strategy.") Integrating digital advances such as machine learning (ML) and natural language processing (NLP) into strategy and practice can pragmatically improve how capital is allocated—or in private equity, how deals are sourced and developed, leading to long-term health and agility.

Leveraging a private equity-style approach to strategic direction entails moving from long-term to a targeted analysis based on a start-from-scratch (i.e., clean sheet) model. In a from-scratch model, where no sacred cows are allowed, advances in digital can help leaders de-bias their decisions and take actions that align with the investment thesis in short, intense time horizons. In such situations, having a fixed ambition combined with a hunger for truly differentiated sources of value creation and agreement on priorities can make the difference in value creation and value capture for the business. In sum, adopting a PE-style approach means taking a three-pronged approach. First, start with a bias for action, followed by a clear *basis* for action. Second, define a lucid investment thesis—in other words, how your company will become more valuable within a certain time horizon. And third, clarify what needs to change in your organization and, most importantly, what needs to remain intact.

Organizations powered by digital advances can provide fast-paced and high-precision assessments, insightful analysis and reporting for objective decision making, or focused action planning in a time-bound and outcome-oriented manner. But it wouldn't be a complete approach without the use of measurable metrics. A PE-style approach demands that leaders leverage digital advances to measure what they can track and measure what matters to a partic-

How Digital Advances Can Improve Strategy

How Digital Advances Can Help	How It Works
Foresight	AI can sift through a vast array of data to reveal trends and unexpected insights, learning as it goes to suggest possible strategic futures or opportunities.
Scenario modeling	Data and AI can be used to model multiple possible strategic futures.
Strategy microexperiments	AI and analytics can help rapidly bring strategic choices to action, learn from the experiments, and formulate ways to scale the results.
Speed and responsiveness	AI and analytics can speed decision making and empower those closest to the customer to rapidly adapt to changing conditions.
Strategic decision making	AI can be used as part of the strategic decision-making team, casting a vote, or informing executives' decisions.
Rapid resource allocation	AI can infer skills of the workforce and rapidly match them to work.
Strategy execution	AI can rapidly analyze a company's operating models' information and workflow to reveal alignment with strategy. It can also analyze whether the organization's key performance indicators (KPIs, a reflection of their strategy) are the right ones to maximize. AI can then prioritize those and determine how effectively they are being maximized based on financial, customer, market, competitor, and workforce data.

(continued)

How Digital Advances Can Improve Strategy (continued)

How Digital Advances Can Help	How It Works
Bottom-up strategy	With the help of digital advances, everyone at all levels can suggest and refine the strategy. They can use AI to run experiments, use digital advances to collaborate in hack-a-thons or innovation idea jams, and use advanced analytics to uncover innovation brokers or energizers who can infuse and spread new ideas throughout the organization.
Dynamic governance structure	Data analytics and AI can help make who is doing what and when transparent. It can analyze the quality and impact of a person's decisions, using this analysis as a basis to gradually grant the person more decision-making power.
ESG/stakeholder capitalism	New sources of data and AI can help better measure the value created for various stakeholders on a real-time basis, enabling the organization to adjust course as needed.
Purpose	Digital nudges can be used to help remind people how their purpose is connected to their everyday work.
Investment or portfolio company selection	AI can crunch massive amounts of data to suggest companies ripe for investment.

ular part of the business. In other words, human judgment combined with the power of AI can help even the most experienced executive or investor avoid a "gut feel" approach and instead, be relevant, targeted, and simple.

Fuzzy Accountability

When there is leadership engagement that reflects visible willingness and expressed support for a chosen strategic direction, then there's hope for the organization's people to fall into alignment as well. Such a purposeful, common direction allows organizations to continually outperform competitors through consistent execution. At root, it goes to the heart of the way a company's senior leaders make money and run the business—clear decision making and the commitment to allocate resources that constantly drive premium results. Companies that can apply such agile approaches to identify and allocate resources swiftly are the ones that will be best positioned to handle uncertainty and change at a metabolic rate.

But to do that, companies also need something else—a dynamic governance structure. That means empowering small teams, especially those on the front line, to engage in rapid decision cycles on business-critical issues. For example, Tencent Holdings helps its small teams to develop products by giving them complete autonomy over day-to-day decision making (top management checks in only when it comes to resource allocation and overall strategy).[26]

Setting a successful strategic direction also involves something else: the ability to forecast future bets and the benefits of investments. Today's companies can do this by making use of sophisticated algorithms combined with human judgment.

While some companies are using machine learning and AI to enhance productivity of existing business practices, others are taking advantage of new digital advances such as natural language processing. NLP enables rapid analysis of operating models' information and workflow, while improving the decision effectiveness of business and investment decisions. Indeed, to explore the consequences of a decision before making it, some investment firms are, in fact, "appointing" algorithms to their board of directors, as demonstrated by Hong Kong venture-capital fund Deep Knowledge Ventures. Focused on age-related-disease drugs and regenerative medicine, the company assigned an AI system called VITAL to its board of investors, giving it a vote in every investment decision. How does a machine make decisions? VITAL does it by scanning prospective companies' financing, clinical trials, intellectual property, and previous funding, and then casting a vote to reflect the most probable advantageous outcome.[27]

Thus, Deep Knowledge Ventures and others like it are ensuring engagement and accountability around strategic direction by integrating smart machines into their top management decision-making bodies. Whether an organization is publicly traded or backed by private equity, the machines' digitally enhanced insights can help CEO, staff, and others make optimal decisions and take on more considered, targeted work.

Culture Clash

Leading companies are constantly refreshing their ability to build a distinct organizational identity and culture—a key focus for chapter 2—that supports execution and has the most impact on overall performance. To be sure, the relentless pursuit toward assessing, evolving, and building distinctive capabilities—the specific internal advantages that a company possesses that are hard to replicate— is a cornerstone to the holistic view of taking stock and leveraging the organization's health. Whether those advantages include an efficient supply chain, or a set of patents and a proprietary software code that can enable executional leadership, or some other advantage, problems arise when a company's established culture clashes with the new strategic direction. The resulting misalignment can stymie growth.

For example, Zappos, under the leadership of its late founder Tony Hsieh, was on a quest to become more entrepreneurial, more self-organized, less hierarchical, and more responsive to customer needs.[28] But its established operating model and culture were set up to resist such changes. Zappos finally was able to transform only after it focused on the company's distinct capabilities by reorganizing purely around roles and responsibilities.

In other words, purpose-driven leaders know how to identify talent skills and gaps, and when to adapt their organizational design for new product lines or geographic expansion. By rectifying structural holes, such leaders keep their companies competitive. When combined with equitable and inclusive workplaces, these are the companies that raise the competitive bar another notch.

Namely, they boost innovation and align to the greater good, ensure workforce well-being and productivity, and unleash workforce passion and potential by committing to a higher purpose. They do this by establishing a set of leadership or operating principles deeply embedded in how the leadership team makes decisions and fosters a culture where openness and dialogue are highly valued.

At Google, I experienced such an alignment between culture and action firsthand. The company embraced full transparency, so employees and outsiders alike could clearly see that, while annual objectives and key results evolved depending on market dynamics, Google's quarterly objectives and key results did not waver.

Organizational health and agility are top of mind for executives today and will only grow more important as it becomes key to companies' ability to scale and grow in the 2020s. As businesses contend with increasing uncertainty, volatility, and the eventual rebound from COVID-19, companies that have purposefully developed the organizational aspects of their enterprise—in essence, those that have institutionalized organizational health under conditions where the speed and unpredictability with which events can unfold abound—are most likely to survive and thrive.

Defining a clear purpose as the bedrock of an enterprise's strategic direction is only the beginning of a company's journey toward organizational health. The next step is to activate the purpose-led strategic direction throughout the organization by using it to shape and reshape the enterprise's culture and identity—becoming something that affects every employee's day-to-day experience.

A tighter integration between the business and culture shaping agendas—a key focus of the next chapter—allows companies and investors to seize opportunities to create new business models, transform operations, and scale their ways of working more quickly and efficiently.

Checklist for Agenda Setting

- Infuse purpose into strategic direction and seek to create value for all stakeholders, not just shareholders.
- Mobilize employees at all levels with purpose, helping them use it as a guiding light to rapidly respond to changing business conditions.
- Constantly evolve and adapt short-term strategies, but set a broad and enduring strategic direction based on purpose, value-creation drivers, and aspirations to serve as a stable guide in an ever-changing environment.
- Turn a purpose-infused strategy into action by defining clear priorities, establishing, and clarifying accountabilities, and building or evolving capabilities.
- Integrate the power of data, AI, and machine learning into strategy and practice, improving decision-making effectiveness.

2 ■ Culture

Craft a Shared but Adaptive Identity

To thrive in the digital era, organizations will need to break with their traditional views of culture, creating a new digital culture— or even a set of microcultures—that unleashes speed, innovation, belonging, agile teaming across people and smart machines, and a continuous renewal of individual mindsets to keep them fresh and relevant.

Of the seven conditions of healthy organizations, culture is the bedrock—the foundation beneath the foundation that the other six provide. Culture is what holds an organization together. While a company's identity comprises its visible, public dimension—often captured in public documents, websites, and press releases—culture is something different. It's what shapes that identity in the first place and provides the narrative that is told to new members of the organization and outsiders.

Culture is the deeper spirit of the organization felt at the unseen or unconscious levels of organizational life, forming the proverbial iceberg beneath the waterline of identity.[1] With this distinction of organizational identity as a public dimension and culture as an often-unseen dimension, we can see how leaders get themselves into trouble. The best leaders mind both dimensions, above and beneath the waterline. If they pay attention only to the identity that the organization displays publicly, they risk inadvertently—and disastrously—colliding with the underlying organizational culture. Think about iconic brands and their failed or lackluster mergers, such as Daimler and its merger with Chrysler, or the megamedia merger of AOL and Time Warner, or the Brazilian mining company Vale when it bought the Canadian iron ore giant Inco.

Fortunately, culture is increasingly at the top of the CEO and board agenda.[2] More and more leaders are talking about culture in their proxy statements, for example, as a way of describing their company's health. Between 2010 and 2016, the percentage of the world's largest companies that talked about culture in their earnings calls increased by 14 percent.[3] In 2019, 22 percent of Fortune 100 companies highlighted some of the ways they were integrating or measuring culture (beyond compliance with codes of conduct or executive pay considerations). Fifty percent of the companies that discussed culture initiatives focus on employee surveys and benchmarking reports, employee town halls, unconscious bias training, leadership off-sites, and inclusive messaging and feedback via onboarding processes, performance reviews, and exit surveys.[4] While proxy statements may not be the primary source for people and organization-related disclosures, they represent a start.

Similarly, culture is top of mind for institutional investors as well. Influential institutional investors like BlackRock and State Street Global Advisors are making company culture a business priority. Further, culture is by far the most-mentioned talent-related topic in investor conversations, with nearly 700 different companies talking about it in 2016 alone.[5]

Why so much emphasis on culture today? One reason is its link to success: in one study, companies that paid attention to culture were found to be five times more likely to perform exceptionally in the market than their non-culture-focused counterparts.[6] But also, a healthy culture is proving key to digital transformation as well as to the great management reset brought on by COVID-19. A digital culture helps to speed up decision making, fostering autonomy and empowerment among employees and ultimately making the culture attractive to more talent.

Further, given how the pandemic affected the way businesses deliver value and operate, culture becomes important for effective functioning. As researcher Fons Wijnhoven notes, "The higher the complexity and dynamic nature of the environment employees are operating in, the stronger the [cultural] norms need to be. The greater the extent of matching between the [cultural] norms and the organizational requirements, the greater the speed of functioning and output delivery."[7]

In other words, to adapt, leaders must enable the unlearning of outdated cultural norms to facilitate the learning of new ones that will increase speed and improve execution in a digital context. CEOs and senior leaders have seen and continue to learn that a distinct culture and organizational identity is difficult to replicate. In a world in which technology, processes, and even business strategies can easily be imitated by others, culture may become the defining difference between companies that outperform the market and those that don't. (See the sidebar "Culture Pays Dividends.")

This chapter will explore how to lay the foundation of a shared culture for your company that is distinctive yet adaptive—and how to overcome some of the stumbling blocks you might encounter along the way. But first: Just what kind of culture should organizations be trying to create today?

Every Culture Should Be a Digital Culture

Before digitization, existing corporate cultures were enough for companies to succeed in terms of competition. But now digitization has brought new business and organizational related requirements for culture. In the digital age, then, every business must be

Culture Pays Dividends

Shaping or transforming culture presents an opportunity to leverage it as an asset to create value. Why? Because it plays a key role in how leaders make decisions to achieve their growth objectives. This is particularly true for hypergrowth companies, where people and their judgments are the chief assets. Just as every company is a portfolio of assets with an objective of achieving financial health, so too is culture a lever that can be used to augment a company's strategy and organizational health.

Few companies, however, fully capitalize on their culture as a portfolio of assets—primarily because they view culture as hard to calculate in dollars and cents. Meanwhile, companies that do invest in and measure culture have demonstrated clear bottom-line impact when they've aligned mindsets and behaviors with strategies and operating plans. Indeed, companies such as Microsoft and Netflix have not only proven it's possible to earn a measurable return on investments toward shaping organizational culture, they've also shown that executives should and can *expect* such returns.

Consider research on culture and performance conducted by John Kotter and James Heskett. Studying the largest firms in 22 different U.S. industries, they showed that firms with strong cultures outperformed—by a large margin—those that did not have strong cultures. In fact, over an 11-year period, firms with strong "performance" cultures—or cultures that promote decisiveness and standards of excellence and ensure direct accountability—increased revenues by an average of 682 percent versus 166 percent for firms that measured lower on these attributes. Furthermore, such firms grew their stock prices by 901 percent (versus 74 percent) and improved their net incomes by 756 percent (versus 1 percent). Kotter and Heskett also make the point that while business strategy can be mimicked by competitors, culture is very difficult to replicate.[8]

In my own research on culture-shaping initiatives, I have found they can be divided into four distinct asset classes (or subcultures), based on the type of value the initiatives create, the optimal way to manage these activities, and the nature of investments they require. Note how this schema clearly shows culture as a balanced mix of assets that has the potential to improve returns, depending on the extent to which they do each of the following:

- **Enable strategy.** These subcultures (what I call "strategy enablers") facilitate superior performance by enhancing the top line with breakthrough innovations. Consider General Electric's move to separate and then fold in its digital business. GE established its Silicon Valley–based software center, part of GE Global Research, initially as a startup that separated digital teams from the main business, thereby enabling the digital unit to operate with a distinct culture and practices such as agile methodologies. After achieving some success, GE only then combined all of its technology efforts with the software center to form the GE Digital business unit and appointed chief digital officers for GE's other business units. It hired a talent acquisition leader who brought in differentiated hiring practices and made some policy and compensation changes to the traditional GE model to be competitive. It then rolled out many of its agile practices (later dubbed FastWorks mode) to other parts of the organization.
- **Multiply talent.** These subcultures ("talent multipliers") elevate brand equity and trust by creating a distinct identity built around a company's employee value proposition to society. One company that took the talent multiplier stance to heart is BMW's Project i. Founded in 2011 as a BMW sub-brand that manufactures plug-in electric vehicles, the group operated with an entirely

(continued)

different culture and set of metrics and incentives. As Ulrich Kranz, its leader until mid-2017, explains, "I had the freedom to assemble a team the way I wanted. The project was not tied to one of the company's brands, so it could tackle any problem. We were allowed to completely break away from the existing structures."[9]

- **Enhance efficiency.** Such subcultures ("efficiency enhancers") improve effectiveness and productivity by, for example, reducing overhead costs associated with a reorganization, ensuring the ROI of restructuring costs supports current and future business needs. Qantas launched its subsidiary low-cost airline, Jetstar Airways, in response to the threat posed by low-cost airline Virgin Blue. Since its launch, Jetstar has had an entirely different cost structure, culture, and operating model and has performed with success and higher margins than Qantas. Recently, the two organizations have worked on creating more synergies by improving cost efficiencies and embracing a first-mover advantage in 5G network capabilities.[10]

- **Mitigate risk.** These subcultures ("risk mitigators") reduce risk by identifying, quantifying, and proactively managing risks of poor decision making. For example, in 2013, State Street created a new business called State Street Global Exchange—a business devoted to data and analytics that clients buy independently of the company's core services.[11] It operates with a distinctively agile culture and generates several hundred million of the total State Street revenue.

a digital business. Being a digital business requires not only external and internal focus—companies need to be able to invent totally new, disruptive, digital business models. Digitization therefore cannot be thought of in terms of silos; it requires cross-company collaboration to cover the different aspects of digitization and to make digitization a company's guiding strategic and culture agenda.

That's why being a truly digital company today means creating a digital culture. In practice, this means that leaders will be called upon to leverage five keys to shaping and nurturing cultures that encourage, among other things:

- A challenger mindset
- Innovation and decision making at lightning speed
- Empowered, agile teams augmented and enabled by intelligent machines
- Radical transparency
- An obsession with the ethical use of data

And they must be able to do those five things at the individual, team, and enterprise level. (See the sidebar "Strong Cultures Need Strong Leaders—and Operating Models.") In other words, today's businesses—already operating at an unprecedented scale and level of exponential change—are being forced to innovate and evolve their operations and management practices to meet new digital and societal demands.

Unfortunately, organizations are falling short of those expectations. Research published by the MIT Sloan School of Management reveals that out of over 4,000 executives surveyed across 120 countries, just 12 percent strongly agree that their leaders have the right culture and mindsets to lead them forward in the digital age.[12] For example, not enough company leaders are truly equipping and empowering their people to make decisions and execute tasks. And many leaders retain a shortsighted focus that limits the organization's potential to engage in digital.

Organizations that hope to evolve and reach their full potential, therefore, need leaders who can connect the dots to reveal a clear picture of the business landscape—and what the recent flurry of changes represents for their companies. Specifically, to prosper in a high-speed, disruptive environment powered by digital technologies,

Strong Cultures Need Strong Leaders— and Operating Models

Culture puts a premium on leadership. As Ed Schein, MIT professor emeritus and the pioneering author of *Organizational Culture and Leadership*, points out, culture is largely set by the leaders of an organization, and the only real thing of importance that leaders do is shape and manage the culture.[13] Leaders need to be intensely aware of how they can leverage culture—at the enterprise, subculture, and microculture levels—as an asset to optimize how leaders run and grow their business.

Thus, culture, and all its facets, is an intangible asset, made up of things like the capacity to innovate, the ability to develop a deep and diverse leadership pipeline, the ability to match talent with new opportunities, the capacity to create and sustain a brand that has appeal to both customers and employees, and the dedication to excellence that comes across in every customer encounter. Top managers must carefully cultivate and manage these intangible assets while resisting the tendency to place them into neat buckets as they do with accounting assets. Why? Because these assets are embedded in *human* relationships—the ability of capable talent to find one another, crowdsource new information, and combine insight and advanced data and analytics into new platforms and services. They are embedded in talent—the discretionary effort that individual contributors, teams, and teams of teams willingly apply to work that takes them from good to great.

Again, here's where the investor mindset I describe in the introduction and chapter 1 becomes critically important. When considering culture, leaders must adopt the mindset of a portfolio investor whose assets are multiple cultural assets that must be managed. When such investment management is done well, a company's culture and identity can truly realize their full potential as the company outperforms its competitors.

Leaders and the cultures they build are the engine for innovation and growth in the digital world. For example, innovation is not a tangible asset until it produces a tangible outcome such as software as a service that can be consistently replicated and easily consumed. No one doubts that providing on-demand cloud computing platforms and APIs to individuals, companies, and governments on a metered pay-as-you-go basis is an astonishing innovation that has generated admirable cash flow for Amazon Web Services (AWS). But Amazon's market valuation is not based solely on the projected revenue from its AWS platform; it is based heavily on what the market expects in terms of Amazon's ability to launch more products and services like the AWS technology and business. The market is betting that Amazon not only has a capacity to innovate, but that its innovations will differentiate it in the cloud wars. Investors are betting on Amazon's culture.

Culture also puts a premium on processes in the operating model. Consider how National Grid sought to alleviate pain points in the processes of its Electric Distribution Operations (EDO) business and to mitigate challenges such as delays, multiple handoffs, and unclear responsibilities. To take this challenge head-on, CEO John Pettigrew leveraged business process redesign to shift and embed its newly desired behaviors in three ways.

First, expert and process teams engaged in culture audits, assessing *core behaviors* such as collaboration and teamwork as well as accountability against key business and HR processes to identify and close gaps. Second, once the audit was completed, the company redesigned its processes to include the desired shifts to new behaviors such as taking responsibility for one's actions, decisions, and results and building alignment that delivers outstanding teamwork. Lastly, the process teams assessed HR support for critical areas such as the employee value

(*continued*)

proposition. Specifically, HR needed to help prospective employees understand what made National Grid unique. It also needed to align the performance-management process with desired culture and leadership qualities for nonunion employees. And HR also needed help with integrating and encouraging desired culture behaviors in performance management systems and talent practices, such as recruitment, selection, and leadership development. Making these changes enabled HR to simplify its own processes to increase accountability and to reduce pain points. The outcome was a culture that supported internal customer service standards and a better employee experience. Ultimately, all of these shifts enabled EDO to foster a culture of accountability and collaboration relatively quickly.

To summarize, then, both the organization's leaders and operations must have a hand in the way culture unfolds and transforms. Leaders must understand that changing culture is about changing behavior. And the most effective way to modify behavior is by designing an environment in which people's work throughout the organization is easier to observe and manage. By putting in place the appropriate structure, process, and metrics, leaders have a better idea of both the observable and more hidden aspects of behavior, which can be harder to influence—such as attitudes, beliefs, and unwritten rules.

companies will need to break with traditional views of culture in three ways:

- First, leaders of companies today will need to evolve their view of culture as a monolithic construct and instead see it as a "culture of cultures"—or multiple subcultures and microcultures that may need to differ based on the goals and needs of a particular group. Why? Because as companies mature and shift from small-scale experiments to wide-scale adoption, organizations need a culture condu-

cive to the execution of their strategy, which may vary
from one business or product area to another.

- Second, leaders will need to embrace a view of culture that
is distinct from but related to organizational identity,
expressed in public opinion about the company and the
way people within the company internalize the cultural
norms to identify themselves as part of that group or
organization.

- Finally, leaders will need to view culture as a set of intangible assets that ought to be managed as vigorously and
rigorously as the economics of the business.

Consider Google, which is well known for its very strong, distinctive culture. At its core, Google's startup and "university"-oriented
culture is pervasive, characterized by campus-like design features,
experimentation, speed, and a flat hierarchy. Yet, as the company
has matured and moved into new businesses over the years, subcultures across its portfolio of businesses have emerged. For example,
the "creatives" group at YouTube or the "enterprise" group at the Cloud
formed because a specific type of culture was needed to achieve the
businesses' outcomes.

Some observers have even speculated whether, given how many
different cultures exist within it, Google has outgrown its corporate
culture altogether—that perhaps the company is going through a
kind of midlife identity crisis.[14] What those pundits aren't considering, however, is the underlying but strong and commonly held
representation of Google's subcultures, as I experienced directly as a
Google employee. In these subcultures, individual perceptions create a sense of identity, identification, and belonging shared within
that particular group. For example, people who work for Google are
"Googlers"; new employees are "Nooglers"; and older Google employees are "Greyglers." Even employees who leave the company retain, to
some extent, their Google identity as an "Xoogler" or "Ex-Googler."

In other words, identity at Google adapts as the context shifts.
Why does this matter? To start, leaders (and investors) place a great
emphasis on both their ability to invest in, grow, or select promising

companies as well as their capacity to add value through financial, governance, and operational engineering. While important, it's not enough. What is required is greater attention to cultural engineering and a reality check that an organization's identity may need to evolve over time and be dynamic rather than static.

Note that particular company cultures can actually help define the success of the organization. Nonhierarchical, collaborative, speedy cultures—like Google's, Haier's, and Unilever's—can support an organization's ability to quickly pivot and adapt to fast-changing business conditions. Indeed, as Leena Nair, Unilever's former chief human resources officer, observed, "culture is the new structure"—the glue that binds people together when boundaries dissolve and cross-functional teaming emerges.[15]

But even in organizations that haven't fully adopted this kind of speedy, flexible culture throughout the enterprise, sometimes micro-cultures of teams that are responsive to businesses can emerge to tackle novel issues and challenges, complete with identities and names to mark their distinct culture. Think the U.S. Navy's elite SEALs special ops force or its flight demonstration squadron, the Blue Angels.

Moreover, as a company grows and changes, the importance and type of culture of its business will shift over time. (See the sidebar "Inflection Points: Evolution and Revolution Revisited for the Digital Age.") That is, culture is important in different ways at different developmental stages of an organization.

Shaping Healthy Cultures

Today, change is the new normal—or "never normal," to be more precise. To embrace disruptive change in a digital and AI-first context, senior leaders, whether they are CEOs or investors, must fully engage in a deep shift in the way that they think about their business models and culture. Clearly, stagnant mindsets yield stagnant outcomes. Change, especially culture change, teaches valuable lessons. Often it requires a *reset of deeply ingrained mindsets* buried in the managerial psyche that have become part of the company's

Inflection Points: Evolution and Revolution Revisited for the Digital Age

Here's what seems to be an immutable law of organizational evolution: Most companies don't make it past the startup phase. Those that do manage to grow and mature must overcome a variety of organizational challenges along the way. But many don't make it. Why? The answer is simple: culture.

Every culture, like every company, is unique. Successful companies, whether they are publicly held or venture capital or private equity backed, experience periods of evolution punctuated by moments of challenge. Depending on the funding life cycle as well as the maturity and size of the organization, companies often face similar cultural challenges and implement similar solutions:

- **Startup.** In this stage of the funding life cycle, companies experience growth through creativity, innovation, and spontaneity. But over time they need to develop repeatable practices, and management structures are put in place, ultimately changing the role of the founder. At this stage founders, and leaders more generally, develop a unified set of initial cultural principles. They make investments with care, emphasizing cultural fit with any new addition to their business portfolio. The cultural architecture at this stage should support companies that are growth-oriented and branching into new markets, but that aren't looking for rapid entry or first-mover advantage.
- **Early.** In this stage, replication accelerates scale, but as the organization grows the founder or leader is called upon to focus more on the challenge of leadership, on motivating and inspiring employees and preparing them for managerial roles. The cultural architecture at this stage may require leaders to empower teams, since

(*continued*)

the organization will most likely thrive in a culture shaped by those who are closest to the operations involved. Leaders therefore see great value in keeping culture local, relying on the use of processes and structures to delegate responsibilities.

- **Growth.** In this stage, a company's diversification (and delegation) unlocks the next wave of growth, aided by more formalized rules about operations, resource allocation, promotion, and the like. However, complaints tend to multiply at this stage about bureaucracy and red tape impeding fast decision making and entrepreneurial growth. In this stage, leaders architect cultures and pursue outcomes through a process of give and take among independent businesses, and between independent businesses and the enterprise or corporate center. Leaders may often operate as brokers and connectors when expanding digitally to access new markets or to orchestrate and integrate new talent and new ideas. They are more concerned with the quality of the ecosystems in which they engage and less concerned with speed and efficiency in the short term.

- **Mature.** In this stage, sometimes referred to as the unicorn or pre-IPO stage, better collaboration through a clearer division of labor between headquarters and the growing array of operating units helps solve the problem of red tape. But organizational identity emerges as a challenge, particularly the question of how to maintain the centrality of founder values when the founders' hands-on involvement diminishes. In this stage, leaders tend to focus most on the organizational structures and processes that tie their business or portfolio of businesses together. As scope and scale increase, leaders view process, structure, and governance as the most immediately useful levers for fostering a unified culture across the company.

While these stages represent a continuum rather than a set of binary choices, they shed light on distinct patterns that frame a "culture of cultures"—meaning that, more and more, leaders are being called to engage in culture shaping as "portfolio investors" and to manage a portfolio of independent subcultures across an enterprise. Shaping culture, let alone microcultures, at each stage of growth and maturity is essential for the success of companies pursuing digital transformations and risky investment strategies. In fact, culture shaping has become one of the most important areas to explore and discuss in founder and investor circles, and by extension, boardrooms. When founders and investors approach this task with a portfolio mentality, leaders can attain a stronger grip on the many cultures that range across their portfolio of businesses and the required focus at every stage of organizational maturity.[16]

"organizational identity," forged to help companies and their people make sense of the organization as a whole.

To thrive, organizations and their people need to continually challenge and adapt their mindsets to keep them fresh and relevant. (See the table "Why Mindsets Matter and How to Understand Them.") That's why healthy cultures often contain mental maps or assumptions, values, and artifacts that speak to the organization's experience of change and transformation.

Consider retired U.S. general Stanley McChrystal's perspective, described in *Team of Teams: New Rules of Engagement for a Complex World*,[17] that small, agile teams are at the center where targeted action is enabled through rapid cycles of learning and doing—a practice at the heart of fast experimentation. The core idea is to move from a historical command-and-control model to leading teams to an adaptive paradigm that emphasizes speed and agility. He and his coauthors share at great length what enables the effectiveness of the team-of-teams strategy—a general shared belief underlying the shared

Why Mindsets Matter and How to Understand Them

In Ryan Gottfredson and Chris Reina's research, they describe mindsets as "leaders' mental lenses that dictate what information they take in and use to make sense of and navigate the situations they encounter." The following table describes a number of common mindsets.

Mindset Type	Description
Growth mindset	Belief that people, including oneself, can change their talents, abilities, and intelligence
Fixed mindset	Belief that people do not change their talents, abilities, and intelligence
Learning mindset	Belief that people are motivated toward increasing their competence and mastering something new
Performance mindset	Belief that people are motivated toward gaining favorable judgments (or avoiding negative judgments) about one's competence
Deliberative mindset	Belief that one should develop a heightened receptiveness to all kinds of information as a way to ensure that they think and act as optimally as possible
Implemental mindset	Belief that people should focus mainly on implementing decisions, which closes them off to new and different ideas and information
Promotion mindset	Belief that people should be focused on winning and gains
Prevention mindset	Belief that people should focus on avoiding losses and preventing problems at all costs

Adapted from Ryan Gottfredson and Chris Reina, "To Be a Great Leader, You Need the Right Mindset," *Harvard Business Review*, January 17, 2020.

identity: "Purpose affirms trust, trust affirms purpose, and together they forge common experiences that bond individuals" to coalesce as a team. By being conscious and explicit about the culture and shared identity, people can become more aware of what mindsets still work and which need to change. This allows them to transform far more easily to overcome a disruption, move from one stage of growth to another, or scale and surmount an obstacle to thrive and grow.

Another example of shaping healthy cultures emerged from one fast-growing company with which I worked as it reshaped its culture and scaled its operations to achieve a new chapter of growth.

How One Tech Company Reshaped Its Culture for Tomorrow

As companies move to recover from the carnage of the global pandemic, some of their current ways of working—including things that have fueled their success—will prove to be liabilities. For example, a fast-growing tech company that I will call OpCo recently found itself at a crossroads when it reached a new stage of growth and maturity. It needed to find a way forward that would align with its goal and north star: to achieve profitable growth.

To determine what OpCo might need in order to scale responsibly, the chief operating officer engaged me to conduct an independent due diligence of the company's performance across a number of organizational health dimensions. Notably I focused on leadership, culture, and the organization's design and their overall alignment to the company's strategic direction. After various alignment workshops, offsites, deep structure interviews, and focus groups to gather feedback and refine the mindsets and behavioral definitions, I then partnered with top management, high-potential senior managers, and selected employee representatives to design a portfolio of targeted interventions, such as structural clarity and prioritization, decision rights, and behavioral nudging to put those new cultural principles into practice.

After a series of deep structure interviews with OpCo's top management, a review of performance and organizational data, and in-depth discussions and executive counseling sessions, the challenges OpCo faced became clear. To achieve a bold new growth strategy and improve the company's operational prowess, OpCo needed to overcome at least two cultural challenges:

- Its workforce was not well coordinated, and its overall structure and how it prioritized and deployed resources to match its growing scale and complexity needed further development.
- At the same time, OpCo needed to improve subpar relationships with its partners.

OpCo was pretty good at spending time on the "what" of its work—the objectives and the key results of its efforts. This included things like launching new products and services in new global markets, strengthening its policies to create a better user experience, delivering business plans to shore up up-and-coming creative employees within the company, building an infrastructure to support scale, and so much more.

Yet, as an organization, OpCo's top management and its respective business unit teams spent less time on the "how" of its work. For instance, some individuals and teams in OpCo had become increasingly focused on optimizing for their individual silos across the team, rather than solving for the business as a whole. To be successful, OpCo had about an 18-month time horizon to find ways to refocus on "how"—by aligning the top management team, encouraging each member to role model the desired shifts, and integrating a new set of mindsets and behaviors into the ways of working and policies of the company.

OpCo's COO also identified a few additional problems. One was cultural rifts between the product and engineering teams that were creating problems. The tensions brewing between these two groups and other factions across the business were being felt throughout the organization and contributing to a divisive culture. In addition, the performance management system rewarded individual contributions, which reinforced a cultural norm and set of existing practices focused on individualized versus shared incentives. This led many inside OpCo to question the business's ability to achieve expected growth.

Fortunately, the COO understood that to restore confidence and ease the tension, OpCo needed to unite around a shared set of cultural principles at every level—while somehow retaining the unique set of subcultures within the company. OpCo's leadership accomplished this feat by partnering closely with the company's ecosystem of creative artists, which enabled the company to adapt swiftly and stay fresh and relevant in response to creative trends as they emerged and shifted.

What soon became clear to the entire top team was that the way the company had built and invested in operations would not ultimately enable the business growth it needed down the road. Organizationally and culturally, OpCo was at a tipping point. While the COO and his managers saw themselves as the foundation on which the business was built, their operations were too brittle and incomplete to bear the burden of growth. For example, a weak technological infrastructure inhibited the platform's ability to expand and support a growing number of users.

To combat this challenge, the COO invested heavily in improving OpCo's organizational health, starting with chartering a new path forward for executional excellence. For example, the COO wanted to make a shift in his own role. Although he would continue as the operational muscle for the business, he would streamline the number of handoffs where platform improvements were needed. This move would decrease the amount of coordination required while enhancing the speed by which teams could troubleshoot platform glitches. The COO would also restructure a number of decentralized partnership teams to act as a single team, with a dedicated leader, which created a direct line of accountability and decision making to support and power the next generation of growth as a strategic partner. Essentially, the COO understood that the organization, beginning with the top team, needed to be explicit about what guided it as a whole, the collective behaviors and mindsets that informed its key decisions, and the social contract between individuals across units, the organization, and with each other.

To move toward becoming efficient at scale, the company needed to invest far more than it had in the past in robust tools and rigorous processes and metrics to track risks. More substantively, what

OpCo was missing and needed desperately were the essential inter-operative protocols for interdisciplinary coordination, accountability, and support.

Working with OpCo's COO and top team, my colleagues and I quickly defined a new set of mindsets and behaviors and developed a culture-change plan along with it. This required OpCo's top team to turn broad themes—its "first" or "cultural" principles—into a set of clearly defined mindsets and behaviors for improved focus, clarity of purpose, cross-team collaboration, and teamwork and accountability. For example, to build the executional muscle needed for scale and consensus around new ways of working, the managers tasked their teams with forming small working groups, which would decide how best to integrate and embed the new principles into their teamwork. Essentially, the new mindset brought the top team together with the next layers of management below it to craft a plan for embedding cultural change. Thus, the teams collaboratively developed a "culture change plan" that would ensure alignment, instill confidence across OpCo, and deliver quick wins and long-term operational improvements. Because the culture needed to evolve into one that was comfortable with ambiguity while sustaining high-speed change, OpCo needed to focus on proactively balancing responsible growth with the real risks of employee burnout.

In the end, OpCo rolled out its cultural transformation companywide. To speed execution and adoption, change workshops ensued worldwide, and "change champions" at all management levels were empowered to embed the new culture principles. The result of this cultural transformation? In a surprisingly short amount of time—months rather than years—OpCo improved its operational performance and made significant strides toward achieving its objectives and key results around profitable growth.

Culture in the Digital Age

Digital disruption, new consumer expectations, the great reset due to COVID-19, and an exponential pace of change continue to prompt companies to renew their focus on growth. In a digital and AI-first context, that means the journey toward scaling and growth rests on a company's ability to create space for experimentation to scale innovation at speed. Companies will also be called upon to adopt automation as a strategy for optimizing costs and efficiency, and to create learn-it-all, customer-centric cultures that embrace AI and advanced analytics to drive agile and evidence-based decision making. And of course, companies will need to encourage a challenger mindset to drive disruption and transformation.

Over the past decade, digital and AI technologies have shifted how businesses shape their cultures and the way they operate. (See the table "How AI and Digital Strengthen or Transform Organizational Culture.") But it turns out that organizations themselves also must change their cultures as they transform into digital businesses. This is especially true since 2020, when digital transformation picked up even more momentum across all sectors and industries. While this focus on a digital culture did not start with the wrenching changes brought on by the global pandemic, racial protests, and economic turbulence, it nevertheless was certainly accelerated by those things. Accordingly, companies began to reappraise and, in some cases, fundamentally change their corporate identity and culture.

Yet culture itself sometimes inhibits change. "The way we do things around here" can be the best excuse for not transforming. That's why strong, healthy cultures are the ones that develop their muscle memories for organizational resilience. Just as the way we ride a bike gets stored in the body and remains available for future use, so too must companies craft corporate identities and supporting cultures that become second nature, enabling leaders and everyone across the business to continuously embrace change, bridge the culture divide of moving from analog to digital, and prepare for the next stage of growth. So, what keeps companies from doing that?

Five Stumbling Blocks to Culture Change

First, companies are often held back because they've adopted a silo mentality, either failing to embrace a true system of interdependency or obsessing over a core business or function while ignoring other businesses. The latter can lead to complacency and reticence to move

How AI and Digital Strengthen or Transform Organizational Culture

AI or Digital Technology	How It Strengthens or Transforms the Culture of Organizations
Digital nudges	Digital nudges use familiar online technologies such as SMS text messages, email, push notifications, mobile apps, and gamification to encourage people to take desired actions that can influence and reinforce the culture.
AI-based talent selection and matching tools	Data-based algorithms can help organizations screen people based on cultural fit for an organization or a team (identifying employees who can work well together) and match them accordingly.
Sentiment analysis	Sentiment analysis (also known as opinion mining or emotion AI) uses natural language processing, text analysis, computational linguistics, and biometrics to identify and quantify the emotional states of employees and subjective view of culture.
Organizational network analysis	By using digital technologies to mine data regarding who is connected to whom and the nature of their relationships, organizations can better understand their culture and identify cultural influencers and change agents in a scientifically and business-proven way and identify the informal network and/or the informal influencers too.
AI collaboration tools	A slew of technologies designed to enhance collaboration and bust silos through transparent information sharing can help create a more agile, open, and collaborative culture.

beyond the status quo in how the businesses beyond the core operate, which stagnates growth. Consider the inability of Digital Equipment Corporation (DEC) to evolve its business model and fully shift to personal computers as a means to ensure the company's survival and overall longevity. Simply put: DEC's leaders failed to anticipate and see what was emerging in personal computing.

Second, a company's reluctance to change creates a tendency to not look outside enough and to ignore minor threats that can sometimes become major issues. Consider Blockbuster's dire mistake of ignoring the rise of new digital channels like Netflix. Once considered the crown jewel of video rental, Blockbuster went bankrupt in 2010 because it failed to disrupt its business model and take a short-term profit hit for a long-term gain—a lesson that is all too familiar for those who miss out on first mover or early adopter advantage.

Third, excitement over new things creates habitual routines of going after shiny objects and then quickly abandoning them when interest is lost. Remember "New Coke," which later became Coke II, and then was removed from the market altogether in the early 2000s?[18] To move to a desired future, companies need to place strategic bets, or as former chairman and CEO of the Coca-Cola Company Roberto C. Goizueta said, "take intelligent risks" and stick with them.

Fourth, companies can fail to make fast, evidence-based decisions if they don't evolve to embrace analytics, digital technology, and data. That is what happened to old stalwarts such as Sears, Toys "R" Us, and others across the retail landscape. Slow to shift from traditional physical experiences and launch their digital transformations, they were unable to fully embrace omnichannel experiences in a timely way.

Finally, companies that have not developed a mindset of questioning the status quo or learning quickly from their mistakes ("failing fast") will find themselves continually stumbling. Think of Nokia, when its operating model and internal politics left it unable to embrace the shift from being a product-based company to a platform-based one.

As we move into the next iteration of the digital age of business, many of today's organizational cultures—especially those driven

---

Cultural Shifts Needed for the Digital Age

From:	To:
Gut-feel driven	Data and AI driven
Insular thinking	Outside-in entrepreneurial thinking
Traditional workforce	Flexible, gig-like workforce
Risk averse	Agile and disruptive

---

solely by a competitive, profit-making motive rather than by what benefits the organization as a whole—might no longer be fit for the future. They will be outdone by those with a bias toward purpose and speed-driven cultures that put people and intelligent machines at their center. Consider, for example, how larger welding companies are implementing employee-performance or welding-monitoring technologies that provide real-time feedback to welders. In an industry in which performance was once almost exclusively subjective ("you know a good weld when you see it"), applying objective criteria to performance is allowing welders to automate their performance evaluation and feedback.

All of which is to say that, to thrive in the digital age, most leaders will need to completely reshape their cultures. In my executive experiences and consulting work advising companies across a wide range of industries (including both big and small tech) to help them scale and grow, I've seen a number of ways that companies can change to best embrace the future. (See the box "Cultural Shifts Needed for the Digital Age.") To maximize their full potential, cultures need to become more data- and AI-driven, entrepreneurial, gig-like, agile, and optimized to move fast. Key will be adopting an investor style of thinking—such as attracting top-notch talent, employing a fresh look at value creation, and adopting what may at times be painful short-term measures that catapult the company to mid-term advantage.

Both leaders and investors need to shift their mindsets about the value of culture and how it should be managed. In my experience, companies can benefit from applying an investor mentality by managing their culture-shaping and evolution practices as if they were made up of a portfolio of different assets, where each part of the portfolio creates a distinct type of value and where each asset needs to be managed individually. These culture-shaping practices are spread throughout the entire deal's life cycle or stage of organizational maturity.

To sum up, culture matters; organizations with higher-performing cultures create three times the return to shareholders as organizations that do not have such cultures.[19] That's why it's important for leaders and organizations to make culture a top priority and see it as a "culture of cultures." Thus, they embrace the view that organizational identities adapt as companies mature, and that cultural health ought to be managed as rigorously as financial health, and as one of the most essential drivers of business performance.

Ultimately, however, any change in culture becomes possible only to the extent that the organization fosters forward-thinking leadership—as we will explore in the next chapter.

Checklist for Agenda Setting

- Adopt an investor mindset of managing and shaping a "culture of cultures," with culture made up of a portfolio of distinct assets that need to be managed differently.
- Apply the same rigor and discipline that you use to measure and optimize financial health to measuring and optimizing your organization's cultural health.
- To thrive in the digital era, start transforming culture to become more data- and AI-driven, entrepreneurial, gig-like, agile, and optimized to move fast.
- Use new digital advances and AI—such as employee performance monitoring software that can analyze and interpret on-the-job trends for productivity improvement—to strengthen or transform culture.

3 ■ Leadership

Be Agile and Human-Centric in the Age
of Intelligent Machines

Today, no leader can go it alone. The turbulent business environment of the 2020s demands a new form of leadership—the ability to lead *collectively*. More and more, leaders will form ensembles
that band and disband around opportunities and problems as
they arise. Practicing agile decision making and judgment will also
be key to realizing the full potential of people and technology.

Companies can't afford to skimp on top talent. That truism takes
on magnified resonance when we consider the hyper-transparency
of the digital world. Today, how capable a leader is (or isn't) becomes
apparent pretty quickly, both inside and outside the organization.
Consider, for example, the general practice of social media sites like
Glassdoor, where active and former employees are willing to share
their views on companies' compensation and diversity practices and
rate the performance of leaders as senior as the CEO. We thus
can think of outstanding leadership as the anchor on which our other

six organizational conditions rely: without it, nothing much else can function correctly. And the stakes are high indeed: an analysis of 180 portfolio companies by Blackstone's former operating partner Sandy Ogg showed that "getting talent right in the first year achieved 2.5 times return on investment for those organizations."[1]

But what does getting leadership right mean, exactly, in the age of intelligent machines? It means being agile. Think about it: even the most advanced, AI-enhanced decision support systems won't help an organization whose leaders can't act quickly. In the new world, where algorithms can call the shots with a simple click of an app or tap on a touchscreen, a company's leadership must be nimble if it hopes to evade disruptions in the market—much less to capitalize on them.

Call it a case of slow organizational reflexes. Data platforms, AI, and autonomous learning loops can provide a company with the foresight to spot an opportunity to create and capture value or market share. But that opportunity may evaporate if leaders can't act quickly to allocate resources and deploy top talent with the right experiences and skills to take advantage of it.

This chapter will explore how the upper echelons of organizations can learn to act with both speed and accuracy to make better decisions in the digital era. Key will be learning to share power by leading collectively and staying focused on the human beings behind the machines.

How Can Leaders Become More Agile?

Top management in hypergrowth companies must be capable of agile decision making and what Noel Tichy and Warren Bennis characterize as the fundamental essence of leadership: judgment—that is, "the extent to which leaders can frame issues, make smart calls, and ensure that they are well executed."[2] But judgment isn't just an approach to be applied in times of crisis and environmental jolts; these days, it's a hallmark of top-performing publicly held companies and private equity firms that recognize and capitalize on the opportunity during intense times of massive reset. Simply stated: top management must know the domain in which they play and where their real value resides.

Thus, the answer for many leaders to the question of how to gain agility is first to *master the art of judgment.* For example, Kewsong Lee, CEO for private equity investment firm the Carlyle Group, sees judgment as dependent at least in part on cultivating a diverse and inclusive workplace.[3] Says Lee, "We are in the judgment business. Great investing requires great decisions. And in order to make great decisions and great judgments, you need a wide variety of perspectives and diverse backgrounds, diverse experiences, and creativity that you can pull into your investment process and say, 'How can we make the best decisions possible?'"

Such a mindset triggers better performance in companies. "You can't be great investors without this intellectual curiosity to want to understand different views, different perspectives, or different ways to look at a situation," Lee says. "Our investment ethos at Carlyle is one that actively seeks out different perspectives and different points of view, because we believe that it makes us better at making informed investment decisions."

Today, with advances in AI and analytics bringing greater speed and accuracy, leaders will have more time and capacity to make better judgments by cultivating relationships and making evidence-based decisions. Which means, ideally, more decision making that is both socially desirable and financially defensible. (See the table "How AI Can Unleash a Healthier Leadership Team.")

Second, *create an "investor mindset."* Having a cadre of leaders at the helm who possess a private equity–like investor mindset, rooted in judgment and commercial savvy, to focus on key drivers of business performance and investor returns is both a source of strategic differentiation and risk mitigation. Again, as CEO of a private equity firm, Kewsong Lee naturally relies on an investor mindset, which he sees as inextricably linked to the Carlyle Group's values of equity and inclusion. "I am a firm believer in the word 'and,' not 'or,'" he says. "Our job is to drive performance and deliver great returns, and have positive change and positive impact. You can do both. . . . We are not doing good just for the sake of doing good,

How AI Can Unleash a Healthier Leadership Team

How AI Can Help	How It Works
Improve decision making	AI and analytics can bring greater speed and accuracy to decision making, helping leaders make well-informed, evidence-based decisions—and in the zone of action needing their focus.
Improve emotional and relational intelligence	"Affective computing"[4] can generate insights into leaders' emotional responses and patterns and make suggestions for how to improve them at the individual or team level. Likewise, AI can reveal relationship patterns and interactions, making suggestions to leaders on how to improve them.
Find novel, disruptive insights	AI filters the signal from the noise of the nondigital world, generating space and thinking time for leaders. By letting algorithms work on a vast landscape of data, they can generate unexpected insights and report back only what leaders need to know and when they need to know it.
Create greater top team diversity	By putting AI on the leadership team, the team can gain greater diversity of thinking and better hone the skill of judgment.
Build leadership bench strength	AI can help develop stronger demand forecasting capabilities; identify potential next-generation leaders across the entire enterprise based on data-based indicators, behaviors, and performance; and surface critical insights such as an executive's readiness or flight risk when performing succession planning.
Develop leadership skills	AI can act as a leader's personal advisor, providing insights that can help develop critical leadership skills such as communication, self-awareness, and time or priority management.

but because it is the smart thing to do. . . . If you have that mind-set, you will see that diversity makes you perform better."

Third, *create ensembles of leadership* that shapeshift and reconfig-ure themselves as needed based on the evolving demands of the busi-ness. A number of company leadership teams already function this way, as I'll describe shortly.

These three leadership principles apply equally to leaders in blue-chip organizations, hypergrowth startups, and investors in venture capital and private equity firms. Having the right leaders who know how best to partner with investors and board directors to shape a strategy to deliver on the investment and execute on a transforma-tion is essential to driving business results. Successful VC and PE companies typically invest over a five-to-eight-year horizon to align their top management teams—deal teams, operating teams, and portfolio company management—with their investment proposals, the value-creation plans within those investments, and the orga-nizational levers they can pull to optimize them. This ongoing exer-cise in leadership and organizational alignment—typically requiring engagement with the board—involves much more than risk man-agement or crisis management.

Consider: When the eye-popping disruption of the pandemic hit, one sports media company with three different businesses across its portfolio experienced the pain dramatically. The company's manage-ment and its PE owners knew they would have to recalibrate toward a future in digital. The challenge, however, was the level of fragmen-tation that existed across its pool of analytics talent. "They had three or four people in analytics across different parts of their busi-nesses, and to be fair, most of these people were doing reporting, not analytics," said one PE human capital advisor I interviewed, who was hired to understand the health of the company and recommend improvements to the company's organizational design.

He determined that, to become digital-centric, the sports media company would need to hire (and/or hone the abilities of) team members to reflect different skill sets—such as advanced data ana-lytics and software engineering—to upgrade the algorithm across their integrated platform. As the advisor put it, "What that means is that the CEO and board needed to think differently about how they were going to do analytics organizationally." In the end, he sketched out an operating model for the CEO and board that consolidated all of the analytics talent into a centralized analytics capability. It would be placed squarely inside the digital organization with a leader for the analytics and a matching corporate transition plan to get there—all of which would make it easier to communicate with the business and drive impact with speed.

As we saw in the case of strategic direction in the last chapter, such leadership alignment requires improving a portfolio company's organizational health across a wide array of probable scenarios. It also means gauging how well the top team can make decisions and orchestrate action across several fronts:

- How top-line growth and operational value are captured and integrated into the firm's business model
- How culture and organizational identity are shaped to meet a company's needs, both now and in the future
- How diverse talent is sourced, developed, and deployed
- How organizational designs match the business strategy and objectives and key results
- How employee well-being is tracked and improved to boost productivity
- How high-stakes change is directed and managed across an enterprise
- How the top team aligns its leaders and employees behind the key strategies

For leaders, such decisions often hinge on complex and ambiguous issues. That kind of uncertainty requires leadership deliberation, judgment, and wisdom that can be tapped as needed.

Ensemble Leadership

As a business grows ever more complex and changeable, a company can no longer rely on single individuals—or even a single team—at the top. True leadership agility means having a repertoire of standing individual teams and quickly assembling temporary groups to meet specific challenges, like leading a digital transformation. That's why nimble organizations are increasingly pulling together fluid, temporary teams of experts that configure and reconfigure themselves according to the task at hand—what Bob Thomas and I refer to as "leadership ensembles." That is, a group of executives who embody various kinds of perspective or expertise. They are brought together in intentional combinations, depending on the specific decision or business situation at hand. And since they share a set of common understandings, they can reconfigure as needed and spontaneously for effectiveness.[5]

Simply put, such ensembles comprise the right people (typically, the top 1 to 2 percent of executives and influential leaders or experts, irrespective of differences in racial or gender diversity, on the one hand, or on the other hand, functional, technical, or business diversity) in the right configurations. That is, small agile teams or working groups, management groups, or executive committees who can respond effectively to the variety of situations that a complex digital world can churn up.

The types of configurations can vary widely. As one former executive vice president at a French industrial company put it, "Sometimes we have to make quick decisions that enable us to stay on par with our competitor's pace and speed . . . even though our collective management team may not always be available at the same time. Other times, we need to convene a much larger group, an extended leadership group of sorts, to vigorously debate our options."

For example, due to the global health and economic crisis brought on by COVID-19, many companies developed temporary response teams, followed by remote work or back-to-work teams to deal with shifting realities. In some cases, racial equity project offices were set up to reckon with the corporate reforms for Black and Brown professionals in response to the protests brought on after George Floyd's killing.

What all this means is that public and privately held company leaders and boards of directors can no longer assume that top management must be organized in the typical hierarchy of executive bodies, such as an executive leadership team, an operations team, and perhaps a cross-sectional committee of high-potential middle managers. Better instead to think in terms of an agile, adaptive *network* of capable, experienced leaders who can come together quickly to apply their expertise (e.g., sector knowledge or functional expertise) to work on value creation and execution strategies, while blocking and tackling emergent challenges.

Let's look now at how such leadership agility functioned at a company I'll call HosCo, with which I worked to help it prepare for its next chapter of growth and geographical expansion. In this case, the organization, its culture, and ultimately its leadership were critical pieces to the puzzle of achieving profitable growth.

The Case of HosCo

This is the story of how HosCo, a large company in the hospitality industry that weathered dramatic organizational change for years—and which comprised multiple brands that historically operated as separate business units—succeeded in improving its organizational health. Moreover, it's the story of how a seasoned CEO and executive committee used their accumulated experience and wisdom to build a powerful network of leaders and instill an agile mindset.

HosCo's ability to create fluid, temporary teams of experts to solve problems enabled it to thrive in a hyperdriven, dynamic business environment. The company's approach to leadership and governance provides us with four valuable lessons—specifically, the need for:

- Setting the right tone at the top
- Ensuring the right talent at the top
- Enabling transformation at the top
- Creating teams at the top

Tone at the Top: Setting the Context

In the late 2000s, HosCo, a holding company of five distinct hospitality brands, was a high-performing company with strong management, a successful track record of growth, and a set of assets in the premium and deluxe segments across the hospitality industry. These included a range of guest services, from luxury all-inclusive experiences for couples to amenities, dining, and transportation fit for a large family reunion. A robust market presence across the major consumer markets allowed HosCo to derive economies of scale in operation, which enabled the company to improve its operating efficiency and margins. Some of HosCo's businesses, such as its premium brand that attracted world-class chefs and entertainers, were very profitable, while other elements of the business weighed down profitability—its short, guided tours, for example. The company's guest experience was considered best in class, which was proven repeatedly, given how favorably a new class of consumers responded to its stellar guest experiences. Yet HosCo faced several challenges to its strategy for growth.

At the time, the industry was growing at a compound annual growth rate (CAGR) of 8 percent. However, environmental legislation and regulations were affecting HosCo's operations, forcing it to increase its operating costs. While the company had an opportunity to capture a new consumer segment in an emerging market, it was wrestling with the changing demographics across its three primary growth markets—which had deteriorated consumer confidence and discretionary spending. A weak economic outlook for the primary markets of its businesses and rising labor wages in North America put the company's top- and bottom-line growth at serious risk.

HosCo's success had always been driven by a simple strategy: deliver a superior customer experience and a steady stream of innovative new products and services. Yet, to management's frustration, it continued to lag behind its peers in terms of valuation. The company's capital investments in its aging facilities were delivering diminishing returns, increasing indebtedness, and downgrading its ratings, leaving HosCo with an unclear path to future growth.

HosCo's leaders knew they had to determine which drivers of the company's profitability would demonstrate growth. Specifically, HosCo set out to achieve the following ambitious goals:

- Improve return on invested capital (ROIC)
- Control operating expenditures (OpEx) and capital expenditures (CapEx)

- Use new digital technologies to enhance the customer experience
- Protect and strengthen the company's brands
- Expand HosCo's footprint in new markets

To deliver on these goals, HosCo's executive committee would have to somehow scale the business and reach the desired revenue targets while simultaneously preserving the legacy culture and values that had enabled the company's success thus far. The solution would involve a keen focus on organizational health, whose decline in recent years coincided with the shortfall in growth. As a first key step, the CEO and the board of directors worked to form a strong partnership, focused on building a diverse championship team that could deliver on the aggressive growth strategy and digital transformation needed for change. Such agile, inclusive leadership and alignment at the top were critical for tackling questions such as: What is the right "portfolio" of businesses to balance cash flow next year with investments to generate profitable growth in three years? Which of these businesses should we be in and why? Can we run these businesses effectively? Do any of these businesses have important organizational capabilities that can be leveraged in other businesses?

Reaching the full potential of HosCo's various businesses and generating breakthrough profitability through revenue growth meant that the operating committee of senior leaders had to make each decision count, day to day. Thus the top management team committed to flexing a set of new skills, behaviors, and ways of working—such as making decisions that benefit the overall enterprise (not just any one business division's interests) and making tough talent decisions—all while leaning into the discomfort that such changes would inevitably generate.

Talent at the Top: Establishing the Right Team and the Right Culture

HosCo's senior management team, beginning with the executive committee, engaged in a high-touch approach comprised of a series of targeted executive forums and coaching at the individual and team levels to drive a step-change in growth and adopt new behaviors and ways of working. The forums and coaching were aimed at deeply understanding the individual and group dynamics at play amid the broader strategic and organizational context, optimizing its ways of working, building solid partnerships across its portfolio of businesses, and planning for executive succession.

The growth and behavioral changes that resulted from the coaching and forums led HosCo's leadership to make three important shifts: acting with disciplined agility; making decisions based on active foresight; and employing "synthetic intelligence"—a term used by developmental psychologist Howard Gardner to describe the ability to "take information from disparate sources, understand and evaluate the information objectively, and put it together in ways that make sense" as a prelude to action.[6] (See the box "Establish the Right Leadership Team and Culture.")

Establish the Right Leadership Team and Culture

First principles for disciplined agility:

- Deploy the right leaders, in the right configuration, with the right data and analytics, in the right areas.
- Stay aligned around the team's unique role and responsibilities.
- Employ simple rules to guide behavior.

First principles for active foresight:

- Bring the future into the room to cultivate "outside the box" thinking.
- Encourage the use of algorithms and a digital mindset.
- Develop a bias toward "coaching" the next generation of leaders.

First principles for synthetic intelligence:

- Embrace irreconcilable differences.
- Prioritize rich and robust debates over speed and efficiency.
- Encourage diversity of thought styles.
- Apply contextual reasoning to frame the right questions before attempting to seek the right answers.

Disciplined Agility. Achieving true leadership agility requires a new level of discipline: clearly defining the unique role and responsibilities of leaders in the management team. That kind of clear charter not only reduces the amount of duplication of efforts by leaders—something that too often occurs on management teams, leading to competing agendas and endless frustration; clarity of roles also enables organizations to move at speed.

For example, one former retail CEO described how the company's leadership delegated day-to-day decisions to cross-functional committees. The committees' job was to make quick decisions and elevate the particular problem to top leadership when that wasn't possible. She noted that the arrangement helped to "centralize the strategic discussion and decision making but decentralize the preparatory work, strategic recommendations, and tactical decision making." That division of leadership roles thus saved busy executives from spending time trying to solve problems that would be better managed by someone else. It also allowed the committees to execute decisions without constantly worrying whether executives higher up in the company would intervene.

Similarly, HosCo's executive committee was committed to working more effectively as a team and engaging with the broader operating committee. While the committee was meeting its sales targets, the CEO saw that the committee would sometimes get stuck on procedures and policies. He asked the committee to take a step back to reassess how it was functioning as a team. As it turned out, the committee members didn't even have a common definition of the word "team." Their work, therefore, began with clarifying the rules that would guide members' interactions and how they made decisions. Ultimately, they wrote those guidelines into an Executive Committee Charter that they agreed upon and ratified. As one leader noted, "Our management team meetings should focus on framing and answering strategic questions and making judgment calls—not on policy and procedure. If all we do is the latter, then that's a waste of our time and talent."

Foresight. Agility also means staying in tune with what's happening in the world, both today and in the future. To achieve its growth goals, therefore, HosCo's leaders knew they'd have to develop the capability to understand megatrends in the market. But historically, HosCo executives had little, if any, exposure to the kind of leadership assessment and development that would help the company's next layer of leaders cultivate the skill of foresight. Therefore, they were less ready to hear hard truths than executives who had had such experiences. The CEO had also long occupied the corner suite, and the company did not conduct formal performance reviews for the top and senior leader positions. Therefore, executives interested in preparing themselves for the top job had little opportunity to take on stretch assignments to hone their learning agility and grow as enterprise leaders.

To stay more in tune with market megatrends and to develop next-generation leaders—two key tenets of foresight—HosCo's top managers needed to open the lines of communication between themselves and front-line employees, who typically observed changes in the market firsthand. Engaging the broader organization and adopting a more inclusive leadership style to get input from up-and-coming managers became a top priority, specifically for topics about digital developments. For example, the executive committee began to seek out the advice of managers and employees, asking "what-ifs" about particular digital solutions that could potentially transform the business.

All of this led to a shift in the organization toward a new kind of culture that was highly collaborative and performing better financially than industry peers. Not coincidentally, HosCo also improved dramatically in terms of the enterprise's health, as measured by customer satisfaction and employee retention.

Nevertheless, the company still had work to do. Its leadership understood that future HosCo leaders would need to be more sophisticated than ever. When it came to thinking and acting digitally, new leaders would need the agility and judgment to know when to stay (or revise) a course of action, depending on the competitive circumstances. They would also need to have far more focus on their customers than HosCo had traditionally engaged in. Moreover, up-and-coming managers needed to unlearn behaviors that historically made HosCo's leadership slow to act on investment opportunities because of the "cost"—even when the company turned a healthy profit.

To accomplish those goals, the CEO appointed senior leaders of the company to several future-focused action teams that would help develop teams of high-potential managers. Charged with enhancing revenue through cross-business unit synergies, the teams would explore ways to balance shareholder return today with long-term performance tomorrow. For example, HosCo's success depended partly on expanding in two key markets, which it would accomplish through investments in digital and technology over a five-year period. During that time frame, therefore, the action teams worked in months-long intervals, rotating among themselves to identify new revenue streams outside of the current core businesses, while capturing cost synergies across HosCo's current businesses.

Synthetic Intelligence. Leadership agility also requires synthetic intelligence.[7] Thought about in the context of ensemble leadership, synthetic intelligence means that multiple minds, properly focused, can solve problems that one mind alone either can't solve or can't solve as quickly or efficiently.

If we take Gardner's concept into today's digital era, we can see how individual leaders and their top teams can draw on AI to augment their decision making and create what Tom Malone coined as "superminds."[8] For example, HosCo's top management created, in effect, such a supermind when it established a clear charter and set of rules for working together as a team and included the use of data and analytics about their consumers' spending habits to help with decision making and mapping out future scenarios. Thus, these leaders achieved a higher level of insight that enabled them to transcend previously irreconcilable differences, such as deciding whether to optimize for a specific business versus for the enterprise as a whole, or whether to invest more in growth markets versus developed ones.

Returning to the concept of synthetic intelligence, HosCo's top executives practiced such collaborative, ensemble leadership in a number of different ways. First, they actively incorporated diverse perspectives into the framing, deliberation, and execution of decisions. They started by applying an intuitive or context-relevant understanding—a practice many successful venture capitalists use to underpin their investment strategies[9]—to interpret the influencing factors in their industry, the broader environment, and major elements across the company's network of partnerships, including suppliers and an extended sales force to create breakthroughs in revenue growth. This meant framing and agreeing upon decisions regarding strategic choices and key actions to bring before the board of directors. To get at the practicalities of embracing differing perspectives on how to grow the business, the executive committee hosted a variety of strategy meetings that sometimes were closed to others and sometimes were opened up to other critical groups of company leaders.

During these meetings, people were asked to reach a broad consensus on each item in the company's list of initiatives—namely, whether to move forward on particular initiatives, eliminate them, downsize them in some way, or expand them. At other points, certain members were assembled as advocates for their business unit and tasked to examine the impact of potential investment decisions. Data and analytics very often informed those debates and discussions, which centered around questions such as: What should HosCo's target market share/size be based on the attractiveness of the geography in question and the demand of the markets it will source from? What high-level product offerings and distribution considerations must HosCo address to successfully meet this market share/scale target?

What made these meetings and working groups successful was their focus on the HosCo holding company as an enterprise, versus what needed to be optimized for each business unit. Productive debate and idea generation being table stakes, high-potential managers learned invaluable lessons regarding the challenges in other business units—providing them not only with where to collaborate on how best to offer support, but also providing them with venues to expand their thinking, skills, and relationships with one another. HosCo's executive committee understood the importance of breaking down silos by creating collaborative, interpersonal connections across the business—and how this approach could enable faster, more effective decisions based on collective judgment.

Another way HosCo's top executives practiced synthetic intelligence was by engaging in fast experimentation across their teams, applying judgment by testing ideas and learning from mistakes and thereby reaching better conclusions. It can mean collective learning from actual field experiments. Still, it can also mean employing "thought exercises" as a means of deliberation to rapidly incorporate lessons learned that better focus ideas and actions.

For example, my colleagues and I regularly asked members of the executive committee and the broader management group to stop and consider how each member of the leadership ensemble adds value and why. We would ask questions such as: Are you making that statement because of your role in the business unit or your role as a functional leader of HR or finance? Are you anchored in the responsibilities and the perspectives of the enterprise leader and looking at the whole of the company? Prompting leaders to explicitly state their assumptions and evidence behind each contention helped them better test and refine their ideas. The goal was to move ensemble members of HosCo's executive committee, and by extension, the leadership group as a whole.

Transformation at the Top: Governance and Change Matter

Top teams need to be agile—that is, capable of adjusting the way they think and whom they draw into the decision-making processes. HosCo offers a compelling example of a company using its leadership to focus on value creation as it charted its international expansion and transformation journey. Specifically, the company created top teams within top teams that were tasked with anticipating new trends and consumer needs to identify and seize opportunities quickly, and which were complemented by the right governance and decision forums. Such networks allow managers to make decisions in a style that matches the situation, challenge, or investment at hand. For example, in situations where the opportunity to enter a new market or expand in an existing one presents itself, generating a multitude of ideas requires a facilitative and coaching-based management style. In other situations, however, the agreed-upon operating principles about how decisions should be made for a routine "yes" or "no"—such as launching the quarterly business review—require less divergence on the part of the management team and more convergence to get things done. That's where a management style centered on quickly delivering results is warranted. Moreover, HosCo's leadership understood that developing judgment skills in the next generation of leaders would not happen overnight. It therefore made a deliberate commitment to focus beyond its executive leadership team and to engage and develop the next layer of top senior executives in cross-functional teams. These teams enabled the executives to solve problems with speed—including making critical decisions such as how to grow, scale, and run the business or allocate capital. As a result, HosCo was able to pivot to digital, expand its presence in new markets, and double its revenue—driving step-changes in its total return to shareholders.

Publicly held and private companies alike can and should embrace a similar approach to leadership and governance. In other words, they need to create top teams within top teams that are complemented by the right kinds of oversight. Such companies can do that by staying aligned through clear responsibilities and simple rules. To accomplish such transformation at the top, public and private companies can learn much from the way private equity companies do things—adopting an investor mindset that shifts their thinking. (As an example, see the table "Traditional and Investor Mindsets at the Top.")

Similarly, improving a private equity firm's capacity to optimize the value of its assets would require an evolution in its leadership and governance model. Deal teams, operating teams, portfolio company management, and boards of directors must work together to ensure top performance. The interactions among those three groups need to align around a set of operating principles in which all three groups feel like equal, value-adding contributors to an enterprise. Thus, agile leadership requires a diversity of configurations, decision styles, and ways of doing business.

Teams at the Top: Creating Fluid Leadership Ensembles
Digital is changing not only how organizations create value and how they operate. It also shifts mindsets and behaviors at turbo speed: users are likely to adopt the latest digital trends before most compa-

Traditional and Investor Mindsets at the Top

Traditional Company Mindset	Investor Mindset
"Which of our brands is most profitable?"	"Which practices or capabilities inside one brand could help make other brands more profitable?"
"Which markets are underperforming?"	"Which markets are the right long-term investments, and how can we accelerate the long-term into the near future?"
"Which assets are showing negative return on invested capital (ROIC)?"	"What are we providing to our customers now that they value less, so that we can drive new value to our customers that they would happily pay for?"

nies even know they exist. That's why organizations today need to elevate the user experience—and align leaders at the top, middle management, and the front line to fuel it. Organizations that don't adopt digital at the same high levels that users are will be left behind as radically agile new entrants capture the hearts and minds of users—and ultimately, market share.

But there's a paradox at work here. It's often the leaders who champion an AI-first perspective to scale, grow, and govern their businesses who then find themselves at odds—both culturally and in terms of investment priorities—with the executives who can turn it into reality. Those are the leaders in charge of product management and engineering excellence (or "product and eng")—groups that, in turn, also have competing priorities and perspectives from one another. The impact: organizational strife that makes digital transformation even more difficult than it already is.

So, the question is: How can a company's top management make the most of their divergent viewpoints, while also being decisive and synchronized enough to chart the digital path forward? To answer that question, first consider the varying perspectives that could be latent among each key stakeholder group.

- **The user perspective.** To represent a user perspective, chief product or chief digital officers are often tapped to design and drive omnichannel experiences and services that are relevant, simple, and meaningful for the user. They understand that the digital world we live and work in has given rise to active users. These product or digital chiefs err on the side of prioritizing investments in the digital user experience, both to seamlessly interact with users across digital channels and to better understand their habits behaviorally, using analytics. This user experience (UX) perspective can, at times, be at odds with the finance perspective.

- **The finance perspective.** CFOs are ruthlessly focused on the financial health of their business, and rightfully so. Coming off the shock of the global COVID-19 pandemic, new investments are scrutinized a lot more. However, that view may be shifting. While CFOs may have historically been forced to determine how to integrate industrial-era practices with digital-era technologies, they may routinely ask why digital technologies should be deployed to improve the user experience, as opposed to being deployed for operational efficiencies that would improve margins. No matter the calculus, quantifying digital investments in machine learning and AI, cloud platforms, and robotic process automation to attach a dollar value to them can be a doubtful undertaking. It can force CFOs to shift from what may have inadvertently been demeaning the importance of digital transformation, especially in the eyes of those who champion it, to embracing it as the way to leap ahead and remain relevant, useful, and most of all, competitive.

- **The CEO perspective.** And what about the chief executive? With all the critical items on the agenda vying for attention, it's unreasonable to expect the CEO alone to be judge, jury, and executioner. While some CEOs might be accustomed to such roles and are confident in their digital knowledge, other CEOs might fall short in understanding intelligent machines. In either case, CEOs need to understand that investing in digital is not a binary this-or-that function. Instead, they must accept the responsibility of infusing digital into *every aspect of the business and operating model,* creating a digital ecosystem that includes people, process, and technology—in short, considering all the various perspectives from their top management.

Digital transformation must almost always start with the team at the top. While there is no textbook formula as to who must lead it, logic would hold that the CEO, CDO, chief transformation officer, or a combination of C-level executives could lead the transformation, depending on its context and full potential. (For more on the muscle required to lead effectively, see the sidebar "Four Key Leadership Qualities for the Digital Era.") In all cases, though, leaders need to put differences aside to decide the path forward and collectively drive it.

Digital transformation therefore presents an inherent tension: on the one hand, many competing perspectives must be recognized and considered, but on the other hand, top management must work together in a synchronized way to drive sustainable change across the organization.

Every company's approach to top-management team effectiveness is different, so there's no single roadmap. But the companies whose leaders have built agile decision and judgment effectiveness have learned three important lessons:

1. Start with setting a tone at the top to align on a plan for breakthrough revenue growth.
2. Agree on how leaders will work most effectively and lead as a team, and then take stock of existing ensemble leadership capabilities to address gaps and weaknesses through procedural changes and purposeful practice.
3. Determine how to engage the broader organization to achieve critical priorities and goals.

Next, we move from our look at leadership to examining how to improve organizational conditions by unlocking the full potential of your *talent*.

Four Key Leadership Qualities for the Digital Era

Going digital isn't a choice anymore. Digital is the dominant business model today and for the foreseeable future. Business model life cycles are shorter, and unanticipated disruptions are becoming more frequent. That is why building better organizations will depend on leaders who are adept at riding the waves of change in a high-octane environment while also keeping the organization on an even keel by providing clear direction to increasingly distributed and virtual workforces.

What changes, then, will be needed in leadership behavior and mindset? Many considerations form a digital era's leadership foundation,[10] but four essential qualities stand out: purpose, resilience, impact, and partnership.

- **Purpose.** The combined evolution of digital technologies and AI-driven companies requires emotionally intelligent[11] leaders who can recognize, understand, and use emotional information about themselves to lead ethically and transparently amid new, emerging conditions—and do so while communicating a sense of purpose throughout the organization. At the same time, today's leaders should be able to spot opportunities and learn from every quarter: from customers, competitors, employees (both new entrants and incumbents), and from the ecosystems and communities in which they are embedded to build the foundation for creating and capturing value. Increasingly, leaders will have to orchestrate an organization with diverse talent pools, fragmented workforces, and shortened time horizons. That means they must embrace and effectively communicate a deep sense of purpose that appeals to all.

- **Resilience.** The diversity of situations in which leaders lead now—and will lead in the future—demands an unprecedented level of resilience and flexibility. In other words, leaders who can weigh several aspects of change—its complexity, scope, and horizon—and, once decided, model the passion to improvise and experiment, and to encourage followers to do the same. For example, in fast growth contexts, leaders tend to get thrown into new roles and circumstances; those who are most effective are able to learn while doing. Why? In part because they are adept at asking the right questions with the right data and right algorithm on the one hand, and, on the other, are equally comfortable taking risks and bouncing back from failure.

- **Impact.** In a world that is increasingly results-oriented, leaders will need to demonstrate impact—on the company's bottom line as well as on society. Despite the clamor and noise of building and running a successful business in the platform-economy world, leaders and their teams will need to stay laser-focused on performance and obsess about growth. Investors expect to see measurable returns on their funding contributions. Against this backdrop, leaders need to make commitments and then make good on them. But to do this well, they must also understand the health of the organization and use key levers at their disposal to carry out the company's strategy.

- **Partnership.** In a digital world, leaders will find it difficult to deliver the best to their customers and users without partnering with an increasingly diverse array of organizations, including both private and public enterprises. The best leaders understand how partnerships both encourage the gravitational pull of success and serve as ecosystem orchestrators. Differences across platforms, business models, and operating styles between ecosystem partners will require leaders to be more flexible and creative in establishing and curating a network of partnerships.

Checklist for Agenda Setting

- Develop and practice the art of judgment as well as disciplined agility, foresight, and synthetic intelligence.
- Adopt a private equity–like investor mindset of focusing on the key drivers of business performance and investor returns, setting a tone at the top to align on a plan for breakthrough revenue growth.
- Agree on how leaders will work effectively together in leadership ensembles, complemented by the right governance, conflict-resolution norms, and decision forums.
- Practice inclusive leadership and create a plan to engage the broader organization to achieve critical priorities and goals.
- Use new digital advances and AI to strengthen leadership health, including the ability to make well-informed, evidence-based decisions.

4 ■ Talent

Unlock the Full Potential of Your People

Too often, the full value of a company's talent remains locked in the organization, thanks to stale talent management practices, lack of development opportunities, or unclear roles. To tap your people's ability to innovate products and services, delight customers with a human touch, and fuel your company's growth, learn how to leverage this fourth condition of healthy organizations in the digital age.

Talent and how companies manage it has become a hot topic, not only for the C-suite and investment leaders but for boards and the broader investment community as well.[1]

Between 2010 and 2016 alone, the portion of the world's 1,600 largest companies (by market capitalization) that emphasized talent management with investors increased by 15 percent.[2] And the boards of the most successful companies—those with 10 percent or more revenue growth compared to their peers—are 1.7 times more likely to hold the broader C-suite accountable for workforce strategy. They are up to 2 times more likely to publicly report diversity and well-being metrics. And they are 3.4 times more likely to lead organizations that excel across all workforce capabilities, such as recruiting, learning and development, employee engagement and experience, and talent retention.[3]

All of this is to say that C-suite executives and investment leaders have a new set of questions to consider today: Are we truly effective at attracting A-level talent and unleashing its potential? Have we taken stock of our growth objectives, competitive landscape, operating performance, and the dynamics of our industry—and translated that into a strategy for our workforce? Do we know enough about the quantity and quality of talent in the current pipeline? Can we calculate, in numerical terms, the talent we'll need in the future?

Granted, most boards and C-suite and investment leaders are very comfortable when it comes to picking the right CEO and top management team. And investor leaders have a well-developed capacity for setting capital aside to procure robust management assessments during due diligence or shortly thereafter.

But today, such tasks have taken on a whole new tone and nuance. People making decisions about their organizations' talent, at every level, are reaching beyond old-school employee assessments and hiring practices. Institutional investors increasingly understand the link between building healthy companies and achieving higher performance.[4] And they recognize that the digital age requires a new set of talent management capabilities—such as implementing and overseeing AI-based real-time feedback about things like job fit and performance or even progress along a particular career path and development plan.

This chapter will explore such emerging digital capabilities and how some companies are already using them to acquire employees and manage their people. Along the way, we will look at the specific challenges and needs of today's global business environment. But first, let's start with an overview of the current thinking on people management.

What's at Stake and What's Needed

To fully understand the breadth of the issues surrounding talent management, both now and looking to the future, I reviewed the works of organizational scholars like Rob Cross and Amy Edmondson, along with seasoned executives like Sandy Ogg and consultants at firms like McKinsey & Company. All point to the need for companies to dig deep and get a handle on how their organizations actually create value—and how their people contribute to it.

"Identifying and quantifying the value of the most important roles in an organization is a central step in matching talent to value," according to one report.[5] But it's not just a matter of hiring the right people into these roles. One particular talent-related practice is most predictive of winning against competitors: *frequent reallocation* of high performers to the most critical strategic priorities.

LinkedIn, for example, hires people for jobs with specific learning and business objectives, based on a limited "tour of duty" lasting four years before moving on to another role.[6] And the Blackstone Group, according to its former operating partner Sandy Ogg, found that "moving swiftly on building out strong management teams and deploying senior executives into roles where they were a better match with work to be done made the difference across 22 of Blackstone's most successful portfolio companies."[7]

Such flexibility and movement among organizational roles not only avoids burnout for employees, it also keeps the organization fresh and vital. Indeed, regularly revisiting whether particular jobs and individuals represent a good fit—and making changes whenever necessary—has proven profitable for organizations. In one study, "fast" talent reallocators were 2.2 times more likely to outperform their competitors on total returns to shareholders (TRS) than were slow talent reallocators.[8]

Other emerging practices and tools include AI-based real-time feedback on individuals' work, which enables people to rapidly learn and adjust. We know, for example, how technology such as Fitbit and other fitness trackers has revolutionized the wellness industry. But other industries too are embracing AI technology to enhance their employees' productivity—from welding and manufacturing to corporate communications and governmental agencies. Technologies vary and include wearable devices as well as keystroke-measuring software to encourage employees to stay on task (via products like Hubstaff). There are also programs that measure collaboration rates within organizations (such as Isaak, a tool from the U.K. firm Status Today). There's even machine learning software (such as programs from Enaible) that measures speed and productivity around particular tasks and then suggests ways to improve.[9]

Another example is a digital program that analyzes people's personal and social networks and measures patterns of interaction by examining the frequency, length, and topics included in posts. This allows companies to understand information flow and help creative people and teams to spread their ideas, thereby unleashing innovation across the organization. Similarly, as more and more PE and VC firms start adopting AI for investment decisions, the significance of platforms such as AngelList, Crunchbase, and several other such investor and company databases will increase, boosting overall user engagement, data input, and network effects.

It has to be said, of course, that these new technologies aren't without controversy or critics. Indeed, concerns over "Big Brother"–type organizations keeping track of our every move are not completely unwarranted. No doubt AI and other technology can and have been used for unethical ends or to monitor employees' personal lives in ways that go beyond on-the-job concerns. But companies that keep the tenets of organizational health front and center understand that unsavory use of technology will ultimately backfire. The most successful companies, therefore, use digital and AI tools responsibly and with transparency and consent from their people—most often to the benefit of both employee and employer.

To make their organizations healthier, more adaptive, and, ultimately, more competitive in a world that continually seems to shapeshift, C-suite executives and investment leaders know they need the right set of talent practices—including the vital developments in AI and other digital technologies—to bring out the best in their people. Before we explore some of those practices, let's look more closely at what organizations in the digital age are up against when it comes to finding, keeping, and managing people.

Talent and Today's Core Business Challenges

Leaders running businesses today confront an array of core business challenges unlike anything that they may have faced prior to the pandemic. First, there are increasing obstacles to rapid revenue growth, such as potential legislation against big tech firms found to be wielding monopoly power.[10] For example, the concern U.S. lawmakers have regarding the disproportionate share of such technology firms' influence over digital advertising "setting and often dictating prices and rules for commerce, search, advertising, social networking and publishing."[11]

Second, stakeholder expectations for economic gain are soaring—as they were even before the pandemic. Consider how in 2017 Kraft Heinz rescinded its bid for Unilever. As reported by London Business School's Julian Birkinshaw and several industry critics, the potential coming together of these two companies marked not a clash of culture but of ideology when it came to capitalism. The Kraft Heinz view of capitalism focused primarily on providing profits to owners, whereas Unilever focused on delivering profits to owners while demonstrating a commitment to society as a whole.[12] The question of which ideology ultimately "wins" in the end will always be a subject of debate. But clearly the ideas as presented in this book about organizational health in an AI era, in particular, lean toward "both/and": that what is good for people and society ultimately will be good for profits too.

The point here, however, is that regardless of what the larger core business challenges are—be they ideological or legislative—having good talent in the workforce matters more than ever.

Talent in the 2020s

Along with the larger business challenges I've just outlined, today there are some very big developments and questions around the topic of talent itself. Among these changes are the rallying calls from around the world for our institutions, including businesses and C-suite executives, to take a stronger stance than they ever have before on issues of racial inequality. Leaders are being asked to reshape talent practices to create more just, equal, and inclusive workplaces. As already explored in previous chapters, this worldwide racial justice movement is forcing many people in positions of power to take a hard look at themselves and their organizations and to act on inequities. This includes inequities that have previously gotten less attention, such as the many forms of below-radar racism and microaggressions that so many corporate environments and society writ large have ignored or minimized for so long, thereby creating conditions that prevent businesses from fully unlocking the potential of top talent.

Simultaneously, the global pandemic placed its unique pressure on issues of talent. COVID-19 forced leaders to meet unprecedented demands to redeploy people, establish remote workforces, build needed capabilities, prop up distressed supply chains, contribute to humanitarian efforts, plan for reopening amid uncertainty, and choose among firing, furloughing, or retaining employees. Consider Delta Air Lines, which offered early-departure packages to employees with an average of 25 years of service. This enabled the company to reduce the number of layoffs, lower payroll costs, and retain more junior staff.[13]

Then, as businesses started opening up again during the pandemic, another talent issue surfaced: staffing at many businesses, especially places such as restaurants and other food-service venues, came up short. It turned out that many workers who lost their jobs amid business closings decided not to return—at least not under the same kinds of working conditions and wages they might have tolerated in the past. Some observers see that labor shortage, however temporary or industry-limited it might prove to be—as pointing to a renewed need for businesses to learn and practice better strategies for finding and keeping their people.[14]

So, what does this all mean for C-suite and investment leaders in the future? How do they lead and invest in a world made so raw and uncertain? Amid this wide variety of challenges and developments—

from the legislative and ideological to the organizational level, one thing remains unstoppable: the rise of digital in the workplace. Everything else is a backdrop to the inevitable march of business toward an AI-first context. Fortunately, AI offers a number of solutions to the very issues that are challenging organizations today.

AI-Enabled Talent = Solutions to Today's Toughest Challenges
Contrary to what some people believe, digital transformation actually offers a boon for talent. That is because digital is far less about technology—which anyone can buy—than it is about people. Think about it: when it comes down to the basic facts, technology is all about giving people the ability to effectively use next-generation skills, judgment, and insight. As routine work becomes more automated, enabling people to carry out their daily tasks more quickly, our uniquely human capabilities will rise to the fore and ultimately set individuals and their organizations apart.

"AI . . . is not playing out like anyone expected," says Greg Brockman, the CTO of the research lab OpenAI, as quoted in the *New York Times*. "It is replacing no jobs. But it is taking away the drudge work from all of them at once." The article, titled "AI Gains, but It Still Needs People," stressed that AI programs still are unable to reason in the same way that humans can. Indeed, as many users of Siri, Alexa, GPS programs, and other consumer AI tools know all too well, robots, chatbots, and the like "replace only a small part of what human experts can do."[15]

Even so, there are no easy answers when it comes to addressing the array of perils that businesses are bumping up against in the digital age. In fact, the only appropriate response might very well begin with more—and more uncomfortable—questions, such as:

- Has your business leaders' interest in scaling and creating a more profitable company contributed to stagnant organizational health in the company and across its portfolio?
- Has the talent in your business—and the talent management capabilities designed to help top management

> develop and thrive—evolved to meet the very real chal-
> lenges your business faces in a digital world?
> - Or, perhaps more to the point: Have your top people
>   outgrown their effectiveness? Are there instances where
>   your talent practices are outdated and, therefore, blind you
>   to the realities of your business context today?

Once organizational leaders can answer those questions honestly,
they can begin to tackle some of the issues. Only then will they truly
be prepared to do business in an AI-first, platform-based business
context. What follows is a primer on where and how to begin such
a talent transformation.

How AI Can Unleash Talent

As already discussed, when it comes to maximizing the potential of
digital and AI, having the best talent in place will matter more than
it ever has. But the opposite is just as true: an array of emerging AI
and digital tools will allow your people to function at their best.
Consider the following areas.

Talent Acquisition. AI and analytics can help assess talent—from inside
and outside the company—spot high potentials, and match them to
the right opportunities in your organization. And digital programs
such as Quid can go even further through the responsible scraping
of web data from text and images/videos from profiles on social media platforms (LinkedIn, Facebook, Twitter, and many others) to
identify and initially source A-level talent. This data can then be
used to model and build a psychologically based talent profile of an
entrepreneur or individual that your company might want to target
for hire.

Employee Experience. German e-commerce giant Zalando offers a fitting example of how digital can enhance employee experience. The
company has implemented various digital tools for top management
to capture and respond to topics of interest from all employees. These
include zTalk, a live-chat application; zLive, a companywide social

intranet; and zBeat, a tool that enables companies to survey employees about their current work experiences.[16] New tools can also optimize social capital, not just human capital. For example, Michael Arena, the former chief talent officer at GM, used his expertise in predictive analytics and network analysis to take "ideas from people in the entrepreneurial pockets of an organization into its formal structures so that they can be funded and scaled to drive" innovations—something he calls creating an "adaptive space."[17] And Laszlo Bock, Humu founder and former Google chief people officer, mines employee surveys using AI to identify and push out targeted behavioral nudges to employees or leaders to encourage certain types of behavior or to provide information.

Performance and Team Collaboration. Data and AI can be used to identify the behaviors that drive improved results, and they can coach employees to adopt these behaviors. In one study, researchers experimented with an AI tool designed to improve their teamwork. During the team's various processes and stages, such as determining team composition and launching the team itself, team members were asked to complete a brief survey using a mobile-enabled bot. Based on individual and team answers, the bot used AI to suggest targeted ways that the team could improve.

About halfway through their work together, team members completed a team effectiveness questionnaire across several different dimensions of teamwork—for example, how well they were managing conflict and making decisions. Then, based on the diagnostics performed on the team's unique survey responses, the bot interface was able to offer a summary of strengths and areas for improvement for the team.[18]

AI can also enhance teamwork by providing intelligent digital coaching that is personalized for the team's particular tasks. And AI can forecast the potential performance of teams based on team composition, which ultimately helps identify the right kinds of team members that will help the group achieve its goals. Along with machine learning software already mentioned, other human-machine collaboration tools include virtual assistants by Microsoft and others that can "facilitate communications between people or on behalf of people, such as by transcribing a meeting and distributing a voice-searchable version to those who couldn't attend," according to *Harvard Business Review*. "Such applications are inherently scalable—a single chatbot, for instance, can provide routine customer service to large numbers of people simultaneously, wherever they may be."[19]

Assessment and Development. AI programs such as peopleHum and Lattice Performance Management can collect and analyze factual data on people's behaviors and performance. This results in fairer (i.e., unbiased) employee assessments. But such smart machines can also provide your people with continuous feedback and customized learning opportunities that ultimately help them improve their own performance. For example, they can match people to on-the-job learning and development opportunities as well as internal gig projects in an area that could help them grow and develop.

Talent Solutions from an Investment Mindset

When it comes to investors, particularly in the rarefied world of private equity investment—in which limited partnerships buy, restructure, and transform companies that are not publicly traded—the topic of talent is paramount.

Kewsong Lee, CEO for PE firm the Carlyle Group, is on the record for adopting a talent-first mindset, which includes creating a more diverse and inclusive culture that attracts diverse talent as a competitive differentiator.[20] To address the debate around EID, in particular, Carlyle's portfolio companies (employing a total of about 900,000 people) start with a focus on making their boards and management teams more diverse. And more than half of Carlyle's companies are run by women. Lee gives credit for the firm's diversity to the "collaborative and partner-oriented spirit running through the halls at Carlyle. That lends itself to real inclusivity. Having an inclusive culture that brings in people and makes people comfortable and want to share is exceptionally important."

Ensuring a pipeline of diverse leaders throughout Carlyle's portfolio, Lee says, isn't a matter of using just one method. "It's about a whole bunch of different things such as recruiting to find the right talent, but also providing the right mentorship and the right professional development," he says. "It's about making sure your organization gets rid of unconscious bias. It's also about compensation and alignment. It has to be more about something that is cultural versus one program or one recruiting initiative."

There's no question that today's portfolio company leaders backed by PE firms now need new suites of skills to deal with talent levers associated with everything from growing regulation and rising operating costs to the complexities of acquisition and an ever-sharper focus on innovation and technology. What is less obvious is that elements of the organization's design and talent system may need to be remodeled to compete with the demands of not just looking digital but being digital. That means identifying and sourcing talent with digital skills, ranging from data scientists to software engineers, and creating a workplace environment that allows this specific talent pool to thrive and do their best work.

For example, many organizations today hope to magnetize and keep Gen-Z talent, among other generations, by investing in amenities like ping-pong tables or spaces designed for social meetings and special creative events. Simply put: what once was a nice-to-have perk is now a must-have for all employers—not just tech companies—who hope to attract and retain the best people. (For more on this topic, see the sidebar "The Employee Experience Factor.")

The question of talent, then, is no longer not "just" an HR issue to be solved with leadership development off-site or team-building exercises. It is a strategic business issue and deserves an investment mindset. The key to your talent strategy? A focus on matching people with potential to the most critical roles that create stellar value for the business, and then developing that talent. That means investment leaders and portfolio top management teams need to think hard about the qualities and skill sets that will matter most and in which parts of the business. They have to rigorously assess their talent to determine whether they've got the right people in the right roles, and

The Employee Experience Factor

The future workforce—and increasingly, employees today—will expect a level of personalization and flexibility not unlike what they've grown to expect from the businesses they patronize, especially online. Like the targeted products and services that consumers today enjoy, the employee experience is becoming more and more tailor-made for the individual. That's because, when it comes to shaping an employee experience, evidence shows that one size does not fit all. Today's business leaders, therefore, are investing in hyperpersonalized employee value propositions to give employees what they want and get what the business needs. And they are using technology to help them get there.

Personalization in the workplace takes many forms, such as merit-based promotions and compensation, flexible compensation systems tuned to differences in life stage and lifestyle, customized learning opportunities and career flexibility—allowing, for example, for time away from the job without sacrificing the option to return.[21] Business leaders know that creating an experience in the organization on par with employees' experiences as consumers will improve both engagement and productivity, which pays enormous dividends in business results. (See the box, "Engaged Employees: A Win-Win for All.")

Such personalization is especially important when it comes to attracting and retaining employees from varying age groups, who often have different values and frames of reference, especially regarding technology. According to one *New York Times Magazine* report, today is the first time in history that any given workplace might employ five distinct generations of people—traditionalists, baby boomers, Gen-Xers, millennials, and Gen-Zers.[22] The article cites an example from the Virgin hotel chain, which sought talent advice from consultants with specific expertise in generational differences. For example, to attract millennials (people born between 1980 and 2000, who expect diverse work environments), offer collaborative spaces and cultural diversity. And to attract Gen-Zers (people born between 1997 and 2012, who deeply embrace personalization), the hotel learned it should individualize everything from the letter of acceptance (ideally, make it a video) to the platform used to send Gen Z employees the company news. Gen-Zers also value work-life balance, so offering flexible vacation policies and work hours along with the ability to work a "side-hustle," like driving for Uber or hosting a podcast, can give companies an edge on attracting and keeping talent.

Engaged Employees: A Win-Win for All

Findings from Gallup's longtime, large-scale studies of employee engagement indicate a strong correlation between engagement and a healthy organizational culture. What's more, such cultures with engaged workforces perform better than those where employees were less engaged on the job. The studies reveal that business units in the top quartile of engagement outperformed bottom-quartile units by 10 percent on customer ratings, 17 percent in productivity, 20 percent in sales, and 21 percent in profitability. Top-quartile units also saw significantly less turnover (24 percent less in high-turnover organizations and 59 percent in low-turnover organizations), 41 percent less absenteeism, 70 percent fewer safety incidents, and 40 percent fewer quality defects.[23] In short, the connection between healthy, engaged employees and strong performance remains a fundamental tenet of organizational life.

to gauge whether their leaders and most productive talent are developing in the right ways, helping to scale a business that can deliver value while being agile and growth-oriented.

One way to focus an investment mindset on talent is to think in terms of various "strategic futures"—actions to take, depending on the stage of the organization, among other factors, that will (1) support growth, (2) boost returns on capital, or (3) improve management quality. Each of those actions comes with distinct implications for talent.

Here we will examine how those three sample scenarios might play out in a single company. Although the scenarios could each be applied to many types of maturing business, here they are in the context of a private equity firm with a company in its portfolio that makes a major domestic acquisition: a large B2C technology business that has a new product line in an area outside its traditional area of operations.

Scenario 1: Supporting Growth

First, we will look at the kind of talent-investment action that will help build this firm's business lines and strengthen the company's reputation as an employer.

Talent implications. The acquisition would mean much greater responsibility for the current CEO, or it might open up the potential for a new C-level role to lead the new business, presuming the business is a separate product area or perhaps even an operating company. Success will require getting all the essentials right, from vision, mission, and purpose to business model, strategy, and assembling the right team. Most of all, it requires that leaders craft a compelling employer brand that attracts top talent and gives them the opportunity to live their purpose and contribute positively to society while pursuing the enterprise's goals.

Talent actions. The portfolio management team and the investor leaders alike should be ready not just for all the mechanical issues of making such a momentous acquisition but for all the big cultural and organizational challenges that come with it. They will need to understand the talent they need, the talent they have, and how to navigate the gap. In other words, they will need to create a talent strategy based on enterprise and business unit plans and extrapolate the skills needed to do the work.

Second, imagine if the PE-backed company were to expand further in an emerging international market through acquisition of a key product or an industry service provider.

> **Talent implications.** In this case, the portfolio management team or investor leaders would need to quickly elevate talent to take on greater responsibility. For instance, they might need an international managing director role and organization to direct and oversee country managing directors in each market portfolio. The role would assume significant responsibility for international regulatory and government affairs.
>
> **Talent actions.** The business's leaders will need a growth mindset and learning agility to successfully enter new geographies. They will be respectful of the host country's culture and open to differences in how people learn, and they will be adept at bringing out the best in people and teams. They should also enlist the support of their HR or talent chief to mine the organization's HR systems and external professional networks (such as LinkedIn) for analytics on the existing workforce's core skills, applied skills, and future aspirations.

Scenario 2: Boosting Returns on Capital

In this scenario, the focus is on a push for cost efficiency and optimization. Potential hires, therefore, must demonstrate deep capabilities in finance, enterprise performance management, and knowledge of AI robotic process automation, which brings significant savings quickly and frees up manual process time. Such hires should understand more than yesterday's approach to cost control or staffing/talent allocation. They will need a profound understanding of digital profit and loss (P&L) control systems that use near-real-time feedback loops and AI algorithms to make sense of patterns that humans cannot easily see. They will also need to know how to effectively use contingent workforces/e-lancers. While digital technology and data analytics enable work to be more easily performed temporarily, thereby reducing costs, they do not make work temporary by themselves.

Talent implications. Shared finance and enterprise performance capabilities call for a new leadership structure. The separation of revenue management and cost-optimization responsibilities requires new roles and skills or, in some cases, upskilling.

Talent actions. Leaders must take advantage of the continued fragmentation in the labor market and seriously consider growing an agile or gig-like workforce composed primarily of part-timers and e-lancers who have demonstrated their interest in the organization and who represent a good cultural fit.

Scenario 3: Improving Management Quality

What if top executives or other critical senior talent with a disproportionate impact on the business retire, decide to leave the company, or, worse, are fired? Or worse yet, what if the workforce grows increasingly disintegrated and fragmented?

Talent implications. Most important will be having emergency and interim successors for all lead and critical roles—both current and future roles. Different skill sets may be required of the understudies, depending on the strategic options (and roles) pursued. It may be necessary to introduce new roles, like chief digital officer or chief transformation officer. In fact, given the digital world, the very idea of "workforce" may give way to something more like "talent pools" that flexibly band together to solve business problems—and then disband—irrespective of where they may reside on an organization chart. Such flexibility requires advanced analytic capabilities to identify individuals across the organization that are able to quickly band together and disband.

Talent actions. In today's world, it is crucial for leaders to have a learning orientation, intellectual openness, and the ability to adjust and respond with nimbleness. It also requires leaders that will understand the nuances of generations and geographies. Such leaders should not rely on academic reports on generational preferences; rather, they should analyze their company's organizational/ workforce data to gain impressions of the employee experience and more accurate pictures of what's really going on. Improving management quality would also mean: (a) honing the ability to rapidly allocate talent on a project basis, in part through developing internal gig marketplaces, and (b) acquiring the ability to tap into alternative talent pools and maximize their potential.

One company that sought to tackle many such "strategic futures" when it came to acquiring new talent was a consumer technology company we will call MediaTech. It had already achieved a strong track record of profitable growth and free cash flow, driven by delivering great products and services and a disciplined approach to operations and investments. But now MediaTech sought to strengthen its portfolio and expand its presence globally. With a focus on growing market share, MediaTech's goal was to invest in assets that enabled the company to compete with media and consumer technology players. It would start by embracing the Internet of Things (IoT) revolution and building digital B2B businesses. But the company recognized that to fuel its ambition, it would have to rely on inorganic growth or growth through acquisition. Here's a detailed look at how Media-Tech transformed its talent base to achieve its goals.

Case Study: How MediaTech Transformed Its Talent Base

To grow its presence in consumer technology, MediaTech invested in a media and gaming company that had a strong competitive track record (which we will call MediaCo) to strengthen its technology, marketing, media, Internet, and commerce capabilities. MediaTech's new chief investment officer, who had a long list of improvements to make in the new portfolio company, began with digital capabilities at the top of that list. Market research and the CIO's own observations strongly suggested that with increasing competition, powering its reach to consumers through digital assets like streaming would be a key growth area.

Yet MediaTech was not meeting consumers' rising expectations of online and customer service. The CIO knew that to continue winning in the ever-changing business and technology environment, MediaTech would need to deliver a superior and differentiated consumer experience. With a track record in private equity of buying and growing businesses, the CIO had witnessed the power of talent as a key lever for value and future business success. She therefore understood that delivering on the company's bold ambition would mean sourcing large numbers of highly skilled leaders and digital talent—everyone from software engineers to e-commerce specialists.

Her strategy for attracting that talent, as well as investors, was grounded in communicating MediaTech's unshakable sense of purpose and clear strategic direction. The company's bold ambition, she was sure, would magnetize the people MediaTech needed to its doors. But because the company had used only limited analytics when making talent decisions in the past, MediaTech had never been very proactive when it came to people analytics and long-range planning. The CIO began, then, by tasking one of her most trusted and experienced leaders, her portfolio talent lead, to do three things: (1) shape a comprehensive talent strategy; (2) focus on attracting and developing top talent, especially across its leadership ranks and critical roles; and (3) use analytics to target improvements in the employee experience and make better organizational decisions. Let's look at each of these in turn.

A Comprehensive Talent Strategy

The work began with a review of internal and external market trends, an organizational due diligence to appraise the company's health— evaluating each lever's effectiveness in contributing to the organization's strategic direction and growth ambition—and the development of a set of business-oriented talent scenarios. This analysis revealed a serious shortage of both leaders and digital talent in the company— such as software engineers—and that the company's key talent practices were woefully inadequate. Among the challenges:

- Company recruiters and hiring managers took far too long to fill critical roles.
- The company had low success in developing a pipeline of entry-level talent.
- Managers often avoided conducting difficult conversations with their teams. What made matters worse on this front was the lack of accountability for managerial performance.
- Further, an outdated set of cultural beliefs—such as that employees needed to be colocated for collaboration to occur—hampered the company's potential to foster growth and develop talent.
- Finally, the environment and general mood in the organization post-deal close revealed that employees from middle management down to line managers doubted MediaTech's commitment to grow and transform the asset; they were likely to resist any talent initiatives the company's new owners proposed.

Working with the CIO, the portfolio talent lead set out to create a three-year talent improvement program to turn MediaTech into a talent-first company. The goal was to unlock the full potential of the organization's people and to identify new revenue streams that were practical and that could take advantage of the company's existing and new digital capabilities to win over consumers and inspire loyalty. The program invested in the company's talent acquisition practices to achieve a number of outcomes, including: building a shared understanding of what "A-level" talent looks like; hiring better talent more quickly; deploying the best talent to the most critical roles and opportunities while managing out underperformers; and shifting from a just-in-time approach to talent management to a longer-term, enterprise-wide coordinated approach to executive development, including regular reviews of leadership and of executive-potential talent as a key focus.

Attracting Top Talent

Early on, MediaTech recognized that its rapid growth required developing and equipping its current and next generation of leaders. To close the leadership gap identified in the diagnostic led by the portfolio talent lead, MediaTech invested in shaping an "executive leadership intervention" rooted in the business and growth ambition. The backbone for the approach contained three elements. First was the creation of a leadership framework. Second was to assess, debrief, and counsel the company's top 100 leaders around the skills they would need to drive profitable, scalable growth. Third was to engage in three-way conversations, where leaders were asked to develop a leadership action plan and review it with their boss and an expert coach.

Improving the Employee Experience

As MediaTech looked toward its future strategic direction, it realized that deepening its relationships with existing consumers would be a critical pathway for growth. Its secret weapon: engaged employees, especially those at the front lines of user transactions and interactions and those creating the innovative products and services of the future. These employees would be critical drivers of improved user satisfaction and loyalty, and thus of business results.

How, then, could MediaTech further optimize its employee experience to drive a better customer experience, thereby improving the user experience and business results? And how could the company implement those changes at scale? The portfolio talent lead's answer: use people analytics to quantitatively measure employee experience, boost employee engagement, and drive a superior user experience. A rigorous analysis ensued of employee engagement surveys, exit interviews, call-center data, and interviews with senior HR leaders across different divisions. Everything pointed to a set of concrete and scalable opportunities MediaTech could begin to capitalize on to further optimize the employee moments that matter. Thus, the company could become more employee-centric, enhance employee engagement across the employee experience journey, and deliver better performance.

Next, MediaTech improved its user experience by doing three things. First, it provided targeted capability building programs for new products, while simplifying processes and tools. Second, it empowered its workforce to take responsibility for delivering a simple, clear, human experience for users at points of sale and service. Third, the company adjusted its compensation structures across the sales workforce to motivate desired behaviors at key interactions, while encouraging the employees to take on more ambitious career paths and growth. Thereafter, the change at MediaTech was dramatic. Its portfolio of businesses improved, and the organization developed a reputation for being a magnet for top talent.

As a result of the talent strategy and leadership intervention by the CIO and portfolio talent lead, MediaTech's leadership pipeline expanded enough to fuel growth and enter into new businesses and markets. Senior leadership also became markedly more effective, ultimately transforming the company into a thriving one and adding millions of customers by scaling new direct-to-consumer businesses. All of this resulted in a steady increase in EBITDA (earnings before interest, taxes, depreciation, and amortization).

Managing Your Company's Talent: Three Key Actions to Take Now

As MediaTech discovered, making wise choices when it comes to talent—both in the C-suite and for other key roles—is a high-stakes proposition. That's true not just with respect to hiring and retention but also for unleashing your workforce's highest potential. That is why talent should be managed as actively as any financial or physical asset on which the company relies, whether that's its buildings or technology.

Specifically, companies can translate organizational health into financial performance by focusing on three key actions:

1. **Create the talent strategy that will enable the growth and the transformation of the business.** The portfolio talent lead at MediaTech created a strategy that ultimately contributed to the company's ability to meet its financial and customer goals. Although the specifics of the talent strategy will be different depending on the organization, most will have some mix of elements such as what workforces and skills are needed, the maturity

levels of the organization's employee experience capabilities, and where those skills and workforces are most needed geographically.

2. **Focus on identifying employee behaviors that will most strongly affect the business and overall customer experience.** Consider engaging a trusted counselor or consultant to serve as a sounding board to gauge employee sentiment, starting with a leader's top team and the broader employee base. It's vital that this person represents an independent set of stakeholder viewpoints across the organization. Why? Because pertinent information about the health of the organization doesn't always funnel up to senior leaders, and your consultant's outsider status could encourage candor.

3. **Gather data about your employees' experience.** Pulse surveys, self-assessments, and multi-rater feedback help organizations understand what employee behaviors and actions have the most impact on the business. This will help the organization achieve its business and financial goals in the most targeted way. Such data-driven information is crucial, especially if your organization is a private equity–backed company in growth mode. Why? Because having data-driven insight in an earlier period of holding will tell you where you need to invest in talent to drive new businesses and maintain workforces throughout a transition. As Holly Kortright, former chief human resources officer of PE-backed Ellucian, shared with me, "Translating business strategy into an executable talent strategy can't be theory; it has to be practical in how a leader puts strategy, backed by evidence, to work."

Talent is essential to the execution of any business strategy. It's always been that way. But many business leaders have not understood how to translate talent strategies and sentiments into tangible business outcomes. Today, advances in digital and analytics have brought newfound clarity. With access to real-time data—and the ability to derive and present analytics-based insights from that data—business leaders can better understand the implications of their talent-related decisions on business success. Indeed, the future will belong to such "super teams" of people and AI working collaboratively and catalyzing strategic growth and value. C-suite executives, investors, and portfolio management teams who take full advantage of the data and insights that new advances in AI and analytics enable will make better decisions about how they grow or transform.

To fully realize that future, however, organizations must fundamentally change the way they've traditionally been designed. By moving from structures based on scale, efficiency, and growth to agile structures and sustainable systems, businesses will become much more resilient and adaptive—the topic of the next chapter.

Checklist for Agenda Setting

- Identify and quantify the value of the most important roles in the organization, and focus on these.
- Reallocate high performers frequently to the most critical strategic priorities.
- Use new digital advances and AI to unleash the potential of an organization's talent.
- Consider various strategic futures when designing a talent strategy, assessing the type of talent needed, whether people are in the right roles, and the types of talent practices required.
- Coach leaders in the talent behaviors that drive impact.
- Use people analytics to measure and improve the employee experience.

5 ■ Organizational Design

Create Structures and Systems for
Agility and Sustainability

Many leaders today are facing a crisis in confidence—if not in fact—in the way their companies function and perform, especially across the tech industry. They wonder: In today's unforgiving and fast-moving environment, can the designs of organizations balance velocity and acceleration? Can they translate strategy into value? Everything hinges on how effectively those designs can shift from a scale, efficiency, and growth orientation to designs that are agile and sustainable, focused on resilience and adaptivity.

If the parade of environmental jolts and economic shocks in the last decades hadn't already cast doubt on the effectiveness of traditional organizational designs, COVID-19 revealed their full vulnerabilities. Combined with unprecedented competition, such conditions are exposing organizations' inability to evolve at speed and scale. Today, no matter how good a company's strategy or business model might be, it will be essentially useless if the organization isn't designed to pivot quickly amid shifting circumstances.

Designing organizations in the past was, to be sure, a lot easier. Traditional organizations rarely needed to adapt in any major way unless relatively predictable changes required it. Design was all about ensuring scale, efficiency, and growth. It was just a matter of aligning the right processes, technologies, and people to deliver a product or service within a particular structure—oriented around either your customers (Amazon and Zappos are examples), your products (like Apple or Google in its early years of Search), or your organization's functions (such as what's found in professional services like consulting firms).

But today's competitive marketplace demands that organizations accept, as a go-forward proposition, that agility and resilience are required—and that they can accomplish that through their organizational designs. By designing explicitly for uncertainty, leaders can reduce their risk. They can build in a design that will support the execution of not only strategy but of strategy that will inevitably evolve based on highly dynamic and fast-changing conditions. Technological disruption, changing customer and user demands, competitive shifts, and geopolitical upheaval will require the occasional transformative shifts as well as multiple, continuous, and orchestrated shifts.

My perspective on design as a condition (the fifth of seven) of a business's health is grounded not only on the work of organizational theorists but also in my experience as an organization strategist working in tech. To bridge the gap between traditional and digital businesses to optimize performance, organizations in the future must be designed to string together a series of momentary advantages.

That implies a design that will scale and deliver growth while enabling *agility* and *sustainability*. By sustainability, I mean organizations that have built-in features that are above all renewable—everything from eco-friendly building materials and healthy workspace design that can serve to rejuvenate employees' bodies and minds. But it also means designing the organization for sustainable outcomes:

ensuring the company's product or service has a favorable impact on society and the environment.

Sustainability, along with the agility that comes with flatter, more collaborative designs, will define successful organizations in the coming decades. And it appears that a number of companies are doing just that. Research done by Gartner reveals that 52 percent of organizations surveyed during the 2020 COVID-19 crisis say they are shifting from designing their organizations for efficiency to designing them for flexibility.[1]

Such organizations are moving from a mechanistic model to an organically self-adapting one with almost human characteristics, morphing as they respond to market dynamics and staying in tune with evolving customer expectations and stakeholder demands. These companies are ensuring that their "structure follows strategy," as the late historian and Harvard Business School professor Alfred Chandler famously advocated—that is, "designing organizations that will support their value creation and value capture."[2]

Indeed, companies that launched their agile organizational design transformations pre-COVID-19 have found that the move helped them survive one of the most challenging tests of our time. By empowering the front line, using cross-functional teams, and acting on clear data regarding desired business outcomes, agile companies performed better and moved faster after the pandemic hit than their nonagile counterparts.[3] (See the sidebar "The Promise of Agility.")

With the certainty that unexpected events like the pandemic will only grow more frequent in the future, many organizations are now following suit by adopting organizational designs that can deal better with ambiguity. These companies are updating their business continuity plans, and they are implementing scenario-planning exercises that include more frequent occurrences of a variety of calamities.

In this chapter, we will look at the specifics of how to design organizations that are sustainable and agile—and how to master that balancing act, as well as how to reshape the organization for its

The Promise of Agility[4]

Agile organizations make timely, effective, and sustained change when and where it results in a performance advantage.[5] Consider:

- **Agile by design.** Agile organizations are resilient, not perfect. COVID-19 revealed agility by necessity (acting). Expect future organizations to become more interested in agility by design (being).
- **Beyond anticipating, prepare for the unpredictable.** Agility is vital to the volatility of today's business environment. Agile organizations establish routines of sensing, responding, testing, and learning, enabling them to bounce back. For already agile companies, agility is not a destination but an ongoing journey.
- **Agile for sustainability.** Successful organizations design to continuously adapt and balance multiple stakeholders' needs to achieve sustainability. More than 2,000 academic studies have examined the impact of environmental, social, and governance propositions on equity returns, and 63 percent of them found positive results (versus only 8 percent that were negative).[6]
- **Agile pays.** Organization agility links to sustainability and profitable growth. Research conducted at MIT suggests that agile firms grow revenue 37 percent faster and generate 30 percent higher profits than nonagile companies.[7] BCG research also reveals that agile companies are up to five times more likely than their peers to become top performers.[8]

own future evolution. We will also examine ways to use AI to transform your design, and I will touch on the unique needs of investment companies. But let's begin with a review of the components of organizational design (or redesign) and why it matters in the first place.

Why "Design" the Organization?

Organizational design isn't like any other management tool. It isn't about moving around boxes on a chart or installing a new structure or governance model. Rather, it's about evolving how the company does business and how it operates. Design doesn't merely change employees' reporting lines and ways of working; it changes the way they work and behave. It is a systematic process, yes, but it also comprises a set of decisions that drive behavior or behavior change.

One hypergrowth business I worked with, made up of approximately 2,500 people, sought to reshape its organizational design to compete globally. Top management's challenge was no longer as simple as "think global and act local." An enterprise-first mindset that balanced the polarities of global consistency versus local autonomy would need to be adapted in order to lead change collectively to offer more customized services. And new mindsets—and incentives to reinforce those mindsets—would need to be prioritized to usher in new organizational behavior to lead toward the future and deliver in the present.

Organizations implement new designs for a variety of reasons, such as:

- To make structural changes to support collaboration
- To decrease costs
- To improve productivity
- To create opportunities for A-level talent
- To enhance decision making and management reporting, or make them faster
- To sharpen customer focus with improved levels of service
- To streamline business processes, such as eliminating non-value-added activities

Two very good reasons to pay attention to your organization's design are, first, because neglecting design or creating a poor one can lead to poor organizational health, and, second, because an effective design will help your company scale and grow.

Design and Your Company's Health

When I launched Google's Change and Design Forum in the latter part of 2019, our mantra was "Reorgs are about today's problems; organizational design is about tomorrow's possibilities." In other words, leaders need to design their organizations for what they need tomorrow rather than modify what the organization is today.

Healthy organizational culture—the positive evolution of a company's mindsets and behaviors—is the direct product of a good organizational design. But most such designs don't succeed: as many as 80 percent of organizational redesign efforts don't achieve their intended value.[9] (See the sidebar "The Roots of Failed Organizational Design.") And the cost of failure is high, including productivity decline, organizational overload and complexity, talent attrition, lack of agility, and diminished competitive advantage.

Common stumbling blocks that high-growth companies may experience—such as poor organizational alignment, duplicative capabilities, a lack of coordination and inconsistent management spans and layers—prevent many companies from mastering the art of organizational design. After all, high-growth companies are either exploring possible investments or they are exploiting the assets within their portfolio to scale or expand their suite of products and/or services. Typically, they have created a lot of slack because of having to move fast and rapidly adapt their organizational design to execute and deliver to their consumers. But at some point such companies need to stop and decide when to either start pruning or else put mechanisms in place to create a more planned structure.

Consider the case of a financial services company with which I worked as it focused on organizational design elements to improve performance—and ultimately, the health of the organization. "FinCo," a U.S.-based company, was already in the bottom quartile of its industry performance when it decided to expand its geographical footprint with an acquisition in Asia. Now it needed to establish a new operating model that would help pay for the acquisition and improve overall performance, while working within a new culture and set of laws.

The Roots of Failed Organizational Design

Research and experience have shown me that organizational design efforts that stall or fail altogether to deliver on their value proposition rarely do so because of execution. More often, failures can be traced to three key root causes: (1) structural problems (confusion over decision rights and roles and responsibilities, for example), (2) breakdowns around metrics and incentives processes (poor performance management and management reporting), and/or (3) problematic people and organizational processes (culture, competencies, and standard operating procedures). The organizational challenges that result from one or a combination of those fundamental issues follow a few familiar patterns, including:

- **Poor alignment.** Lack of clarity and alignment around priorities and their link to strategic imperatives to preserve and/or create business value can undermine an organization's ability to execute on its strategy.
- **Unclear structure and roles.** Siloed priorities as the organizational design evolves with the company's growth—usually to accommodate geographical, customer, business unit, and product complexity—can create design challenges. That's because there is little clarity around who is accountable for key decisions and what people's roles and reporting relationships are. All of this gets in the way of value creation.
- **Duplication of individual and organizational capabilities.** In a fast-growth context, companies may hire talent and build institutional capability too quickly in one specific area of need and not enough in another, which may mean underinvestment in key areas. This often results in redundant staff or shadow functions across line organizations, teams that lack the right

talent to sustain growth ambitions, and team members who aren't sold on or excited by their plan to deliver value.

- **Conflicts surrounding coordination and leadership.** Leaders and managers may lack the ability to balance big-picture thinking and hands-on execution. This can lead to a host of challenges, such as a failure to orchestrate coordination, cooperation, or collaboration across different product teams or business units, and missed opportunities for true synergy.
- **Inconsistent spans and layers.** Underutilized high-cost talent and resources, bureaucratic processes, or the proliferation of special committees and task forces can hinder operational effectiveness.
- **Rigid, tightly defined roles and processes.** This can prevent employees from adapting to changing demands at speed. It can slow down their decision making, preventing employees from identifying and addressing unseen problems and opportunities for customers, the workforce, society, and other stakeholders to create new sources of value and sustainability.

Meantime, top management had also embarked on a change program to shift the organizational culture of FinCo from a volume-driven mindset to more of a value-driven mindset. But so far it hadn't been a success, and communication was breaking down. For one thing, middle managers in Asia were hesitant to fully trust the new executives, who lacked industry experience of doing business within the Asian culture. Further, these employees did not completely accept the Western-based profit and customer-value orientation that their new top managers espoused.

To achieve FinCo's goals, including the desired culture improvement and need for elevating the company's performance to the top-quartile position, our advisor group recommended a systematic process of designing and redesigning the organization. Ultimately, FinCo would develop true agility, sound execution, and sustainability (beyond compliance) to improve its industry performance. Among the steps the company took in its redesign were the following:

- To minimize its high-cost structure and increase employee productivity, it consolidated physical locations and the spread of its regional head office in Asia. It also cosourced and outsourced all noncore activities. For example, top management sought to minimize the company's high-cost structure and increase employee productivity by focusing on tasks that were core to its business model.
- To improve culture clashes and overall efficiency, it streamlined its governance and decision-rights model. For example, it abolished unnecessary and duplicate approvals of certain kinds of decisions, including consolidating contact centers across its customer operations footprint based on ongoing optimization and performance improvement. This not only helped to smooth over cultural differences around legacy and inconsistent ways of working to a shared set of norms and operating practices, but it also eliminated the lack of clarity around roles and responsibilities, thus improving the lines of communication between different management levels.
- To focus on customer-centricity, FinCo's new structure included a new position, chief digital officer, who would put more emphasis on analytics and new technologies that enhanced their ability to serve their customers better.
- To expose and eliminate unproductive expenses while centralizing procurement processes, rationalizing its supplier base, and standardizing demand specifications, the company created a new zero-based approach to budget management. This meant that removing unnecessary complexity and investment required top management to focus on investments and priorities that drive the greatest business value from a clean sheet.

- As part of its sustainable location strategy, FinCo made plans to move employees into "green" buildings. It also began to lay the groundwork for a more agile operating model to support a pending digital transformation.

In the end, FinCo's intensive organizational design effort—over a period of about nine months—helped the company set a course that would enable it to achieve $30 million in annual cost savings. Equally important, the steps that upper management took to improve the organization's overall health went a long way toward easing intercultural tensions, strengthening its strategy, governance, and innovation, and improving cooperation and collaboration among all management levels within and outside the Asia region to focus on the customer.

Design and the Organization's Ability to Scale and Grow
It's one thing to develop a growth strategy; it's quite another to execute it effectively. Disruption accelerated by the COVID-19 environment is driving many companies—both traditional and hyper-growth—to do what all of today's organizations should be working on as well: improving their agility and sustainability. Sixty-two percent of organizations say that, since the pandemic hit, decision making has improved in their organization and more of it has moved to the front line. Nearly three-quarters of employees report that their teams are working with greater agility since the pandemic hit, and 19 percent of employees indicated that decentralized decision making will be one of the top three permanent changes they expect once the pandemic is over.[10] Moreover, nearly half of Fortune 500 CEOs say the pandemic has accelerated stakeholder capitalism in their companies—for example, by serving employees through efforts such as creating new work-from-home policies to alleviate long commutes or providing flexibility in a given work week to manage childcare. In contrast, only 18 percent of such companies believe that efforts for stakeholders such as employees are slowing down as companies focus on short-term financial pressures.[11]

Meanwhile, newly formed companies are organized from the start into platform-based ecosystems that can quickly form and adjust.

Think DoorDash, the takeout and food delivery service, or Compass, the real estate platform, which are examples of modern enterprises that can scale up to meet customer demand. Against these incumbents, established companies will need to double down on agility if they hope to meet today's dynamic needs. They must have rapid, assured access to required data and analytics and adopt new organization models that enable adequate flexibility, coverage, and speed. If they hope to scale, such established companies must be prepared to take any number of steps.

For example, they could launch new products, incubate new businesses while protecting existing ones, or strike the right balance between centralized and decentralized responsibilities and reporting lines. Alternatively, established companies could optimize physical assets and equipment more efficiently, or protect long-term value by better responding to customer and user demands while thwarting competitive threats. But whatever solution they choose, leaders of established companies today are finding it necessary to redesign their organizations and move from acting agile out of necessity to being agile by design.[12] To meet the execution demands of scale and growth, especially in hypergrowth contexts, organizations must differentiate between "brilliant improvisation"[13] and a repeatable dynamic capability[14]—in other words, capabilities that enable the company to adapt and evolve with rapid speed. Apple, for instance, has been masterfully successful due to its ability to "market technologically based products to consumers and developing features that people value."[15]

Pursuing designs optimized for dynamism and agility doesn't mean giving up stability, however. This is a false trade-off. As *New York Times* columnist Thomas Friedman aptly put it, "You have to build an eye that moves with the storm, draws energy from it, but creates a platform of dynamic stability within it."[16] Organizations that have passed the startup challenge must manage the inevitable tension between stability and change. They must produce and deliver well enough today to generate profits—but also plan and prepare for tomorrow. They must manage the complexities of multi-stakeholder demands and the responsibilities that come with doing so.

The organizational designs that can operate in faster and more uncertain markets and environments will be flexible and agile, and they will be sustainable. But how do you create such designs?

How to Design Organizations for Agility and Sustainability

Every organization's design, of course, needs to be tailored to the business's goals, strategy, maturity, and geographic and line-of-business footprint, among other factors. So, although there's no one-size-fits-all design or approach to design, advances in digital technologies and AI are forcing business leaders and investors toward opportunities for greater speed, cost reductions, and operational efficiencies as companies scale. Such advances will ultimately lead to organizations that are designed to flex and roll with uncertainty. (See the sidebar "Principles for Organization Building.")

Key Organization Building Questions on Leaders Minds
As a first step, leaders whose business and operating models aspire toward digital must ensure that their organizational designs harmonize with the overall value business strategy or value-creation plan. Leaders can begin, therefore, by asking themselves several critical questions and considering all their implications.

Are we properly organized and aligned to execute our strategy for growth? Although every organizational design is set up to help a company compete, not every such design actually succeeds in making the company competitive. Many companies can master the essentials where they have a stable, predictable situation. But only companies that can pivot fast enough to string together momentary advantages will succeed in the current environment. One study found that organizations designed for high responsivity—such as open information and data sharing, plus a decentralized structure with dispersed decision making—were better able to meet their business goals than those not designed for responsiveness. These companies had higher degrees of innovation, increased employee engagement, and more satisfied customers, and they were better able to respond to market changes.[17]

Principles for Organization Building

Investors and business leaders need to employ principles of organization building to take concerted action and ensure that they can add value to their companies, outperform the market, and enable organizational designs that can reliably produce exceptional returns. In my view, any attempt to make real changes in the quality of an organization's design must start with six basic principles.

1. **Think, speak, and act with one voice (and be clear about deviations).** Leaders at all levels need to be aligned and engaged. It's important to keep going back to the basics and continually ask the question: Why are we doing this? As you do this, pay attention to the energy level of the top management team; expect dips after certain intense periods and plan accordingly.

2. **Commit to universal criteria to improve the organization's design and break ties.** Design criteria, grounded in strategy, provide a clear, consistent mechanism for organizational growth and navigating change. Having a leader who doesn't sit back and observe but rather owns the design criteria and holds other leaders accountable about how they run their businesses against these criteria will ensure durability and a one-team, one-org mindset. Once design criteria are established, organizations can be designed more intentionally to directly support their strategy.

3. **Be pragmatic and worry more about changes that are directionally correct and supported.** While leaders may start with the "art of the possible," deliberate deliberation and constant calibration are required to stay on task and determine the feasibility of strategy execution based on timing, rigorous planning and cadence,

and understanding what change the business can truly absorb.

4. **The more global, the messier the change.** Cultural sensitivities, country-specific labor laws, and drawing on local knowledge are key to successful strategy activation and execution. When in doubt, just ask. Don't assume you know what people will need; ask them and enlist them in the solution.

5. **Change management is not optional, and it is inadequate without change leadership.** Build time for different layers of management to learn about and reflect on the standing up of a new organization before communicating it to their direct reports. Doing so will lead to better dialogue as organizational transitions make their way through the organization.

6. **Don't just design the organization of the future, model it with confidence.** Whether a company engages in a reorg, acquires a new business, undertakes a transformation, or simply wants to know how people spend their time and how much activities cost, design requires top management to get a single version of the truth. Digital platforms with visualization technology enable massive amounts of data to be consolidated, analyzed, and reported on in an instantaneous, visual, and compelling way. These and other platforms like it help top management teams engage in organizational modeling live in meetings, to not only get an integrated and accurate view of the organization but to rapidly identify key areas of improvement—like reducing silos, process inefficiencies, and managerial workload and complexity to avoid bureaucracy (based on span-of-control analyses)—and make faster and better decisions.

When we look at what became possible at some companies in the pandemic, we can see clearly how such alignment and responsiveness allowed those organizations to creatively access new capabilities at a speed and scale never seen before. Some fast responders rapidly switched out manufacturing lines for in-demand products, doubled production output, or crafted new remote in-home services in a matter of days. Some built new, innovative partnerships, like a household goods company partnering with doctors and universities to build ventilators. Employees in apparel companies like Brooks Brothers and New Balance quickly turned to making surgical masks and gowns. Meanwhile, U.S. automakers Tesla, Ford, and General Motors—after idling their automotive plants due to plummeting consumer demand—retooled their factories to produce ventilators from car parts.[18] More recently, Ford has been looking to bring the same speed and agility it brought to ventilator production into developing new capabilities for its next-generation automated production.[19]

Do we have the right governance to make better, faster decisions? And are we focused on the right decisions in the first place? The goal is to move leaders and, by extension, the management team as a whole, from single-loop learning to double-loop learning. Take, for instance, how the CEO of a Latin American airline tasked a group of senior leaders with answering the question: "Why aren't more of our countrymen taking advantage of our company's low fares?" Questioning their assumptions, the group of leaders realized that taxis to the airport were too expensive for the average customer—sometimes 40 to 50 percent the cost of the airfare—and transit services were too infrequent. The team, therefore, decided to implement free and frequent airport shuttles. As a result, passengers were booking more than 3,000 free bus rides per day to the airport, making the Latin American airline the fastest-growing airline in its home country.

While such double-loop learning helps make *better* decisions, the key to *speedy* decisions, according to McKinsey research, is to hold fewer meetings, with fewer decision makers present at each one. It also found that leaders need to encourage real-time, high-quality debate over high-stakes decisions with the potential to shape the company's future (big-bet decisions)—and they need to delegate noncritical decisions to empowered employees and teams. The research further shows that slow decision making most strongly separates slower organizations from faster ones. Indeed, firms that make a special effort to gain speed outperform others by a wide margin on various outcomes, including profitability, operational resilience, organizational health, and growth. That explains why, during the COVID-19 pandemic, executives and directors reported that their firms were making changes to increase how quickly they adjust strategic direction, make and implement tactical decisions, and deploy resources.[20] Other research echoes McKinsey's findings; the 15 percent of executives who said that their organization was "very prepared" for the pandemic were twice as likely to recognize the importance of organizing work to facilitate rapid decision making.[21]

What is the most effective way to structure and govern the organization? Clearly, organizations in the digital era must be structured for agility—collaborative, team-based, open and transparent, and minimally hierarchical. In one survey, 74 percent of executives said their transition to just such a team/network-based organization has resulted in improved performance.[22] The trouble is that many agile designs focus mostly on performance and not on outcomes—specifically, sustainability. That means embedding sustainability into the DNA of the organizational structure rather than siloing it as a project, a corporate initiative, a department, or a position. Companies whose success includes sustainable outcomes focus on providing different stakeholder groups a meaningful voice in governance and decision making. For example, a co-op company, which is typically jointly owned and democratically governed by employees, might include employee stakeholders in their board meetings in order to ensure that the economic, social, and cultural needs of the communities where they operate and do business are met.

How do we run a business within a business (run a core business in parallel with a new business)? In today's world of constant disruption, organizations must constantly reinvent themselves—experimenting with and creating new businesses for the future without abandoning their core business.

And they must know how to continually calibrate investments to grow new businesses at precisely the right time. Accenture research has found that for a small group of companies, expanding into new businesses while driving continuous transformation of existing operations has become the new norm. These "Rotation Masters" are constantly reinventing themselves by radically transforming their legacy business, while at the same time seizing new business opportunities. And it's paying off: 64 percent of Rotation Masters have achieved double-digit growth (more than 10 percent) in sales, while 57 percent achieved the same growth results in EBITDA.[23] Similar research has been done by others; Bain calls this "Engine 1; Engine 2," Deloitte calls it "ambidextrous leadership," and the book *Lead and Disrupt: How to Solve the Innovator's Dilemma* calls it an "ambidextrous approach."[24] Organizations must embed structural ambidexterity in the organizational design to account for core and new businesses. An approach recommended by John Kotter is to create a dual operating system—one built for reliability and efficiency, and another built for agility and speed to leap into the future.[25]

Another way to build such ambidexterity into the organizational design is to create a series of microenterprises with unique mechanisms and ways of working to best support each engine. That approach has been refined by Haier, the $35 billion China-based appliance maker—the world's largest with more than 75,000 employees globally. Having long viewed bureaucracy as a competitive liability, Zhang Ruimin, Haier's CEO, built a company where everyone is directly accountable to customers (a policy he describes as "zero distance"), employees are entrepreneurs, and an open ecosystem of users, inventors, and partners replaces formal hierarchy. Haier accomplished those things by evolving from a few monolithic businesses into some 4,000 microenterprises (MEs), most with just 10 to 15 employees. With MEs free to form and evolve with little central direction, they all shared a common approach to target setting, internal contracting, and cross-unit coordination.[26]

We can think of Haier's distinct businesses as modules—discrete capabilities that can be "plugged and played" at will based on well-defined, standardized interfaces. In this way, enterprises operate as actual platforms with multiple autonomous businesses within a business, simultaneously transforming the core, expanding into adjacencies, and growing new businesses. Even support capabilities can become business modules that can efficiently plug and play with companies inside or outside the organization.

Creating new businesses and optimizing the core business depends on fast experimentation. It means using today's unprecedented amount of data to continually test and refine hypotheses and pursuing multiple paths of investigation to reach a more refined conclusion. As the world grows increasingly uncertain, organizations are shifting to creating multiple possible scenarios and as many possibilities as they can through active experimentation.

To be sure, according to the 2019 book *Everyday Chaos*, "the best strategy in a capricious world might be to avoid planning for any one particular scenario and instead create as many possibilities."[27] Some companies seem to be heeding that advice: Deloitte found that prior to COVID, 23 percent of organizations were focused on multiple scenarios for the future; during COVID, the number climbed to 47 percent.[28]

How do you craft your organizational design to accommodate not one but multiple future scenarios? One way is by employing active thought experiments, prioritizing the right *questions* over right answers, and balancing action with learning. In other words, to better focus ideas and actions, leadership teams might try deliberating through thought exercises. The mode of dialogue can itself be important, as MIT researchers discovered when studying the collective intelligence of groups. They found that the more even a dialogue tended to be (that is, the less dominated by a single individual) the higher the group scored on tests of their combined smarts. The MIT researchers also found that including AI as a group member enables collectively intelligent human groups to get even smarter.[29]

Achieving the Balancing Act

In what seems like a bygone era—that is, pre-pandemic—when disruptions tended to hit one at a time, pursuing an organizational design or redesign response to business or economic shifts could work, because the competitive dynamics were relatively predictable. Back then, business leaders could afford to make deliberate, localized decisions, which often affected only a specific segment of the business.

But today enabling growth requires a deliberate focus on elasticity: building agility and sustainability into the design of the organization while creating confidence that the business can meet its performance objectives far into the future. In fact, companies need to adhere to the evolving societal standards and operate using sustainable business practices to scale and drive growth. Opting in or opting out of sustainability is no longer an option.

Consider ESR, one of the largest Asia-Pacific-focused logistics real estate platforms, spanning across China, Japan, South Korea, Singapore, Australia, and India. The company focuses on sustainability through green design initiatives to develop and manage energy- and resource-efficient buildings.[30] This provides long-term benefits for tenants and local communities while also driving value to capital partners. Other companies are achieving the balance between sustainability and agility by developing things like ethical, energy-efficient supply chains and ethical labor relations.

Sustainable organizations expand the term "performance" to optimize environmental, social, and governance (ESG) outcomes as well as financial results. Since the relative emphasis on these outcomes changes over time along with the methods for achieving them, there is no sustainability without agility.[31] Indeed, the digital era has revealed the implications for the effective design and implementation of agile and sustainable organizations.

Take Patagonia, a company that fuses its structure and design with purpose, agility, and sustainability. Patagonia embraces a flat organization model to actively ensure that employees have more freedom in making decisions and pursuing goals. Additionally, taking a stand on environmental issues has made them the envy of many companies seeking to become certified B Corporations—businesses that balance purpose and profit. By risking profit for purpose, they have led the industry in ethical and environmental investment, while blazing a path of steady and continued growth: from 2008 to 2015, Patagonia had a compound annual growth in revenues of 14 percent, while profits surged 300 percent during this period. From 2017 to 2019, Patagonia set new sales records each year, approaching $1 billion in annual revenue in 2019, up from $750 million in 2015.[32] It also contributes 1 percent of annual revenues to nonprofit organizations that promote conservation of the natural environment that their outdoor-customer base loves.[33]

Designing Sustainable Places
More and more, organizational design typically includes a company's "location strategy," which encompasses physical assets such as buildings and equipment that an organization uses. Increasingly, however, because the future of work appears to be a hybrid workplace, organizational design also needs to encompass assets pertaining to remote work. Studies during the pandemic indicated that there could be three to four times as many people working from home than before COVID-19. This change would have a profound impact on urban economies, transportation, and sustainability.[34]

As organizations shift to more remote work operations, therefore, companies will need to understand the critical competencies employees must have to collaborate digitally—and they should be prepared to pivot within the strategy according to employee experiences. Broadly, to be sustainable, organizational design should address such remote-work issues as transforming existing offices into meeting spaces where employees can come into the office only as needed for collaboration or, alternatively, gather together one or two days per week and work from home on the other days.

Indoor spaces where employees work, learn, play, eat, and even heal (with offerings such as massage and on-site health clinics) will also factor into organizational design choices and decisions. Why? Healthy buildings can have an outsized impact on our performance and well-being. They affect creativity, focus, and problem-solving ability, and they can even make employees sick, jeopardizing the organization's future in many ways, including dragging down profits. Study after study has found that performance dramatically improves if you are working in optimal conditions: with high rates of ventilation, few damaging persistent chemicals, and optimal humidity, lighting, and noise control. Research from Harvard's School of Public Health shows how buildings can both expose employees to and protect them from disease. They reveal the Nine Foundations of a Healthy Building and show how tracking what they call "health performance indicators" with smart technology can boost a company's performance and create economic value.[35] Simply stated: healthy buildings are an aspect of healthy organizations.

Reshaping Your Organization for Its Future Evolution

You developed an organizational design for your business back in the startup phase. Now as the organization evolves from startup to maturity, your design needs to evolve too. That's especially true today, when business life cycles have become shorter. Consider the fact that 93 percent of executives say their companies' very existence is jeopardized by operating models that can't keep pace.[36]

But there is a difference between reactive improvisation (as we've seen in the pandemic) and proactive, continual evolution of organizational design. And I am not talking here about revisiting your design after a reorganization. In fact, rather than focusing attention on a reorganization as a means to scale and turbocharge growth, leaders should consider first proactively looking at the ways their current organizational design needs to evolve along with the business. Such evolution often requires three actions:

- The ability to quickly gain new capabilities
- The ability to evolve from a startup into a mature business
- The development of continuous change capabilities

Gain New Capabilities

Organizations are often missing the capabilities needed to evolve quickly and expand and grow. Sometimes it's a capability that's hard to come by, like a creative imagination. In an article about the demise of Digital Equipment Corporation (DEC), the author notes:

"The first glimpse came when the engineers at DEC saw the Apple II. Had they the imagination, in that taupe plastic box they could have seen the death of their entire industry."[37]

But just as often, the problem is a broken business and operating model that doesn't drive enough profit. Kellogg's, for example, saw its future in the growing segment of the healthy ready-to-eat cereal category and adroitly picked up a vibrant, organic upstart, Kashi—an alternative cereal and nutritional convenience-food maker—only to succumb to the internal battles. To cut costs and increase margins, Kellogg's started making Kashi bars with GMO grains,[38] and today the company faces similar pressures again.

Companies experiencing fast growth must build an agile and sustained organization designed to rapidly deploy and redeploy talent and resources without denigrating operational capability in other areas. Capability building is more important than ever and includes everything from training on how to run virtual meetings and executive coaching to workshops focused on teaching fundamentals around how to lead change. Before the pandemic, 59 percent of organizations said capability building was very or extremely important to their organization's long-term growth; a year into the pandemic, 78 percent agreed.[39] While companies face significant opportunities to expand and realize revenue and profit growth, they may not always readily have the organizational capabilities to do so effectively. Why? For one, external disruptions to a given market (e.g., new regulations, innovations, customer performance requirements) can quickly make current business and/or operating models less viable. In meeting these challenges, organizational designs must be able to outpace disruptive changes of environmental jolts, economic shocks, and more classical reorganizations.

How do you get new capabilities fast? One way is to create an organizational design not just for the organization but also for the ecosystem around it with which it shares interests. Organizations can design in collaboration with a broad range of ecosystem partners, including academic institutions, startups, alliances, and even competitors to acquire new capabilities quickly. Also, they can design their organizations for modularity, and design it to share or rent assets. Take hospitality, for example, where platform-based companies like Airbnb, TripAdvisor, and Open Table have marketplaces that bring together large numbers of producers of products or services and potential customers.

Evolve into a Mature Business

In addition to gaining new capabilities, organizations—particularly startups—need to develop abilities that will make them faster and able to mature. Organizational designs that can operate with speed can successfully scale to enable business growth. But with growth, complexity and complication multiply. As the frequency and magnitude of disruption increases, the comfortable notion of being able to change or refresh your organizational design every so often is obsolete. Organizational designs need constant upgrades, not periodic tune-ups. Faster and more uncertain markets and environments require more flexible and agile organizations.

Develop Continuous Change Capabilities

To continually evolve, organizations need to develop continuous change capabilities. For future-focused organizations seeking to scale and grow, not only should their leaders *inspire* change, they also need to *instigate* change as catalysts. This stance enables companies to take an integrative and future-focused approach to their strategic redesign, allowing them to integrate structure, people, process, and incentives as leverage points to drive scale and growth.

I worked with the leaders of one technology business, which I'll call PSO, who took this stance of instigating change to heart. Driven by an emerging need to reshape a global organization toward a business for the future (just after a period of executive turnover, a series of disjointed reorgs, and a stalled transformation), PSO doubled down on its strategic direction. It also refocused on a portfolio of transformation initiatives that connected business model innovation and scale to enable revenue. Other businesses trying to scale globally would do well to follow suit. Engaging leaders at all levels and aligning mindsets and incentives to reinforce new behaviors go a long way toward executing large-scale organizational design efforts and growing the company.

Using AI to Transform the Organization's Design

While the recent economic crisis served as a potent accelerant for organizations to create more adaptive designs, advances in AI have also accelerated such change, especially over the last half decade. Ninety-five percent of extensive adopters of AI say their organizational structure will change as a result of adopting those technologies, with a full 39 percent saying that AI will change their organizational structure fundamentally.[40] When asked *how* AI will change their organization structure, respondents cited (in order): more continuous learning, the creation of new business units, more cross-functional collaboration, more agile ways of working, and more team-based work.

Tom Malone, director of the MIT Center for Collective Intelligence, explains how AI will effectively change business hierarchies. For one thing, management structures could become more rigid. "AI will help managers track more detailed data about everything their subordinates are doing," he writes, "which should make it easier—and more inviting—to exercise stricter controls." But a deeper look reveals the opposite is more likely. "That's because when AI does the routine tasks, much of the remaining nonroutine work is likely to be done in loose 'adhocracies,' ever-shifting groups of people with the combinations of skills needed for whatever problems arise."[41] Thus AI actually would lead to less rigidity, not more.

Another impact of AI is the notion of "data democratization," which enables companies to integrate data across the businesses and allow a broader range of employees to access and understand data where needed.[42] If data and tools are readily available, employees will be able to extract real value from AI because they will have the information and the empowerment to make final decisions aided by AI and act on those decisions.[43] When companies design their organizations to optimize for AI and an increasingly shifting environment, they unlock the technology's potential to help the business continually adapt.

Let's examine some specific ways that AI will almost certainly transform organizational design.

Organizations Will Become More Experimental

New sources of data and AI enable an organization to experiment and evolve its structure. With advances in digital and AI, companies can leverage critical organizational data and convert it into knowledge, insights, and action, such as new behaviors, initiatives, or redesigned structures and processes, to produce business outcomes that improve financial performance. Consider how one consumer packaged goods company decreased time-to-market by almost a year when it used data analytics to identify employees who were causing delays. It then redirected communications to other employees who were better able to push ideas and products to market.

Or consider how Humanyze, a startup, provides smart ID badges that track employees throughout the office, reporting data to employers on how well employees interact and collaborate during the day. In this and other ways, AI can help increase the predictive power used in team collaboration and innovation at scale.[44]

Consider these other examples of AI's impact on organizational design:

- **AI on the org chart.** Leaders are beginning to view machines—not just employees—as workforce talent. Now that AI is essentially "joining" the workforce, it makes sense to include such automation in the design of the organization too.
- **How work *actually* gets done.** AI and new sources of data can help leaders see how work is done in the organization rather than through the org chart. AI can be used to find the right balance of decentralized decision making, delegating more decision rights to the front lines as they can handle it. But many organizations may fear pushing such major decisions down to workers too far and giving employees too much autonomy. AI even has a solution for this. Take, for example, Klick Health's machine learning technology, Genome, which helps employers manage autonomy. By analyzing every project at every stage in the firm, it rewards more responsibility to people who have

demonstrated consistent competency and success. The AI tracks every decision made in the firm and the context in which it was made. The more a person proves their judgment, the more flexibility the system grants in making bigger decisions.[45] These factors take human bias and politics out of the equation and reward people based on evidence and merit alone.

- **Transcend basic scenario modeling.** Analytics-informed, tech-enabled experimentation and evaluation of organizational data provide organizations with the ability to continuously mine unstructured data like email and online activity to paint a truly connected and "live" view of the organization that surpasses traditional enterprise resource planning systems and HR databases. Organizational design has always been about understanding and reinforcing as well as creating a pattern of interactions among a group of members that help accomplish the organization's goals. What has changed is the availability of fine-grained data about interactions and the computational power to analyze them. Consequently, we need new ways to think about organizational design that link individual actions and interactions to business results.
- **Unleash the productive power of talent.** The biggest opportunity created by implementing AI at scale is not the cost reductions and efficiencies (although they're great too), but rather the new levels of human creativity and innovation you can unlock. Leaders need an approach that puts transparency, iteration, and participation at its core. New sources of data, tech, and AI can help with this— making it far easier for people to access the information they need, enabling them to test, learn, and iterate, and enabling them to network and find one another to create self-organizing teams.
- **Configure and coach teams.** With networks of teams emerging as the dominant building block of the agile organization, organizations can also use AI to help create

the right team compositions and coach them for performance. Saberr, for example, has an AI bot that improves a team's performance with intelligent digital coaching, personalized for each team. It is based on analyzing productivity, relationships, roles and responsibilities, goals and purpose, and decision making.

Investor leaders are also using algorithmic decision-making platforms to increase productivity, reduce managerial errors, and improve the quality of decisions. For example, Ray Dalio's hedge fund Bridgewater Associates, the world's largest hedge fund with $150 billion in assets, developed a "robo-coach" that acts like a personal GPS for decision making. Investment principles are converted into algorithms, which are then automated to guide employee interactions and decision making.[46] In a lengthy interview with *Business Insider*, Dalio aimed to clarify his firm's effort to create an "idea meritocracy." That endeavor has led Bridgewater to create a system in which employees rate one another's credibility on several dimensions, and everyone can see the ratings. The data from these assessments are crunched to create a "believability" rating. Votes by employees with higher believability ratings are given greater weight in decision making. That, Dalio told *Business Insider*, is how a company can achieve an ideal meritocracy underpinned by "radical truth" and "radical transparency."[47]

Bridgewater is just one of many institutional investors that are using rapid insights through automated reporting or drag-and-drop interfaces to enable more value-adding analyses, such as simultaneously simplifying processes and streamlining management layers. Ultimately, reducing layers drives smarter, faster decision making, elevates employee engagement within the organization, and accelerates agile organizational design.

The Unique Needs of Investment Companies

Leaders who perceive their business environment as extremely chaotic and changeable—such as in PE or VC companies—will likely focus heavily on making their organizations agile. Resourceful portfolio CEOs and management teams that thrive in today's challenging business environment will be clear about the structure needed to scale while flexing their managerial muscle to balance the tension between longer holding periods and short-term value creation. That balancing act requires designing new organizational forms that are agile, sustainable, and far more responsive than the conventional analog company. That truth applies both within the PE or VC firm and across portfolio companies with due consideration of current structure, processes, and people capabilities.

Specifically, when portfolio leaders design their organizations to incorporate six key factors, they increase the odds for stronger performance:

- Simple rules and simple measures that delineate profit and loss responsibilities and governance
- Practices that elevate agile structures, agile cultures, and ways of working
- Cross-team collaborative behavior backed by incentives
- Automated or augmented end-to-end business processes with clear customer interfaces
- Hybrid human and machine roles that free up time to focus on more value-added work
- Porous and flexible talent pools and ecosystems enabling rapid resource allocation

Similarly, many leaders agree that the planet can no longer be ignored and must have full standing in all decisions related to innovation, performance, and overall agility and sustainability of a company. As noted earlier in the book, a healthy organization is worth a lot. Sustainability extends this definition of healthy by focusing on the long-term economic and brand value driven by strategies that positively impact the environment and the social community in which a business exists.

Some private equity and venture capital firms promote environmental stewardship across their portfolio companies through procurement of products and services from vendors whose design and manufacturing practices are environmentally and socially responsible.

Others encourage portfolio companies to monitor and measure progress toward achieving corporate sustainability and socially responsible business and IT practices and track the business benefits accrued from doing so.

Growth, clearly, is high on the agenda for investors, founders, CEOs, and business leaders alike across the private equity and venture capital continuum—even as market volatility remains at an all-time high. Investors, boards, and portfolio management teams recognize that their organizational designs must match and stay aligned to the environment to sustainably compete in the digital economy. Consider global private equity firm Warburg Pincus, which cultivates relationships with real estate and environmental consultants that provide on-site visits for energy audits, analysis of energy-efficient capital improvement projects, green leasing options, and other low-cost opportunities to reduce energy use. So, when an investment is posted, that's when rapid day-one organization and governance design reduce uncertainty felt by the broader organization. Thus, it is critical for investor leaders and portfolio management teams to utilize organizational design methods as a management tool to rethink their structure, roles, and sourcing of work activities—and ultimately to scale and grow. They should invest in robust organizational mapping/job mapping processes to customize selection processes and right-size the location of talent and physical assets, factoring in agility and sustainability.

But gaining the agility to compete isn't a one-time exercise. Rather, it's an ongoing process as leaders seek optimal designs to organize and meet the demands of scale and growth. Hence, to succeed in the digital world, a company's organization model or organizational design must be as dynamic as its business model. The right organizational design must be in place and tightly aligned to the value-creation plan and business strategy to enable successful execution. When this occurs, the impact can be big. Privately held hypergrowth companies, like publicly listed companies operating in today's more complex market environment, now face a much more complex organizational challenge. Given the unique needs of privately held hypergrowth companies, which are often financed by PE/VC, the velocity and acceleration of change have ratcheted up while digital requirements have become more complex. Bureaucratic structures are maladaptive to platform-based business and organization models and radical transparency. Digital advances have ushered in the era of machine learning algorithms, which demands both complex coordination of multiple specializations and rapid adjustment to shifts in markets, technology, and the planet. The era of machine learning algorithms demands other items too: increased skills in judgment and data literacy, as well as leaders who are attuned to issues of bias, and data privacy.

Organizations can be designed to fit the ecosystems that continue to multiply as a product of the digital era. The organizational model of a high-growth company should be based on strategy-driven operating requirements that result in integrated structural, people, process, and incentives decisions. Resourceful CEOs and management teams that can thrive in this challenging environment do so by designing new organizational forms that are agile, sustainable, and far more responsive than the conventional analog company.

In the next chapter, we continue to explore the theme of sustainability with a look at the sixth condition for cultivating your organization's health: the degree to which the company practices equity, inclusion, and diversity.

Checklist for Agenda Setting

- Design organizations for agility *and* sustainability to promote environmentally sound and sustainable practices across operations.
- To design for agility, create organizational hubs to manage agility, adopt a flatter network of teams, and use an ecosystems approach to organizational design. Additionally, create greater transparency to empower employees on the front line to adapt to changing conditions, design for experimentation and collaboration, and design to account for core and new businesses.
- To design for sustainability, design sustainable places, provide different stakeholder groups a meaningful voice in governance and decision

(*continued*)

making, aim for triple–bottom line outcomes, and embed sustainability into the DNA of the organizational system and structure rather than siloing it as a project, a corporate initiative, a department, or a position.

- Conduct an organizational audit to spot any issues with respect to the organizational design's alignment with the company's strategic direction; clear but flexible structure and roles; lack of duplication of individual and organizational capabilities or bureaucratic processes; presence of digital talent, mindsets, and incentives.
- New organizational design challenges require new thinking. To ensure continual evolution, focus on gaining new capabilities, the ability to evolve from startup into a mature business, and the development of continuous change capabilities.
- Employ technology advances to radically disrupt business as usual in order to adapt to the market, while infusing digital talent and tools with the use of AI and analytics to transform organizational design.

6 ■ Equity, Inclusion, and Diversity

Adopt a Bias for Radical Transparency and Belonging

To overcome deeply embedded historical practices and craft equitable workplaces where everyone feels they belong, today's
organizations must provide more than window dressing. They
must harness the power of radical transparency to create policies and practices that satisfy new social demands and integrate
respect, empathy, and fairness into the organization's very fabric.

By now, most leaders understand, at least in theory, that to be
healthy—to grow and thrive—companies need to be equitable, inclusive, and diverse (EID). Most leaders have seen the numbers to
support that notion. For example, inclusive organizations are eight
times more likely to achieve better business outcomes, six times more
likely to be innovative and agile, and two times more likely to meet
or exceed financial targets.[1] Moreover, the more diverse the organization, the stronger the impact on the bottom line: companies that
embrace ethnic and racial diversity and inclusion are one-third more

likely to outperform industry norms. And when gender diversity is embraced, companies earn 21 percent more revenue than the other companies in their industry.[2]

In spite of the evidence in support of EID, however, organizations have largely failed when it comes to these issues—so much so that today we're in the midst of a reckoning, both in our businesses and in society as a whole. As already described in chapter 1, the killing of George Floyd in 2020 by a Minneapolis police officer became a spark that ignited mass outrage over injustices, past and current, against African American communities. After weeks of protests across the globe, businesses began to make substantive changes to their EID profiles. For example, JPMorgan Chase made a $30 billion commitment to promote racial equity over five years.[3] Likewise, companies across corporate America as diverse as Home Depot, Procter & Gamble, and Coca-Cola pledged billions to encourage diversity in employee ranks and in the communities in which the companies operate.

However laudable these commitments have been, companies and investors face significant challenges if they aspire to make a difference beyond diversity that's based solely on demographics. Outdated policies, unfamiliar gender designations, cultural, ethnic, and racial differences, and organizational barriers are often just the surface manifestations of bigger underlying issues that need attention. Responding to the challenges of today means addressing equity, inclusion, and diversity by way of "intersectionality," because the interconnected nature of social categorizations such as race, class, and gender often serve to widen even further the equity gaps already experienced by any given individual or group. Real change will require an understanding of all three dimensions of equity, inclusion, and diversity, which together comprise our sixth condition of healthy organizations. Today's digital companies need to deliberately cultivate inclusive cultures that enable all employees to thrive and experience a sense of belonging.

This chapter will look at precisely what's meant by EID and will expand that definition even further. It will explore the wide-ranging challenges that come with incorporating EID into workplaces—

including why the gig economy makes it hard to offer workers a true sense of belonging. It will touch on why EID matters, particularly for investors, such as private equity firms. And it will answer the question of why the digital age is also, necessarily, the age of radical transparency before diving into the ways that AI is unleashing EID specifically and how companies can begin their own such transformations.

Let's start with a closer look at how today's organizations have found themselves confronting a powerful ultimatum: become more equitable or risk their demise.

The "S" Factor in ESG: How Social Issues Intertwine with EID

So, how did we get here? In the last half decade, the #MeToo movement, Black Lives Matter, the peaceful protests to condemn police brutality, racism, sexism, and other forms of bias and discrimination— all of these have amplified the importance of the societal aspect of the trio of issues (environmental, social, and governance, or ESG) that organizations today must address. Accordingly, EID mandates have been rising on the organizational agenda, and there are many compelling reasons that drive people to create more equitable, inclusive, and diverse organizations. These include (but are not limited to) heightened awareness of the need for more just workplaces, a way to provide companies with a sense of purpose, or the promise of funding that an EID focus might attract.

As a result, we're seeing initiatives today such as Salesforce's announcement in 2020 that they would invest $200 million and dedicate 1 million volunteer hours by employees—all targeted at working with organizations worldwide to advance racial equality and justice.[4] Or consider the University of California's investment to incorporate EID into its responsibilities as an employer, asset allocator, and shareholder—an initiative more commonly called "Diversified Returns"[5]—to make a difference on a larger scale.

But effectively shaping an equitable, inclusive, and diverse organization—one that goes beyond a basic gender or ethnicity focus or metric reporting on diversity demographics—is more complicated than it may seem at the outset. Why? For three big reasons.

First (and predictably), leaders must deal with the sorts of new and evolving identity categories that are becoming more common to any organization's reality. For example, organizations must determine how much to openly acknowledge that their employees' identities may not fit existing categories of gender or race. Instead of rigid categories like male or female, identities today are far more likely to fall across a spectrum of multiple options. Consider how Facebook now lists 71 gender options from which users can choose, including gender neutral, transgender, and gender questioning. Likewise, categorizing people in just one dimension (such as gender) can also be problematic. A focus on women leaders, for example, may not capture the intersectional aspects and increased bias that could also be at play: consider the unique ways in which Black women leaders feel excluded as compared to Asian women leaders. In fact, the increasing recognition of this new discipline of intersectionality (looking at all the characteristics that apply to an individual in combination, rather than considering each characteristic of that individual in isolation) may help leaders address the full complexity of diversity.

And then there are all the other dimensions of people who might be marginalized but that often aren't captured. For example, dimensions such as neurodiverse populations, caregivers, LGBTQIA or LGBTQ+ (lesbian, gay, bisexual, transgender, queer or questioning, intersex, asexual) populations, or people with disabilities, to name just a few.

Given today's increased complexity in all of those areas and more, it's no wonder that business executives and investors might feel stymied when it comes to EID issues. Consider cryptocurrency platform Coinbase's CEO Brian Armstrong, whose policy to discourage employee activism and discussing politics at work resulted in 5 percent of its employees either being offered severance to quit or leaving in protest.[6] Nevertheless, businesses must decide whether to align their organizations with these shifts in societal culture. And they need to recognize that doing so will likely mean eschewing former policies and practices in favor of adopting new ones that reflect a more modernized stance.

A second complicating issue around EID at companies today is that it forces leaders and employees to confront and discuss what makes them uncomfortable. No company can dodge and weave around society's demand for transparency on issues of gender parity, pay transparency, LGBTQIA rights, or the upward mobility of underrepresented minorities—much less capitalize on them— if its top management, board, and investors are less than committed to confront years or decades of exclusionary practices. Today, companies operating in a digital, AI-first context must institute equitable and inclusive practices, while diversifying their on- and off-balance-sheet talent pools, such as gig economy workers, including freelancers, independent contractors, and other contingent workers not fully employed by the company. Organizationally healthy companies will be those that can recognize the benefits of shifting, not just temporarily, their talent composition and therefore expanding the possibilities for performance, innovation, and investing.

Consider the slew of research in recent years highlighting the positive impact that diversity can have on investment outcomes. Diverse investment teams, for example, perform as well as or better than others. And diverse leadership teams operating in an inclusive culture boost innovation, while gender-balanced investment teams have a 20 percent higher net internal rate of return.[7] As noted by one operating partner focused on organizational issues at the private equity firm Blue Wolf Capital: "Beyond the numbers, the value of an investment is often dependent on a company's human capital; people with a particular mindset can make or break the profitability of a portfolio company."[8]

A third challenge is answering a big question that's increasingly asked, especially if you are an investor: How diverse are the entrepreneurs you are talking to in your pipeline? One venture capital firm with $5 billion assets under management is using data and analytics to proactively preempt such a question. This tech-focused VC uses data modeling tools and techniques not only to examine what the diversity of funded companies looks like but also to examine how they can identify potential minority-led/Black founder–led companies in which to invest. Interestingly, in parallel, they are at the early stages of leveraging AI to tap into the funnel of pitches or sources of deal flow, which can also help identify diverse entrepreneurs.

Why EID, Not DEI?

Organizations might well be diverse but not inclusive. In fact, diversity alone does not guarantee either inclusion or equity. Diversity is critically important but merely the "tip of the iceberg for this entire field," as one diversity and inclusion chief in a venture capital firm shared with me. That is why I prefer to *begin* the acronym with the E, for equity, which encompasses "inclusion and diversity." In other words, I and D will more likely follow when equity is the focused priority.

But what precisely do we mean by equity, inclusion, and diversity—and a newer term to join the ranks: belonging? Let's take a closer look at each element of EID-B.

The *E* in EID—equity—includes the combined set of policies and practices that an organization adopts to ensure fairness in treatment, equality of opportunity, and access to information and resources. But don't confuse equity with equality. Equality aims to promote fairness, but it can only work if everyone starts from the same place and needs the same help. Rather than treating everyone the same regardless of need (equality), a more sophisticated or just view of fairness is treating people differently depending on their need (equity).

For example, organizations may achieve equity by giving more to disadvantaged groups who need it, as a way of eventually reaching equality. Fairness is important; research has shown that employees who feel fairly treated in their workplace trust their employer, enjoy their work, and are more dedicated to their workplace.[9] *E* also encompasses parity, or statistical measures that compare a particular indicator (like pay) among one group (such as women) with that of another group (such as men), with the goal of achieving equal indicators (equal pay for men and women). When done right, performance management and compensation systems help ensure pay and advancement parity, and also compliance with the law.

The *I* in EID—inclusion—addresses how welcomed diverse people feel in an organization, and the extent to which an organization's culture cultivates it by actively encouraging the contribution and participation of all who make up an organization's workforce. Inclusive cultures enable all employees to feel supported and respected, able to bring their authentic selves to work each day. Authenticity is a major element of such inclusion, and true inclusion is a step toward belonging. Inclusion also speaks to prospective recruits to the organization, reflecting and affecting the brand and reputation.

D—diversity—is the representation across varied identities and differences, both visible (such as race or gender) as well as underlying, not-visible differences (such as culture, religion, or thinking style). For legal, social, and economic reasons, creating a diverse workforce is now a required capability for organizations that seek to scale and grow. For one, only organizations whose workforces mirror the people in the communities in which they operate can expect to effectively understand and serve their customers. Two, research has long shown that diverse perspectives spark innovation, reduce algorithmic bias, and unleash a whole host of other benefits for organizations, from improved brand reputation to reduced turnover, higher engagement, and faster problem solving. Importantly, and as mentioned earlier, diversity impacts the bottom line. When inclusion and ethnic and racial diversity are embraced, companies are one-third more likely to outperform industry norms.[10]

What these studies and others suggest is that talent (and culture) and how much your people feel they belong are important criteria to consider for winning in the digital age. "At the end of the day, your biggest differentiator is going to be: do you have the best talent?" said Chip Bergh, CEO of Levi Strauss. "So, doubling down on talent is critical. And so, the large investors, BlackRock, Fidelity, the guys that are long-term investors and companies, want to know what you are doing on diversity and inclusion, and what you are doing to drive engagement with employees."[11]

Finally, *B*, for belonging, is an important addition to EID when it comes to organizational health. For all our talk of diversity and inclusion, leaders often fail to recognize that just because someone is included in an organization certainly doesn't mean they feel they belong. A diverse and inclusive organization might not cultivate a sense of belonging in some employees. The result is usually a stubbornly disengaged workforce and high turnover. Simply put: employees who lack a sense of belonging are likely to feel that they are unable to fully contribute and reach their potential. (See the box "CEOs: Does Your Company Make People Feel They Belong?")

The consequences for a workforce lacking a sense of belonging are high indeed. According to research, 44 percent of employees feel isolated at work, leading to lower employee commitment and engagement.[12] Other research has found that belonging correlates to a 56 percent increase in job performance and a 50 percent drop in turnover risk.[13]

Belonging is a feeling and therefore a far more powerful force than any EID strategy could ever be. Belonging is a basic human tenet. If diversity represents the numbers in the demographics of a company's workforce, inclusion is a set of mindsets and behaviors that

CEOs: Does Your Company Make People Feel They Belong?

If you are a CEO leading an organization today, here are some questions you can ask yourself to get a sense of your company's "belonging" quotient:

- My employees are respected for their differences, but are they truly engaged?
- Do the employees who make up my workforce today feel comfortable sharing new perspectives and ideas?
- Do people in my company—across different time zones, geographies, cultures, backgrounds, etc.—actively listen to and value each other's contributions? Or are some employees (diverse or not) brushed off, ignored, or talked over?
- Do my leaders, beginning with my top management team, make all their people feel connected and valued? Do they not only invite their people to the table (inclusion) but go beyond that to encourage everyone to contribute to the conversation or the task at hand?

lead a person in the workplace to experience being included or not. Belonging, however, is a feeling that can be deliberately experienced and reinforced through organizational culture.[14] As Pat Wadors, who is credited with creating the term "DIBs" (Diversity, Inclusion, and Belonging) puts it: "D&I may capture your head, but belonging captures your heart."[15]

While EID is necessary, it is simply not sufficient. As Harvard Business professor Amy Edmondson notes, to unlock the full potential of organizations, they must be supported by a culture that enables all team members to bring their full selves to the table, which she calls a culture of "psychological safety." Edmondson explains: "With so much riding on innovation, creativity, and spark, it is essential to attract and retain quality talent—but what good does this talent do if no one is able to speak their mind? The traditional culture of 'fitting in' and 'going along' spells doom in the knowledge economy. Success requires a continuous influx of new ideas, new challenges, and critical thought, and the interpersonal climate must not suppress, silence, ridicule or intimidate."[16]

Salesforce provides a good example of a company focused on crafting a culture of true belonging, an effort that starts at the top and includes supporting underrepresented communities. "We all know the fight for equality will never be done," CEO Marc Benioff said recently. "We are guided by our core values and are fortunate to have our Office of Equality team leading us and building on our progress."[17] To that end, Benioff appointed Tony Prophet as a CEO of a different kind—a chief equality officer—focused on "ensuring everyone at Salesforce receives respect and fairness, no matter the longitude or latitude," in Prophet's words.[18]

At Salesforce and throughout his career as a Silicon Valley executive, Prophet has also worked as a human rights and social justice champion. He began his career as part of the GM Institute Co-Op, where he started in the company car wash. From there, he quickly moved on to working side by side with hourly workers on the factory floor. In theory, Prophet was learning the importance of doing the best that he could with whatever task he'd been given. But he believes the most important result of that training was the empathy and respect he gained for people across all levels of an organization. He learned what it takes to work effectively, to do the right thing, and what it might take to further equality for everyone in the workplace. In effect, he was taking some important steps toward the role he holds today.

At Salesforce, Prophet is focused on building a workplace that reflects the diverse communities it serves and that advances equality for all. He is also leading the new Ethical & Humane Use of Technology initiative to ensure that the technology developed by Salesforce not only drives the success of the company's customers but also drives positive social change and improves the lives of people around the world.[19] For example, consider how Salesforce's platform helped Experience Matters—a nonprofit focused on connecting the skills and talents of experienced adults/retirees with the diverse needs of nonprofits—to create an integrated view to sync local volunteers' skill sets with local community organizations' needs.[20] Another example of a company driving positive change is JPMorgan Chase. Its racial equity program provides Black-led, Black-owned, and Black-serving nonprofits and businesses with a new markets tax credit (NMTC) investment price as a way to incentivize private investors to increase the flow of capital to businesses and provide financing to underserved communities.

Not all companies, however well intentioned their efforts, have been able to make the kinds of strides toward equity, inclusion, diversity, and belonging that Salesforce has managed. And there's much that can be learned by looking at what can go wrong.

Hurdles along the Path to Equity, Inclusion, and Diversity

When an organization grows, both in size and complexity, things that were previously simple and easy tend to become more difficult. Different maturity levels and growth rates of a company impose different requirements on a company's organizational health. That truism applies especially to equity, inclusion, and diversity in a company: if a leader leaves those requirements until too late, the organization may experience a series of punctuated crises and face difficult regulatory and societal pressures.

And yet, better to address EID deficiencies late in the game as opposed to never. At least then the problem can be assessed and corrections can begin. As James Baldwin wrote, "Not everything that is faced can be changed; but nothing can be changed until it is faced."[21] Organizations attempting to scale in the digital era while simultaneously improving the workforce's sense of equity, inclusion, diversity, and belonging should take note. The first step is to recognize and face the problem.

Ideally, companies should incorporate EID principles and requirements from the outset. Such practices should be part of the culture from the beginning, although as the organization matures, the picture of equity, inclusion, and diversity within the company will necessarily shift as well.

But the question remains: Why do some companies institute clear policies, robust practices, and a culture of belonging with ease, while others have trouble either immediately or down the road? What part of the solution can be dealt with through policies and practices? What part of the solution can be addressed through the behavioral lens, notably the mindsets and behaviors at the board and top management levels?

To be sure, scaling EID alongside a company's growth can be fraught with headaches. As successful VC investor Ben Horowitz famously said, "If you want to build an important company, then at some point you have to scale. So, if you want to do something that matters, then you are going to have to learn the black art of scaling a human organization."[22] Let's look at some of these challenges, not all of which have ready solutions.

- **The hard and soft challenges of EID.** One reason why EID can evoke so much anxiety among senior executives and investors alike is that even companies that are highly adept at managing the "hard" aspects of EID may at the same time ignore or underprioritize the "soft" aspects. And by the time the importance of this omission is made clear, it may be too late. Soft aspects include psychological safety and belonging (as already discussed). Because these can be difficult to quantify, they therefore are often neglected. Hard aspects of EID are akin to the formal policies and practices necessary for organizational health: for example, constructing hard metrics and targets such as dashboards and annual diversity reports, or metrics on supplier diversity and sourcing channels. Consider Monsanto, which provides its HR staff and managers with an automated dashboard to help them make informed people and diversity management decisions. Similarly, General Motors CEO Mary Barra uses a "diversity scorecard" with her direct reports—and ties their scorecard results to their bonuses to ensure they are accountable.[23]

- **The culture challenge of EID.** Instilling equity, inclusion, and diversity into the organization represents a major form of cultural transformation. While such a transformation can potentially hold great rewards, it can nonetheless potentially be painful and take a long time to achieve. Therefore, as companies mature, they must embark on an EID journey that mirrors the evolution of their business practices toward maturity. In other words, they must work toward creating a workplace culture that is inclusive for individuals and policies that span legal and regulatory compliance to ensure fairness and equal treatment of people regardless of their range of differences. Practically speaking, organizationally healthy companies focus their attention on the formal aspects of EID, such as policies, practices, and capability building (i.e., unconscious bias training). They devote as much of their attention to the challenging task of cultivating the informal aspects of EID, such as creating a culture of psychological safety and belonging. Consider software company Rainforest QA, which uses unconscious-bias tests on company executives to encourage them to take into account various forms of bias when they design company policies, programs, and initiatives.[24]

- **Why increasing diversity can sometimes interfere with routine tasks in the workforce.** Consider how one study of financial services firms found that the racial diversity of individuals in the workforce was associated with higher productivity in firms seeking a growth strategy—but with lower productivity in firms pursuing a downsizing strategy.[25] At the team level, another study reveals that the nature of the work performed affects how team diversity can have varied effects on performance. For example, diverse teams are much more capable of recognizing their biases than nondiverse teams.[26] The conclusion? Diversity is often beneficial for activities that require creative problem solving, but it can interfere with performance on routine tasks.[27] The implication? Diversity matters even more in an AI-first world, where work is increasingly nonroutine, agile, judgment-oriented, and project-based, and often completed by self-organizing networks of teams. As work becomes more agile, iterative, and complex, teams will increasingly comprise people with a broad range of backgrounds and talents from across a range of organizational boundaries. For example, Amazon did away with its recruiting algorithm once it was revealed how gender-biased it was.[28] Or consider a video-upload app for iOS launched by YouTube. Between 5 and 10 percent of videos uploaded by users were upside-down because the design team was almost exclusively right-handed. In other words, the developer team had not considered the way left-handed users manage a phone.

- **How gig economies can work against a sense of belonging.** In recent years, the rise of tribalism, polarization, and populism has led many employees to turn to the workplace to find meaning and solidarity. But the simultaneous rise of alternative workforces—gig workers, freelancers, independent consultants, and the like—have left many workers feeling even less like they belong in an organization at all. Layoffs and cutbacks, when they occur, further fray the psychological contract between employees and organizations. And of course, the way many of us use technology can contribute to feelings of isolation, and gig work often revolves around technology. Many people essentially became gig workers during the pandemic when they shifted to remote work. In recent studies, virtual workers cited loneliness, longer work hours, and erosion of feelings of belonging.

While there are no easy solutions to these challenges to incorporating EID and belonging in organizations, leaders still need to consider and weigh them as they explore their companies' organizational health.

Next, we look at the importance of EID considerations in the context of private investment companies.

Why Equity, Inclusion, and Diversity Matter for VC and PE Firms

As part of due diligence, private equity firms investing their limited partners' capital are adept at uncovering and analyzing data like spend, costs, EBITDA (earnings before interest, taxes, depreciation, and amortization), and total addressable market. But what about assessing another critical dimension not represented on the balance sheet? In other words: how diverse is the company, including its board and management team? As private equity grows in its importance in shaping the business landscape, due to the decline in public companies over the last two decades by almost 50 percent, scrutiny will grow over the diversity of top talent in PE portfolio companies. That will include scrutiny over whom it places on boards or management teams.

Moreover, competition for deals will increase over the next five years. Because private equity is now the fastest-expanding asset class within private capital firms—growing at 9.1 percent compound annual growth rate (CAGR) over the past five years[29]—many private equity firms face pressure to improve returns through higher deal multiples and leverage. With so much at stake for different stakeholders, "things like culture, diversity and inclusion, and team effectiveness are critical for success," says Ben Holzemer, the human capital partner at TPG Capital, a traditional leveraged buyout fund.[30] EID issues are a priority for the firm: Holzemer is highly focused on working with portfolio companies to build healthy businesses and develop strong leadership teams.

It's well understood in private equity that great management teams can do great things. Even more, diverse management teams can do remarkable things and boost innovation. Portfolio company performance is strongly correlated with having the right team in place at the outset of ownership. With so much at stake, PE firms need to install the right set of diverse leadership talent right from the start. As shared by a colleague of mine, a chief human resources officer (CHRO) responsible for the people function of a PE-backed company: "PE leaders and boards have discovered that diverse leadership teams are the ones driving the best financial results. So, diversity and inclusion really matter."

Venture capital firms have their challenges as well. For example, Crunchbase found that Black and Latinx founders raised $2.3 billion in funding, representing just 2.6 percent of the total $87.3 billion in funding that had gone to all founders since 2020. Moreover, over five years, an abysmally low 2.4 percent of total funding went to Black and Latinx founders.[31]

Another study focused on whether early-stage investors display gender biases. The researchers used a proprietary data set from AngelList to observe private interactions between investors and fundraising startups. They found that male investors express less interest in female entrepreneurs compared to observably similar male entrepreneurs. In contrast, female investors express more interest in female entrepreneurs. The findings were not driven by within-gender screening/monitoring advantages or gender differences in risk preferences. Interestingly, the male-led startups that male investors express interest in actually underperform compared with the female-led startups they express interest in—suggesting evidence is consistent with gender biases.[32]

The investment industry's narrative, which has historically prioritized financial returns at the expense of equity, inclusion, and diversity, has started to unravel. It is no longer a trade-off between the two; rather, the new narrative is that the two are mutually interdependent. Today, megafunds like SoftBank, large VC funds like Andreessen Horowitz, and select PE funds like Carlyle and Blackstone invest large sums of capital in Black and Latinx entrepreneurs. At the same time, they're introducing new measures to create a diverse and inclusive environment within their own workforces and at the companies they own—all of which is leading to a sea change for diversity at the top. Let's take a closer look at what's taking shape at some firms.

PE firms, which directly and indirectly employ millions of workers globally, wield a significant influence across major sectors of the economy as fund sizes grow. These firms are embracing their role not only as value creators but also as social change agents. Consider the Carlyle Group, a Washington, D.C.–based private equity firm, and its efforts to implement a new hiring policy requiring at least one candidate interviewed for every new role be Black, Latinx, Pacific Islander, or Native American. The firm, whose portfolio companies employ close to 900,000 people, also has committed to ensuring that 30 percent of all board directors of Carlyle-backed companies are gender and racially diverse.[33] Further, Carlyle is making diversity and inclusion a core part of assessments and incentives for rewards and promotions. In 2021, it started asking employees to set personal goals related to diversity and inclusion. As CEO Kewsong Lee says, "In our business, alignment is everything. Where the rubber really hits the road is when you have important issues like diversity, equity, and inclusion become a part of someone's professional career advancement and compensation."[34]

Meanwhile, another global investment firm, Blackstone, has stressed the importance of its commitment to inclusion and diversity both at Blackstone and in its portfolio, which includes more than 200 companies. The firm engaged in several endeavors, including recruiting from historically Black colleges and universities, for increasing diverse representation on its portfolio company boards. It also expanded employment opportunities for people from underserved communities, as described by Joe Baratta, global head of private equity and a member of the firm's management committee. Baratta's take is that Blackstone has an obligation as a leader in the business community to ensure that diverse backgrounds and perspectives are represented at all levels, including on their boards. He believes that not only is championing diversity the right thing to do but that it will also make their companies better. Summing up his beliefs, he explains, "Portfolio company leaders are making important decisions every day, and we want to make sure they have the input of people with different life experiences and perspectives, leading to more inclusive and thoughtful decision making."[35] Even institutional investors like Goldman Sachs have upped the ante to diversify on the exit side, as they sell companies that have the potential to become publicly listed. In February 2020, the investment bank announced that it would not take any company public unless it has at least one diverse board member.[36]

As public awareness of social justice and the challenges to achieving diversity, equity, and inclusion increase, the related demands for transparency and belonging will become even more material to how businesses are led and their valuations. Given the success that venture capital and private equity firms engaged in leveraged buyouts have had in scaling their companies or exiting them into the public markets, this industry can have a profound influence in shaping the composition and practices of companies—both public and private—creating a ripple effect for decades to come.

Next, let's look at how a bias toward transparency in companies of all kinds naturally leads to higher levels of equity, inclusion, diversity, and belonging.

How Radical Transparency Is Enabling EID-B

The digital age is also the age of transparency. Organizations increasingly have access to the technology and data they need to understand things like how diverse their workplaces and customers are or how heavily the business is affected by equity issues. This allows organizations to make more informed choices and decisions about how they might need to evolve, which can trigger a kind of virtuous cycle: the more open and transparent companies become, the more accountable—and potentially attractive—they become to potential investors, prospective employees, and customers.

Every day, digital advances, from social media analytics and web scraping to spend analytics and visualization, enable open access to data, information, and ideas. Financial data, employee grievances, internal memos, environmental disasters, product weaknesses, international protests, scandals and policies, good news and bad—all can be seen by anyone who knows where to look.[37] Federal mandates require that organizations make themselves clearly visible to many different stakeholders, including shareholders, customers, employees, partners, and society. Accordingly, organizations are ramping up efforts to transparently disclose information to the public and key stakeholders about their EID practices and initiatives and the composition of their workforces. And they are actively taking steps to insist on and increase information access and transparency inside their organizations.

Take Ray Dalio, founder of Bridgewater Associates. Dalio codified a set of principles that led to Bridgewater's exceptionally effective culture of transparency and belonging. The principles included adopting radical truth and radical transparency and nurturing meaningful work and meaningful relationships. Dalio also made "learning from mistakes" into a cultural norm. He communicated and modeled this norm throughout the organization by encouraging employees to openly criticize one another's ideas and behaviors, including his own. In a TED Talk, Dalio showed the audience a work email he received from a rank-and-file company employee describing how poorly prepared Dalio was for an internal meeting, and its negative impact on others in that meeting. Dalio describes the resulting culture as a "meritocracy that strives to achieve meaningful work and meaningful relationships through radical transparency."[38]

Salesforce, too, has set a headline-making goal of having "underrepresented groups" comprising half of its U.S. workforce by 2023. And by the company's definition, it's well on its way, with 43 percent of its U.S. workforce currently meeting the criteria for being underrepresented—a category that Salesforce says includes women, Blacks, Latinx, Indigenous, multiracial, LGBTQ+, people with disabilities, and veterans. Salesforce's efforts to improve gender equality have been significant: in 2015, CEO Marc Benioff vowed to close the wage gap between men and women employees, spending about $3 million to adjust unexplained discrepancies in compensation the following year. Since that time, the company has spent $12.1 million fixing gender and race wage discrepancies.[39]

Meanwhile, tech companies from Apple to Facebook are including women in their diversity stats. But it's not just tech. Since the beginning of 2021, investment management firms like BlackRock and Vanguard Group have been tracking the gender, ethnic, and racial diversity in the public companies they invest in. BlackRock is pushing companies to diversify their boards and release their overall company ethnic and racial data. Meanwhile, Vanguard is saying it may vote against board directors at companies with slow progress on diversity.[40]

What do all of these efforts show us? In a fast-paced digital era, organizational health hinges on radical transparency if companies hope to achieve both their ideals and mandates when it comes to EID and belonging. More and more, it's AI that will help companies meet those goals.

How AI Is Unleashing Transparency—and Thus EID

New advances in digital technology like AI, wearables, collaboration tools, and more can enable more transparent (but targeted) information sharing than we've ever seen before. In turn, this enables a whole list of improvements in the ways people work—from self-organizing networks of teams and dynamic allocation of resources to real-time knowledge sharing and dynamic work design optimized for outcomes. Other advantages include improved trust in organizational leaders because of radical candor and open feedback loops that improve companies' ability to quickly adapt based on signals of the future.

New digital advances are now on the brink of transforming EID as well. Consider the evolution of EID, which for many years was especially focused on gender. Over time, the focus of attention shifted to include race and ethnicity. Social justice movements and conversations around discriminatory workplace practices and behaviors then led to greater attention to inclusion than ever before, followed by a new trend focused on belonging. And as of late, the role of AI in mitigating bias to enhance equity, inclusion, and diversity has come front and center, with many new approaches that have been just recently introduced to address this issue, especially in tech.[41]

In the near future, AI may be used to determine fair pay. Infosys is exploring the use of AI to decide when to give employees a raise based on their performance and pay relative to colleagues'. The technology will make pay fairer by taking biases and personality traits out of consideration.[42] Or consider how Intel, eBay, JPMorgan, and Twitter all use the AI-based tool Perception to analyze large sets of written data to improve EID efforts. Perception can sort a company's data by gender and ethnicity to give HR professionals unique insights into how certain minority groups are treated on a wide range of hot-button issues, such as promotions, job security, and hiring practices. Imagine all of the practical implications of such a tool. A person standing up and claiming the organization has bias now has proof with data. The solution can pinpoint organizational deficiencies that are holding women back and make recommendations for positive organizational changes that will help empower and retain women. Perception can be used to analyze performance reviews—for example, to recognize that when a supervisor repeatedly uses the word "good" to describe an employee, that should actually be interpreted as a negative, not positive, sign— signaling that they are politely setting up an employee for a criticism.[43]

No matter what digital systems an organization chooses to improve transparency, any advances a business makes to become more equitable, inclusive, and diverse must begin with the top leadership.

Start from the Top: From Investors to Founders to Boards to Executive Teams

It simply makes sense: organizations that wish to increase the equity, inclusion, and diversity of the business need to have a more diverse representation of humanity not just in the ranks but also sitting at the top table—meaning, the boardroom and executive suite tables.

Racial and gender diversity, in particular, has become a hot button, especially regarding executive succession. More and more, shareholders are pressuring portfolio boards and management teams to ensure that they have the right mix of skills, perspectives, and tenures to execute its strategy. For example, at the beginning of 2019, California mandated that all companies headquartered in the state have at least one female board director (and in some cases a higher number) by the end of that same year.[44]

But apart from government mandates, improving the diversity among the top team members of organizations is simply good business. Companies with executive teams in the top quartile for ethnic/cultural diversity are 33 percent more likely to enjoy industry-leading profitability.[45] Another study suggests that leadership teams with above-average diversity in companies across developed and emerging economies are better at driving innovation and financial performance, such as improved EBIT margins.[46] Other research has established that companies with diverse leadership teams and boards create disproportionate shareholder value. Take, for example, the fact that diversity-engaged organizations have 3.9 times the earnings per share (EPS) growth rate.[47] Publicly traded companies with 2D diversity—inherent diversity such as gender, ethnicity, and sexual orientation, combined with acquired diversity, such as skills and education—are 45 percent more likely to have expanded market share in a year.[48]

For all of those reasons and more, when it comes to questions concerning an organization's stance and practices around EID, it's a matter of when, not if. So whether or not a company decides to take a public stand on such issues, its leaders will at some point need to answer questions about how equitable the organization is.[49] Ultimately, the job of building a healthy business—one where employees, customers, and the community in which the company operates all feel a true sense of belonging—begins with those most responsible for designing the company, the people at the very top of the house: investors, boards, founders, the C-suite, and executive teams.

Making EID a Priority: Practical Steps

Shaping the direction of an EID strategy is difficult, to be sure, because of intersectionality and many other factors that go into fostering an equitable organization, underpinned by a sense of belonging and psychological safety at the individual and team levels. Yet over time, EID in an established or an AI-first organization can be cultivated by taking a disciplined approach. This begins with a rigorous, fact- and science-based baseline of the existing strengths and weaknesses of a company's EID policies and practices, followed by a playbook for action and leadership role modeling.

For companies that are scaling and growing exponentially, focusing on EID effectiveness can occur by taking four initial actions:

- **Conduct an EID audit.** First, take stock of what's working and what's not. Conduct a forensic, evidence-based EID audit to understand the company's unique way of seeing and interacting with differences, human and otherwise. A solid base of facts and insights will give senior executives and investors the confidence to know where they are long and where they are short on EID matters. Sometimes just asking the right questions can lead to greater bias toward radical transparency that can extend for several generations of a company. Armed with a robust audit of facts (e.g., metrics) and sentiment (i.e., mindsets and external rankings), it is far easier to coordinate and orchestrate how to roadmap, plan, and execute targeted EID strategies at scale and with transparency.
- **Develop a playbook to shift mindsets and ensure an inclusive, transparent, and fair talent experience.** Second, develop a clear framework and topical playbooks with a transparent set of specific tactics, metrics, and ROI focused on each E, I, and D domain, which can be packaged, tracked, and shared with leaders and employees (and portfolio companies, in the case of PE firms) and in some cases, even the board as the company scales. A common set of operating principles and practices based on

the EID philosophy and values can be critical for an organization and determine its success or failure on these topics. This is especially true as companies face enormous demands across social, regulatory, and ethical boundaries. By fostering a common set of policies and practices, or a portfolio of initiatives in the case of a cultural transformation, a company can unify its business and operations and overcome the challenges of operating in a siloed and fragile way.

- **Align leaders to reinforce mutual accountability.** Third, align leaders at the board and top management levels to ensure commitment and mutual accountability and help focus a diverse workforce on a tangible set of common goals that are shared and communicated across the organization. These goals help leaders and employees, including off-sheet talent, at all levels and across all aspects of the business understand and accept the imperatives involved in fostering a culture of psychological safety and belonging. This is a critical pathway to follow in structuring a company and cultivating organizational health to compete successfully in the digital age. Organizational health requires alignment throughout the organization on both EID policies and practices and mindsets and behaviors; without such alignment, organizations won't be able to achieve effective adoption and application of both the hard and soft aspects of EID. Organizations should also define and track the health of EID across all other essential elements of organizational health, and strengthen commitment from leaders who will be directly modeling EID and mutually reinforcing a culture of belonging through their actions.

- **Set up the right EID reporting and insights capabilities.** Fourth, to get to the truth, organizations should establish the right EID analytics. Take a data-driven approach that identifies areas for improvement and tracks progress. Use forensic analytical methods—such as voice recognition software, video-recorded meetings, or apps that record feelings and overall sentiment—to create psychographic assessments of each company employee (or a subset of key decision makers) and identify predictors of bias that deliver actionable answers. The same analytics can be used to track success and course correction during a change process and afterward. Successful EID policies and actions are built on facts and insights. They are built on effective change management and communications strategies and tactics that enable persuasion to establish buy-in.

In every human era, the reigning pundits proclaim the challenges of their current age to be the most pressing in history. Our era is no exception. But the evidence is strong indeed that the world has never seen a more challenging business environment than the one companies face today: the devastation of a global pandemic, the protests and social unrest of police brutality within U.S. Black and Latinx communities, the dissolution of traditional industry boundaries, and the blending of uniquely human skills with AI, to name just a few.

Many companies are now moving into a new intersectional or nonconforming era, requiring the cultural dexterity to engage people of all differences in fast-moving markets in a digital world. Income inequality is growing across the United States, and to some extent, the globe, and the diverse talent that hypergrowth companies need to succeed is also increasingly found in locations such as in headquarters or satellite offices.

Can companies continue to attract diverse talent and cultivate the cultures of radical transparency and belonging that they'll need to execute strategy at the speed necessary to compete in this digital era? The answer to that question largely depends on the value of a company's policies and practices, its leadership composition at the board and management levels, its incentives, performance (and consequence) management systems, governance, and clear reporting and insights of performance metrics that matter.

To be sure, AI-first organizations will need many right things and the right people working together to survive and thrive. Sound EID policies and practices can operate like a through line for all of those "right things," enabling companies to achieve their aspirations and fulfill their commitments to their people, communities, and shareholders alike.

A focus on EID is, therefore, a key part of shaping the health of an organization. And it is intimately connected to the final condition necessary for healthy organizations today—your people's health and well-being—as we will see in the next chapter.

Checklist for Agenda Setting

- Create a holistic strategy that addresses not just diversity but also equity, inclusion, belonging, psychological safety, and transparency.
- Transparently disclose information about EID practices and initiatives, along with the composition of the workforce, to the public and key stakeholders, and create clear reporting and insights of EID performance metrics that matter.
- Avoid simplistic, binary categorizations of employees and instead embrace the discipline of intersectionality.
- Harness new digital advances such as AI to unleash equity, inclusion, and diversity in the workplace; create greater information access and internal transparency; and for PE/VC firms, identify and select investments.
- Infuse EID at the top—ensuring boards and management teams are diverse and effectively model EID, and ensuring that investors are not only diverse themselves but effectively source and select diverse top talent in their portfolio companies.
- Plot a plan of action to scale and mature EID as a business scales and matures.
- Infuse EID metrics and practices into every essential of organizational health.
- Get started by conducting an EID audit, developing a consistent EID playbook that can be shared with all, and aligning leaders to enforce mutual accountability.

7 ■ Well-Being

Embrace the Overlooked Essential of an Organization's Health

As leaders struggle to vanquish the many challenges presented by disruptors such as the pandemic, the overall well-being of employees is emerging as a critical organizational priority.

Business executives once looked upon wellness initiatives as human resource issues in which they had little interest. Accountability for employee well-being was "HR's job." No longer. Today's business leaders are finding that their most sophisticated growth strategies stand little chance of being implemented if their people aren't well enough, at a basic level, to adapt and respond to ongoing organizational change. The global pandemic has brought the importance of employee well-being front and center, and leading companies are driving the charge as never before.

When I talk about well-being, I'm not referring to the attention given over the last decade or so to employee "wellness"—meaning physical health. Well-being encompasses physical health, of course, but also mental, emotional, financial, spiritual health, and employ-ability/professional development. As YouTube's chief mental health advisor Jessica DiVento told me: "Well-being is a person's overall quality of life in each area of well-being—physical, mental, financial, social, occupational, and spiritual health." Amid the tumult of change occurring as we embrace the digital era's new normal, it is easy to forget such basic elements of individuals' and society's hierarchy of needs.[1] But we do so at our peril. Few factors will affect the health of an organization in the coming years more than a highly motivated and productive workforce. Well-being, the final in our list of seven conditions for healthy organizations, is arguably the most overlooked of all. Quite literally, employees' overall quality of life in each area of well-being will be a deciding factor in the success or failure of organizations in the future.

Many business leaders have already gotten that important message. Since the early 2000s, employee well-being has been rising on the organizational agenda. Scores of research publications about well-being (and happiness, by extension) all point to the topic's growing focus. Before the pandemic, only 35 percent of C-suite leaders responsible for a business or HR function strongly agreed that their organization was responsible for helping their people become better off than when they started (mentally, physically, financially, and re-lationally, and with a stronger sense of purpose and career prospects). But during the pandemic crisis, a full 50 percent of those leaders surveyed agreed.[2] Indeed, well-being already had risen to the top-ranked trend for importance before the pandemic hit. In De-loitte's 2020 Global Human Capital Trends study, 80 percent of survey respondents identified well-being as important or very important to their organization's success.[3]

Today, COVID-19 has cemented well-being on the organizational agenda. The need to secure the health and safety of employees has prodded companies of all kinds to expand people's ability to work remotely and to implement hybrid work arrangements. Meanwhile, telecommunications companies responded with products that improve the remote-work experience, such as T-Mobile's launch of its "Work from Anywhere" (WFX) campaign and its suite of 5G solutions.[4] One result is that many employees report a preference for working from home either full-time or part-time, citing things like flexible scheduling and less commuting time as benefits, which affect people's overall well-being.[5]

Many studies draw a clear link between strong company performance and employee well-being, including physical health (which often means healthy, happy cultures). Researchers at the University of Auckland and Auckland University of Technology have found that a four-day week makes workers happier, less stressed, and more productive.[6] Similar indications come from Microsoft, whose "Work Life Choice Challenge" experiments show measurable performance improvements when productivity—an indicator of a healthy well-being culture—jumped 40 percent. The compound effect of a four-day work week and reduced time that managers and staff spent at meetings and responding to work emails made the difference.[7] Indeed, Google research shows that people who rigidly separate their personal and work lives are significantly happier about their well-being—and ultimately reap the benefits of higher satisfaction—than those who tend to blur the lines between the two.[8] YouTube's Jessica DiVento summarizes the line between productivity and well-being this way: "High well-being drives productivity. So when a company invests in supporting employee well-being, it really is an investment in creating a productive, sustainable work environment."

There are no quick fixes for an organization's well-being challenges. Developing a healthy and resilient work environment still requires organizational wellness programs—everything from yoga classes and on-site fitness centers to providing nap rooms and healthy lunches and snacks. But most important is creating a culture conducive to individual and organizational well-being. This involves designing well-being into the everyday fabric of work and into the employee experience itself. That, in turn, creates a virtuous cycle that can boost a business's productivity and performance.

But the opposite is also true. When companies overlook employee well-being—and when they don't attend to the root causes that promote it—employees thrive far less ably. This can cost companies billions of dollars a year in lost productivity, not to mention garnering those inattentive businesses a low (or no) position on popular "best places to work" lists. Chief among the root causes of poor well-being? Employee burnout—the consequences of which have been well researched and documented.[9] (See the sidebar "Burnout: The Hidden Cause and Consequence of Poor Well-Being.")

Burnout: The Hidden Cause and Consequence of Poor Well-Being

Employees today are facing a crisis in confidence—if not in fact—in the way many organizations operate. Skepticism is on the rise regarding the effectiveness of traditional organizations, whose design and operating systems were largely built for the second industrial revolution. Traditional organizations are getting stretched to their limits in their ability to improve engagement, decrease turnover, provide meaning, and enhance people's physical and emotional health, thereby threatening company performance. As Stanford professor Jeffrey Pfeffer contends, many of the maladies found among today's managers—such as long work hours, work-family conflict, and economic insecurity—are proving toxic to employees and ultimately to the organization's health.[10]

All of which points to the fact that employee burnout is on the rise. Even before the pandemic, between 2016 and 2019, there was a spike in reported cases. Employee burnout levels in 2020 remained high throughout COVID-19—with a major shift that hasn't been seen before: fully remote workers are now experiencing far more burnout than on-site workers, which we can likely attribute to difficulties separating work time from off-work time.[11] And the problem is reaching crisis levels: 95 percent of human resource leaders admit that employee burnout is sabotaging workforce retention, according to research for the Employee Engagement Series conducted

---

(*continued*)

by Kronos Incorporated and Future Workplace. Moreover, the research reveals that 46 percent of HR leaders believe that employee burnout is responsible for up to half (20 percent to 50 percent, specifically) of annual workforce turnover.[12]

What leads to burnout? A Gallup survey of 7,500 full-time employees found five specific organizational issues associated with the phenomenon:

- Unfair treatment at work
- Unmanageable workload
- Lack of role clarity
- Lack of communication and support from their manager
- Unreasonable time pressure[13]

Burnout is also linked to the physical manifestation of stress. Unaddressed burnout can lead to new or the exacerbation of existing chronic health conditions, which can also increase healthcare costs for a company and lost hours. Workers in fast-moving industries or hypergrowth companies may be particularly prone to burnout. Not surprisingly, leaders in such contexts may feel compelled to focus on getting the product out at all costs—and worry about the cost of burnout or poor well-being later.

Addressing and preventing burnout in any team environment will depend on the degree to which individual employees engage in self-care, and in how much they feel a sense of belonging, impact, and acknowledgment. Fortunately, these are things that business leaders and all stakeholders can foster in their organizations. When well-being is infused into the operating model design, that makes it easier and more natural for individual employees to apply the tools for well-being in their daily work routines.

Fortunately, by understanding the organizational barriers to well-being, business leaders, investors, boards, and HR professionals can foster more effective outcomes, such as productivity, talent retention, and health. They can thwart these barriers and their potential damage by taking three main actions, covered in this chapter, to support employees to experience a stronger sense of well-being. First, they can better understand what well-being encompasses and why it matters. Second, they can make the invisible visible by assessing the direct costs of burnout—and the benefits of well-being. Lastly, they can take steps to renew the organizational "psychological contract"—the implicit agreement between employees and employers regarding what the working relationship should be.

Well-Being and Why It Matters

Well-being means different things to different people, but as I've said, it is not at all the same thing as wellness. It isn't a tacked-on HR program. It isn't office gyms or free fruit baskets in the break room, or even a good health insurance package—although all of those things are important and certainly contribute to aspects of employees' well-being. Rather, well-being encompasses the spiritual, mental, social, financial, and physical needs of employees. And as I see it, today those needs are undergoing a kind of evolution. Changes in digital technologies, as well as new employee-employer psychological contracts (as we'll explore later in this chapter), are making well-being a priority for individuals and for the organizations who wish to hire them.

To outpace the competition, then, organizations are being tasked with investing in and placing employee well-being at the core of their values. Every element of the organizational system—the culture, the structure and ways of working, and so on—must explicitly reinforce well-being practices to boost productivity and performance. If leaders accept this premise, then they no longer can simply bolt on HR wellness programs and initiatives and hope for a positive outcome. Instead, they will need to adopt a new way of approaching organizational health and change. They will need to focus on making the kinds of broad organizational changes that will most affect their people's well-being, treating it as a kind of through line across all other organizational levers.

But what does it mean, in practice, to weave well-being into the very fabric of a business? It means ensuring that your people feel supported in every aspect of individual health.

- **Mental health.** Companies can emphasize mental health as a priority in a number of ways—everything from keeping an in-house counselor to providing health benefits packages that cover counseling and therapy. Perhaps most important, however, is encouraging your people to clearly separate their work and home lives, which supports emotional/mental health, among other things. Top management can lead by example in this area. For instance, they can hold listening sessions to hear the honest and candid perspectives of employees and how they are really doing. They can also invest in robust health promotions and campaigns to reduce stigma. Great programs won't be used, let alone stick, if people are unaware. And even if people are aware of these programs they won't use them if there's stigma.
- **Spiritual health.** Again, communication from the top on the importance of balancing work and home life and helping employees identify meaning and purpose will naturally support individuals' spiritual health as well. But companies such as Boeing and Coca-Cola also offer employees the opportunity to practice Quran or Bible study in voluntary prayer groups.[14]
- **Physical health.** This is another area that individuals can enjoy far more easily when there's an explicit balance between work and play/home communicated throughout the organizational culture and in leadership practices. In addition, many companies (Kimpton Hotels, Nike, and Under Armour, to name just a few) make workouts more convenient for their people by providing them with well-equipped on-site gyms for their use.

- **Financial health.** Individual employees' personal financial problems can add intense stress to a job that is already stressful. Companies like SunTrust Bank have launched an online program geared toward improving employees' financial health. It uses videos, modules, and other learning activities to boost user confidence in personal finance.

Consider the case of Aetna under the leadership of Mark Bertolini, the company's former chairman, CEO, and president. In making the changes he sought for the company, Bertolini was influenced by his own personal well-being journey, which included grappling with the aftermath of a severe skiing accident and responding to his son's cancer diagnosis.[15] He believed deeply that his employees were committed to the health of the organization, and he wanted to reciprocate that commitment and have it go both ways. So Bertolini made well-being a business imperative at Aetna, while also promoting a *culture* of individual and organizational well-being.

In the end, Aetna's change program enabled Bertolini to expand the definition of well-being by giving employees access to workshops in such areas as financial literacy. As Bertolini pointed out, "Your financial situation can play a daily role in stress and have an impact on health."[16]

To be sure, Bertolini's logic—equating things like proficiency in personal finance to individuals' health and wellness—points to a key reason why every leader should focus on organizational well-being: it affects workforce performance, which has a positive effect on a company's bottom line and competitiveness. Several studies bear this out, including research conducted by the HERO Employee Health Management Best Practices Scorecard in collaboration with Mercer, the global HR consulting firm. Based on their own study and others, the authors conclude that a comprehensive well-being strategy and culture positively impact financial performance: "The robust investment in workforce health and well-being appears to be one of the practices pursued by high-performing, well-managed companies. The positive financial results for a company support the need for continuing to cultivate a well-being culture and strategy that is embedded into the ethos of the organization."[17]

Gallup, too, found that there were positive economic impacts linked to well-being: thriving employees have 41 percent lower health costs compared to those who are struggling. They also found 35 percent lower turnover costs in thriving employees when compared to employees who were struggling.[18] Further, there is growing evidence to suggest that organizations with cultures of well-being adapt to change and perform better than those with lower or nonexistent well-being cultures. In well-being cultures, employees are happier and have, on average, 31 percent higher productivity and 37 percent higher sales.[19]

Moreover, well-being can strengthen employee engagement, and consequently, individual growth and agility, while poor well-being impedes progress toward those goals. And it isn't just "kind of important" or "a good thing to focus on." As one chief human resources officer (CHRO) in a hypergrowth company shared with me, "We can't be overly focused on the business. Companies that have programs in place to help employees' well-being can reduce the stressors to productivity and perform better than companies that do not. Employee well-being is the next huge wave that corporate America will have to get on board with and care about."

All of which is to say that business leaders would be wise to give as much thought and funding to the design and execution of well-being initiatives as they are giving (at least today) to equity, inclusion, and diversity initiatives. But this is not easy to do. Engagement and productivity, for example, are often based on individual accountability, even though most well-being initiatives today are organizational in nature. And wellness programs and practices usually focus on individual preferences and experiences while overlooking the critical importance of an employee's well-being against the backdrop of the organizational context from which they operate. Wellness programs and practices also overlook systemic changes that may need to be made to the organization's health to create the right environment so employees can support their well-being; this has to come first before people in the organization will feel empowered to take action at the individual level. IBM, for example, offers online educational resources (e.g., resilience training, mindfulness communities) and confidential support programs such as virtual or telephone counseling to help its employees fight remote work stress. Programmatic efforts like the one at IBM and several others serve as good examples of how employers can execute initiatives to effectively improve employee mental health.[20] The difference-maker in what makes these programs even more successful includes the engagement of people in them. In other words, how people learn about these programs, the time granted to leverage them, how barriers to access are identified and addressed, and assessing the overall effectiveness of their yield and impact.

Make the Invisible Visible

By first determining where their company should focus investments in employee well-being, leaders will have the facts they need to take remedial action to shape the culture.

For example, when Mark Bertolini made an assessment of the situation at Aetna, what stood out in his organization was that, like many other companies, "healthcare costs are one of their biggest financial issues." That convinced Bertolini that innovative wellness programs "aren't just 'nice to have'—they are essential to the success of the organization." He wanted to help employees improve their physical health, yes, but he also meant to improve the bottom line through reduced healthcare costs, improved productivity, and making better organizational decisions.[21]

To fully understand the current state of the organization—including barriers to well-being—means revealing the critical root causes and drivers that both impede and foster it. In other words, leaders must take stock of not just what individuals think and how they act but also why. An independent organizational analysis can identify where there are critical gaps that are—or may become—barriers to individual employees' well-being and, ultimately, barriers to realizing the organization's strategic priorities. Without such evidence and benchmarked data, companies will have a hard time understanding root causes and thus risk going down the wrong path to address problems. That is why hard data is a vital part of planning and implementing well-being initiatives effectively.

One hypergrowth tech company, for example, measures employee well-being scores across its workforce on a regular basis. When company leaders noticed those scores dropping, they quickly saw a correlation with the number of employees taking vacations, which had also dropped. This valuable information indicated that people were not getting enough sustained detachment from work—resulting in elevated depression, anxiety, and burnout risk among its workforce.

To proactively counter barriers such as low to nonexistent levels of detachment, leaders should invest in people analytics such as web scraping of employees' calendars to determine how and where people spend their time. Similarly, biometrics obtained from wearables can give leaders at all levels new tools to collect workforce well-being data and perform rigorous analyses of organizational determinants that are tied to it. As organizations use new digital technologies to track the productivity of physical and remote workers and their well-being metrics, leaders can create a comprehensive and reliable way to understand root cause issues crossing all levels of the organization from top to bottom. Advances in digital enable us to go beyond sampling the perspectives of only a select few, most notably those of the top management team.

Although this approach can offer great benefits to both workers and organizations alike, leaders should take care to gather data in a responsible way. No one wants to have "Big Brother"–type surveillance in the workforce. Employees can voluntarily opt in to digital platforms that promote, track, manage, and measure their well-being, all through the integration of apps and programs (such as weight loss programs to manage obesity in the workplace) into the dailiness of work.[22] To protect privacy, personal data can be made available only to them, with anonymized, aggregated data only available to managers and leaders. Such data—coupled with technologies like mobile devices, AI, and more—can help improve workforce well-being. What's more, based on an individual's data, AI could even act as a personal coach, making suggestions to each individual to improve their well-being. (See the table "How Digital Advances and AI Can Unleash Well-Being in the Workforce.")

How Digital Advances and AI Can Unleash Well-Being in the Workforce

Well-Being Dimension	How Digital Advances and AI Can Help
Physical well-being	A variety of individual wearable devices such as Fitbits or Apple iWatches can monitor physical well-being and safety in the workplace, reveal patterns, and use AI to suggest ways to improve them. Enterprise or individual apps can also support physical well-being.
Emotional and mental well-being	Affective computing can generate insights into employees' emotional responses and patterns and make suggestions for how to improve them at the individual or team level. Such programs include AI-enabled emotion-detecting capabilities, either on a device or through a cloud service such as voice-pattern software that enables agents to recognize changes in employees' or customers' moods in real time. Digital apps that use AI to coach the person in the right direction can also improve resilience, mental health, and well-being.
Relational well-being	Data collected from employees who opt in to being monitored (e.g., via email, social sites, embedded sensors) can reveal relationship patterns in interactions. This allows the AI to make suggestions to employees, managers, and leaders on how to improve interactions.
Financial well-being	AI and cognitive computing such as financial-wellness platforms now make it cost-effective and scalable to offer employees completely customized financial plans and personalized advice that gets smarter and better over time.
Employability well-being	AI-enhanced job-matching platforms analyze online labor market information from multiple job boards to predict upcoming jobs and skill requirements. These platforms can then suggest which skills employees can develop in order to be marketable and employable as organizations evolve, and match them to new opportunities (e.g., projects, training) to help them develop these skills.

Moreover, acting on anonymized and aggregated data across the workforce, leaders will begin to understand workforce behaviors and how they change over time, while reinforcing and optimizing healthy leadership and organizational behaviors. By taking such an objective and quantifiable approach, leaders increase their odds of overcoming the limitations of a subjective analysis and can then produce key indicators that can be tracked over time. What will be key is ensuring the responsible use of data to support well-being by building in the right safeguards with legal that will prevent the nefarious use of this data.

Understand the Organizational Costs and Benefits

Leaders should also consider building and maintaining a normative and benchmarked database of costs associated with these key indicators, allowing for comparison with industry-based practices and benchmarks. Researchers at the Mayo Clinic developed a well-being index that measures multiple dimensions of well-being among doctors, nurses, medical students, and other healthcare workers.[23] However, most organizations don't have readily available costs, nor do they know the scope of any well-being challenges they may face. But chances are that there are employees in any given company who are now experiencing job withdrawal and associated loss of productivity, reduced employee commitment to the job and/or organization, decreased job satisfaction, greater personal conflict with colleagues, or a disruption to coworkers' work. Simply stated: what the International Classification of Diseases (ICD)[24] classifies as burnout risk can be observed as fatigue/exhaustion, cynicism/pessimism about work, and reduced job efficacy. In short, loss of productive, psychologically and physically engaged employees is always expensive for an organization.

The psychological and physical problems (sometimes chronic) of burned-out employees cost an estimated $125 billion to $190 billion a year in healthcare spending in the United States alone.[25] But this is just the most obvious impact of burnout. There are less-direct costs as well. Burnout can impact financial wellness or relational wellness (the degree to which employees feel connected and a sense of belonging). Burned-out employees are 2.6 times as likely to be actively seeking a different job, 63 percent more likely to take a sick day, and 23 percent more likely to visit the emergency room.[26]

The American Psychological Association estimates that 550 million workdays are lost each year due to stress on the job. One company that sought to combat this with an increased focus on lifestyle and preventive healthcare is BMW. Michael Zuerl, general manager for total vehicle quality management at BMW Group South Africa, states, "Our most valuable assets are our employees. Is it not time that we start maintaining our most valuable assets?" To put his belief into action, Zuerl and other leaders asked employees to experiment with a heart rate variability-based analytic tool that reveals the link between lifestyle and performance. This enabled BMW to start incorporating new habits and analytics into its culture. BMW's investments in improving workforce health and well-being not only had a positive impact on individuals but had a positive impact on teams and the overall organization as well.[27]

While this example is clearly notable, it doesn't reveal the true impact of well-being on organizational health. That's because the intervention employed by BMW was based primarily on individual employees rather than considering the ecosystem of support essential to getting employees to adopt new behaviors and make them stick. Companies without systems to support the well-being of their employees have higher turnover, lower productivity, and higher healthcare costs, according to the American Psychological Association.[28]

Make Well-Being an Organizational Priority: Renew the Psychological Contract

When it comes to the well-being of organizations, leaders and other stakeholders cannot afford to ignore the psychological contract—that is, the often unspoken agreement between employee and employers regarding what the working relationship should look like and be.

Historically speaking, the psychological contract was based on a simple agreement: in exchange for employee loyalty and performance, organizations would provide safety and stability in the form of job and financial security and a commitment to career advancement when employees met performance goals. For example, Gen Z values aspects of well-being, such as financial health, over compensation and sees this as an employer's responsibility.[29] Therefore, organizations need to lean into well-being to attract top talent. But today's changing business landscape, along with shifting employee priorities, has nullified that agreement. Workforces now expect far more from organizations: specifically, a balance between work and family life as well as perks around health preferences (from on-site physical fitness facilities and massage sessions to courses on meditation, and more). Most importantly, employees today expect employers to help them stay relevant and resilient in a changing market for skills and jobs, find meaning at work, and design work so that it is integrated with well-being. Failing to do so may cost companies talent and undermine overall performance of the business.

With employee expectations so high, company leaders operating in today's digital context need to invest in orchestrating better human experiences and exchanges between employers and employees. Consider the wellness manifesto titled "It's OK to . . ." that has made the rounds at Google and in a number of businesses and government environments, especially since the beginning of the pandemic. The document's declarations of what's OK at work include: "ask for help," "not check email" after hours, and "put your family before your work."[30]

Returning to our example of Aetna, Mark Bertolini embraced the idea of essentially renewing the psychological contract between the company and its employees. For Bertolini, that meant developing some mindfulness-based programs at Aetna, such as yoga, and encouraging better sleep habits. He used a reward system, paying up to $500 per year to Aetna employees who could document healthy amounts of sleep, such as through use of a Fitbit.

Ultimately, by committing to well-being as a management priority, infusing it into the strategy and daily work routines of Aetna employees, and defining a new domain of individual and organizational responsibility for well-being, Bertolini saw the impact of his investment realized.[31] Not only did these initiatives reduce stress, but they also improved productivity by 69 minutes per month and created bigger profits because they allowed employees to be "present in the workplace" (i.e., not distracted by their own neglected health) and make better decisions.

All of which is to say that aligning employees' sense of well-being with companies' organizational functioning is not only a necessity but a prerequisite for the modern enterprise. To be sure, the shift toward a new psychological contract and a long-term investment in individual and organizational well-being is already happening. Increasingly, organizations are moving from serving only shareholder needs to serving all stakeholder needs—their workers, their customers, their communities, and the society at large—what leaders call "conscious capitalism," "the social enterprise," "responsible business," or most often, "stakeholder capitalism."

Given the increased focus and pressure on organizations to promote workforce well-being, organizations can adopt principles to guide them in a holistic approach, covering areas such as management practices, work week reductions, reporting and insights, and the design of the organization's work itself. Here are five principles leaders might consider when crafting a new psychological contract for the organization:

- **Develop management practices for stress mitigation and resilience development.** This means fostering psychological safety at the workplace, providing a robust set of well-being benefits and programs, and, often, seeking to make a difference in the communities in which company workers live.[32]
- **Consider four-day work weeks or shorter working days.** Organizational psychologist and Wharton professor Adam Grant suggests the COVID-19 pandemic could give rise to "the holy grail of shorter working days."[33] Companies might consider offering workers the ability to work a slightly longer day—say, ten hours—for a shorter, four-day week.[34]
- **Support healthy employee work-life balance.** This is an issue of organizational culture. The best means of shaping and supporting balance is by aligning top management with the change—in both words and behavior—to

promote employee health and time to disconnect from work.[35] Mitigating the pace of work and overall demand will help with this. However, it will be incumbent upon leaders to strike the right tone and balance that there inevitably will be times their people may need to work extended hours and engage in sprints. Be sure to breathe between sprints and avoid creating single points of failure.

- **Measure well-being and its impact on performance.** Encourage managers to evaluate performance in new ways. Most organizations have not yet begun to measure the impact of their well-being initiatives on organizational performance, and if they do, they tend to measure only the impact on employees' experience.[36] But there's a key advantage in measuring the impact on organizational performance: ensuring that there is less absenteeism and greater retention.

- **Redesign work to give employees more control over how and where they work.** One company instituted more flexibility around job design and soon saw the benefit: employees' health, well-being, and ability to manage their personal and work lives improved. Meanwhile, the company itself benefited from higher job satisfaction and lower turnover.[37]

Quantifiable incentives can motivate management and the workforce to think and behave better, but so can encouraging them to feel responsible and accountable for the conditions that help or hinder their well-being. In a healthy organization, these principles form a mutually supportive virtuous circle.

In this moment of change, creating a new psychological contract for the future of work, one that is optimized for well-being, is core for the well-being of both individuals and organizations. That will entail policies and programs that unlock people's potential and opportunity to grow, treat people as humans and not just as employees, and design work structures such as jobs and the organization itself, technology, and experiences around humans to amplify the human element. Once leaders better understand how to track the causes of challenges to employee well-being, they will need to identify the drivers that will lead to better outcomes, such as employee productivity, firm profitability, customer satisfaction, and employee retention.[38]

Checklist for Agenda Setting

- Assess the costs and benefits related to well-being, and measure well-being on a continuous basis to reveal the critical root causes and drivers that both impede and foster it.
- Clearly define the psychological contract or domain of individual and organizational responsibility for well-being.
- Infuse well-being into the operating model design, thereby enabling individual employees to apply well-being in their daily work routines.
- Commit to an ethos that reinforces all aspects of well-being as a management and C-suite priority.
- Use new digital advances to unleash employee well-being, but be sure to do so in a responsible way that protects privacy and benefits employees.

GROW INTO A BETTER ORGANIZATION

Using Digital to Unleash the Business's

Full Potential to Scale and Adapt

8 ■ Invest in Data and Lead with It

Use Digital Advances to Conduct Continuous
Org-Health Checks

> Too many business strategies fail because leaders overlook the
> value of measuring and monitoring the organization's health.
> Part 2 of this book explores how companies can leverage data to
> their fullest potential, directing investments toward growth and
> value. It all starts with conducting continuous organizational-
> health checks.

Most of us have experienced firsthand how wearing a mobile health
monitor changes the wearer's behavior almost immediately. We've
all had that one friend who became maniacally obsessed with "getting my steps in." So we understand how having access to specific
data about our health raises our awareness and ultimately affects our
choices and thus the quality and length of our lives.

We've heard less about how businesses, too, can use advanced data
and analytics to diagnose and manage the organization's health.
Until now, gathering such data directly from the company has been

an untapped resource that can potentially transform organizations. From an investor perspective, failing to capture and use such data is a missed opportunity—leaving executives to rely on intuition and best guesses instead of facts.

Specifically, organizations need a robust set of data regarding both their people and the business in general. That will allow them to measure how well they're doing on the seven conditions of healthy organizations we just examined in part 1 of this book: strategic direction; culture; leadership; talent; organizational design; equity, inclusion, and diversity; and well-being.

Consider the following scenario. You have a potential target investment or two in sight; teams of quantitative software engineers and specialists are creating advanced financial models and crunching numbers. You proceed with caution to avoid tipping off the founders or management team of the target company. So you charter an expert or organizational due diligence team with the explicit purpose of identifying and monitoring opportunities and risks related to the organization's health, such as decision-making practices of top management and attrition over a set period to gauge employee commitment (and by extension, managerial capability). Using the monitor lets you understand which business areas or programs you'll need to prioritize and deprioritize investing in as you move ahead with purchasing an asset—or not.

Just like a mobile health monitor, the insights you gain from organizational-health checkups—such as the data that your expert or quant engineers provide—will give you a quantifiable baseline and the basis for successful organizational redesign and change. These insights can take a variety of formats. At the highest level, a "people analytics" team would extract data concerning the workforce, such as sentiment analysis on employee perceptions about an event or policy, demographic analysis of the talent pool's size and skills of a business prior to a reorganization, and physical presence in an office location versus remote working based on office badge swiping. The team then would do a first pass at analyzing the results and, depending on what emerges from the data, proceed to collaborate with HR business partners and other teams. For example, if the data reveals that talent is a problem, those responsible for talent management would be enlisted to analyze results and craft credible solutions.

At the other end of the spectrum, the most basic level, the organization's leaders would be given an automated dashboard from a selection of key public data sources—less robust than the types of data that can be collected directly from within the organization, but still useful for tracking patterns and the general trend line of the organization's culture. As a complement to either format, an organizational expert—likely someone with a background in psychology or behavioral sciences and experience in mergers and acquisitions (M&A), talent management, and strategy and organizational consulting—would conduct interviews with leaders and employees to provide qualitative richness to the analytics.

Using a robust set of people and organizational data underscores the importance of evidence-based management for leaders when it comes to their debate, agreement, and alignment on critical decisions, particularly at the start of a business transformation or reorganization. Equipped with such information and evidence, leaders develop stronger organizational diagnostic and analysis capabilities. Those capabilities enable them to align around the CEO and leadership team's shared objectives and key results, to ruthlessly prioritize (or deprioritize) value-creating initiatives, to anticipate and measure risks, and to implement future changes. Moreover, in today's digital economy, CEOs and other organizational leaders, deal makers, and chief performance officers can use new technologies, including AI, to improve their decision effectiveness and, in turn, a company's organizational health.

In this chapter, we will look at data showing the link between organizational health and performance. We'll examine what you need to measure to capture health dimensions accurately. We'll also explore new advances in measurement and how to use them. And we'll look at how private equity firms are leading the charge in measuring organizational health, essentially providing a model for other kinds of organizations to emulate.

Let's begin with a look at the ways that many company assessments today fall short on effectiveness—and at two necessary actions organizations should be taking.

Two Actions to Take Now

In many companies I've observed, in-depth analysis of organizational health remains painfully nonholistic, despite its critical importance. Only a few of the seven key essentials ever get systematically assessed—and if they do, it's incomplete. Company assessments typically involve talent reviews, which measure individual employees' performance and perceived potential against their job requirements. Too often, such reviews are based on subjective judgment, not facts, leading to ineffective and often unfair assessments. Consider that 57 percent of leaders believe most organizations assess performance ineffectively; 46 percent of employees, too, believe their evaluations have no basis in objective data.[1] Yet most employees would prefer an objective assessment: 82 percent say having reliable, factual data gathered by new technologies would improve fairness in pay, promotions, and performance appraisal decisions.[2]

Google is one of the early pioneers in using a routine enterprise analytics program to access people and organizational data, providing rich insight into each of the seven pillars of organizational health. This allows the business to create targeted people strategies. Similarly, one senior HR leader I worked with at a fast-growth technology company recommended a change to organizational-health checkups, from optional to mandatory. Because this leader recognized the value of maintaining a quarterly business review cadence that included such checkups, top management was able to focus on strategy execution and ensure that the right incentives and alignment drove the business's performance.

All of this implies two critical actions for organizations to take today. First, build an enterprise-wide organizational-health framework comprising a shared set of consistent, comprehensive principles, practices, and tools—and their accompanying measures and metrics—that are adopted and accessible by all. The framework you choose should define what elements of health the company does well and not so well. Building out a framework is similar to deciding what your mobile health monitor will measure (heart rate? calories burned?) and what constitutes a healthy score. Roughly half the companies I've worked with or observed have taken the important step of developing an enterprise-wide framework. They use it in the operating rhythm of the business or at critical inflection points, such as a merger and acquisition, transformation, or executive transition.

Second, invest in analytical talent and new technologies such as AI to assess—and thereby improve—overall organizational health. The amount of data companies contend with today is unprecedented, and such emerging technologies as AI and analytics will help to mine that data quickly and at scale. Such tools and techniques can promptly tease out insights, substantially improving the accuracy of your organizational health–related decisions. The talent you use to analyze your data can be leadership teams working with organizational experts to make better-informed decisions about topics that range from executive succession and promotions to diversity, equity, and inclusion initiatives and transformation.

Simply put, by employing digital advances in analytics, investors and top management teams will be able to find patterns and draw insights from big data to make better evidence-based decisions about the health of their organization or of a targeted acquisition.

Data, Performance, and Organizational Health

Data-based research has revealed some significant findings regarding the connections between organizational health and business performance. According to McKinsey's research, organizations that do not emphasize health miss opportunities to deliver a total return to shareholders three times greater than their peers.[3] Other researchers have found that organizations with adaptive cultures—a dimension of organizational health—perform better than those with more rigid cultures. In adaptive cultures, managers attend to all of their constituencies, especially customers, taking the right risks and initiating change when needed.[4] Separately, Duke and Columbia University researchers have found that more than half of senior executives believe that corporate culture is a top-three driver of a company's value. Although 92 percent believe that their companies' value would increase if the culture could be improved, only 16 percent believe their culture is where it should be.[5] Complementary indications come from MIT, whose longtime, large-scale studies show that agile firms grow revenue 37 percent faster and generate 30 percent higher profits than nonagile companies.[6] Similarly, another study showed that agile companies are seven times more likely to have sustained above-average profitability than nonagile companies.[7]

In this AI-first era of extreme velocity and volatility, agility is more important than ever. Business leaders and investors alike need reassurances that they are both designing and investing in agile organizations and cultures that can adapt swiftly to unlock new sources of business value. In today's context, however, the key to capturing that value extends beyond the economics of the business. Instead, in both business and investment management, leaders need to apply equal rigor to how they measure the economic performance of a business and its organizational health. In short, realizing an adequate return on investment in a company requires managing those essentials that make up organizational health as effectively as possible— tracking impact and analyzing the effects of any single dimension across the entire business. (See the sidebar "The Case of HealthCo: How an Organizational-Health Check Set the Course for a Comeback.")

To realize the potential of organizational-health checks, companies must consider two critical things: (1) *what* to measure, which includes developing a unique framework of areas that are of material importance, and (2) *how* to measure, which entails using new advances in digital technologies.

What to Measure: Capturing the Key Dimensions of Organizational Health
Many companies could benefit from establishing a complete organizational-health checkup process—a systematic pulse check of the organization and its workforce across all the essentials. What some companies label as "people or organizational analytics" can help your business make evidence-based decisions on setting a clear strategic direction, selecting and cultivating leadership that shapes culture, designs the organization, and attracts and hires the right diverse talent while also unlocking their potential to perform at their best and ultimately execute the company's strategy.

The Case of HealthCo: How an Organizational-Health Check Set the Course for a Comeback

"We are no longer set up for long-term success." That's a harsh statement, but it's what many leaders and the board of a company we'll call HealthCo were worried about. It was also what their investors observed about the fast-growth company in the software industry. Moreover, it was what the evidence confirmed, based on insights from an organizational-health review that the chief performance officer had just presented to the group at the table.

Indeed, the data exposed significant shortcomings compared to peers across the portfolio of companies owned by the investment firm. The intelligence gathered drew from an array of reputable third-party sources to shine a bright contextual light on the company's struggles with themes such as diversity, equity, and inclusion, and a culture closed off to outside ideas. The chief performance officer and her analytic team framed a discussion that could no longer be about any single organizational element in isolation. Rather, the data revealed that the organization was affected by problems to do with all the elements of the business's health in combination, continually interacting with each other.

For the company's top management and investors, the path forward would entail confronting seismic change as they tried to envision how to rewire the organization for the future. As they mulled over the data, they quickly identified a much bigger and more awkward question: Had top management's interest in scaling hurt the business's health in the end? Had that single-minded interest effectively added to its own revenue declines and organizational dysfunction?

To be sure, the company had experienced rapid growth—certainly in maturity and scale. It was quite conceivable that top management missed some things along the way. The focus on profitable growth specifically revealed weaknesses in a culture

(continued)

rooted in competition rather than collaboration, and an operating model that slowed decision making.

Fortunately, the comprehensive health data forced the management team to see the organization clearly in the mirror. With concrete evidence in front of them about where the business was ailing, top management and the team of investors were able to start unpacking those business issues. And by facing the facts, the group at the table began to feel some hope. They could now identify the essential changes that HealthCo needed to make—among other things, changes to its myopic hiring and promotion policies that had contributed to an inequitable, insular company culture. That was just one of the critical issues that had gotten lost in the company's single-minded striving toward rapid growth. Ultimately, the investment team and management team were able to make the step-changes needed to improve the company's effectiveness and take it into the future.

Not only do full org-health checkups help business leaders better guide their investments and priorities, but they are immensely helpful to PE firms as well. Today, such firms are finding more and more often that the leadership capabilities necessary for change and strategic execution—such as strategic thinking, complex problem solving, or learning from experience—will all involve AI. As Emily Amdurer, principal in Heidrick Consulting's New York office and a member of its private equity practice, shared with me: "Some private equity firms are applying AI and advanced analytics to their talent assessment practices. It enables investors to get a quicker read on their companies' leaders' capabilities to be agile and manage through uncertainty. This is important to predicting which leaders in their portfolio companies will be able to lead the growth, enter into new markets, integrate acquisitions and lead under new structures, such as carve-outs. These AI methods are less obtrusive and time-intensive than traditional interview practices. The results inform investors around critical talent and development decisions." As one human capital operating partner at a leading middle market private equity fund shared with me, "There is immense value using [digital] technologies like a social listening capability. Private equity firms are data junkies. We measure everything. So, if there is an environment in which human capital metrics, data, and analytics can flourish, it is in private equity." In other words, the role of advanced analytics is proving increasingly important as the focus on organizational matters in the private markets grows.

Moreover, based on the amount of deal activity across a variety of industries, conducting routine organizational-health checks enables organizations to leverage advanced analytics in a way that improves organizational due diligence and performance initiatives and more closely aligns organizational essentials with the value-creation plan and overall strategy. To accomplish this, leaders must first decide on what they want to scan. (See the table "What to Measure" for examples of types of measurements that companies can capture and potential sources of information.)

To establish what is essential to measure, companies need to build out an enterprise-wide framework. This will give company leaders a consistent guide to monitor changes over time. The framework is a shared set of broad principles, practices, and tools—and their accompanying measures and metrics—that are adopted and accessible to all. Building a framework is akin to deciding what your mobile health monitor will measure (heart rate? calories burned?) and what constitutes a good score. In the case of PE firms, the investment team defines a set of principles and their accompanying measures and metrics—a framework of sorts regarding key areas—which are then adopted by the deal team. Roughly half the companies I've worked with have already taken the important step of developing an enterprise-wide framework and using it in the operating rhythm of the business or at critical inflection points, such as a merger or executive transition.

How to Measure: Utilizing New Digital Technologies

The state of a company's organizational health can mean the difference between its success and failure. But the way that health is

What to Measure

Org Health Element	What to Consider Measuring	Traditional (Old) Data Sources	New and Emerging Digital Sources Mined by AI
Pre-deal: Discovery and Due Diligence *In this phase, the focus is primarily on public data sources, with an emphasis on founders/leaders, culture, and talent in the discovery.*			
Founders and leaders	• Founding team's background • Team completeness • How a company's team stacks up against its main competitor's team • Leadership vision	• Word of mouth • Personal networks • Interviews with founders • Psychometric assessments (due diligence only)	• Digital profiles (e.g., LinkedIn), including companies they worked for, schools they attended, people they know, whether founders worked for a previously successful company, number of PhDs on the team) • Social media customer and employee reviews • Patent registries • Academic publications • Open-source contributions • Company web pages • Blogs and articles • Written or verbal communications (such as meeting minutes, speeches, or media interviews)

Culture	• Employee engagement • Agility • Execution • Innovation • Performance • Customer-focus • Inclusiveness • Trust and respect • Employee commitment to company purpose and alignment with strategy	• Review of engagement and other surveys (due diligence only when the organization provides it) • Interviews and word of mouth	• Video interview analytics (e.g., HireVue, Retorio; due diligence only) • Social media (e.g., Glassdoor) • Public data regarding a company's values
Talent	• Strength in hiring	• Review of attraction and retention data (in due diligence only)	• Job postings

(continued)

What to Measure (continued)

Org Health Element	What to Consider Measuring	Traditional (Old) Data Sources	New and Emerging Digital Sources Mined by AI
	• Top talent attraction and retention • Quality of talent compared to competitors • Skills and skills gaps		• Talent and skills migration to the organization (or out of the organization) and quality of talent in the organization compared to competitors mined from social media profiles, media articles, and other sources for specialist roles (e.g., patents, citations, opensource coding sites, etc.)

Post-deal

In the post-deal phase, it's critical to continuously assess all seven dimensions of org health, with the potential to gather robust internal data through new digital advances.

Org Health Element	What to Consider Measuring	Traditional (Old) Data Sources	New and Emerging Digital Sources Mined by AI
Strategy	• Purpose-driven, with a commitment to creating meaningful impact on society and the environment in addition to profits (i.e., commitment to stakeholder capitalism/ESG goals)	• Human analysis only, based on collecting a variety of data (e.g., financial, customer, market data)	• Text analysis of public documents regarding values and metrics to analyze the extent to which the organization is purpose-driven

	• Product market fit
	• Clarity of strategy and vision, including clear value-creation drivers
	• Competitive differentiation
	• Existence of a data-driven approach to strategy formulation
	• Key performance indicators (KPIs)
		• AI can analyze whether the organization's KPIs (a reflection of its strategy) are the right ones to maximize, prioritize them, and determine how effectively they are being maximized based on data such as:
		  ○ Financial and customer data
		  ○ Demand and market data
		  ○ Competitor data
		  ○ Sentiment analysis from Twitter, geotagged

Culture	• Engagement • Trust and transparency • Collaboration	• Engagement and other employee surveys • Sentiment and engagement analysis as analyzed from internal emails and chats • Speed of work performed as analyzed from corporate digital applications (e.g., calendar, email, social) • Collaboration and information sharing as analyzed through social network analysis and corporate digital communications

(*continued*)

What to Measure (continued)

Org Health Element	What to Consider Measuring	Traditional (Old) Data Sources	New and Emerging Digital Sources Mined by AI
	• Innovation • Agility • Data-and-AI driven • Employee commitment to company purpose and alignment with vision/strategy • Number and type of microcultures		• Audio analysis of business meetings (e.g., for positive or negative words) • Glassdoor or other external social media employer review platforms
Leadership	Individual leadership traits: • Inclusive leadership (listening to employees, customers, and external trends) • Focus on strategic priorities	• Psychometric assessments • Interviews and observation	• Degree of listening and communicating with employees, customers, and expert problem solvers, as measured through digital communications • Time spent on various activities as mined through work applications • Video and audio analytics to infer qualities like learning orientation

	• Agile decision making • Judgment, with the help of algorithmic insights • Learning orientation • Ability to collaborate across boundaries Collective/organizational traits: • Leadership bench strength • Presence of cross-functional top teams		• Social network and collaboration analysis (through collaboration patterns found through digital applications) • Skills and qualities of potential successors, and the number of the potential successors per key role, as inferred from data such as projects, outcomes, or experience
Talent	• Skills supply and skills gaps now and in the future • Top talent in mission-critical roles, and the ability to attract and retain them • Identifying and quantifying the value of the most important roles in an organization	• Systems data (e.g., attraction and retention numbers) • Engagement and other employee surveys	• Inferring skills from work products or projects • Quality and type of team communications, and team alignment and optimal composition as determined through work applications • Talent and skills migration to the organization (or out of the organization) as inferred from sites like LinkedIn • Team communication data on digital platforms

(continued)

What to Measure (continued)

Org Health Element	What to Consider Measuring	Traditional (Old) Data Sources	New and Emerging Digital Sources Mined by AI
	• Frequent reallocation of high performers to the most critical strategic priorities • Employee experience • Team performance		
Organizational design	• Clear accountabilities • Speed of decision making, information sharing, and workflow • Ability to quickly move people to the evolving needs of work • Empowerment and autonomy	• Org charts • Employee surveys	• Information and workflow as analyzed from digital work platforms • Organizational network analysis performed through text analytics of email engagement, company social profiles, contacts directory, and other data sources; or through wearable badges such as those by Humanyze, including connections and the influence at work across the width and depth of their company, divisions, geographies, across lines of businesses (LoBs) and functions, or just within teams • Degree to which management is involved in all deals and details as determined through calendar and digital work applications

	• Effective interaction between the organization and its parts	• Number of meetings and meeting participants as measured through calendar data, amount of time spent on email
	• How effectively the organization obtains resources necessary for high performance	• Project and decision data relative to outcomes
	• Organizational drag (i.e., cumulative effect of needless internal interactions, unproductive or inconsequential meetings, and unnecessary e-communications)	• Enterprise social graphs, mapping workplace connections between employees, people outside the organization, and work-related objects (such as events, tasks, activities, and content)
	• Social and organizational networks	
EID	• Belonging • Inclusion • Microaggressions or actions based on unconscious bias	• Demographic diversity metrics obtained from information systems • Employee surveys
		• Written or verbal communications (such as meeting minutes, speeches, or media interviews) to detect microaggressions or feelings of belonging and inclusion
		• Cognitive diversity on teams, including personalities or beliefs and values as determined through digital communications

(continued)

What to Measure (continued)

Org Health Element	What to Consider Measuring	Traditional (Old) Data Sources	New and Emerging Digital Sources Mined by AI
	• Demographic diversity • Cognitive diversity or diversity of thought (e.g., learning styles)		• Benchmarking pay based on responsibilities and performance (based on analysis of actual work performed), not titles
Well-being	• Emotional/mental wellness (e.g., happiness, lack of burnout) • Physical wellness • Relational wellness (e.g., inclusion and belonging) • Purposeful wellness (i.e., feeling like life has meaning and purpose beyond oneself) • Employable wellness (i.e., having or growing the skills to remain employable) • Financial wellness	• Employee surveys • Data from information systems such as absenteeism	• Emotional computing (e.g., text analysis to detect emotions in emails, social sites) • Wearables and environmental sensors to track physical movements and health • Amount of time spent on work (including after hours) as tracked through work applications

traditionally measured falls short. Self-reported data gathered from employee questionnaires and surveys tend to be unreliable: people often provide the socially acceptable answer (e.g., skewing positive) regarding their beliefs and values, rather than stating how they truly feel and behave.[8]

Today, however, compelling new ways to assess org health make it easier and more effective. Routine organizational checks powered by multidimensional data—both structured (i.e., employee opinion surveys or exit interviews) and unstructured (i.e., collaboration that occurs within and across teams based on calendar scraping)—broaden the number of organizational-health aspects that can be considered. For example, fintech startup QuantCube Technology analyzes customer reviews and social media posts to develop predictive indicators of events, such as price changes and economic growth.[9] Such data helps the company to understand critical moments of growth that can enable leaders to forecast changes in their organizational size and workforce makeup, and thus make better decisions. And at private equity firms, during the pre-screen and due diligence stages of a deal, such data offers investor and portfolio leaders a more precise and accurate picture of the target organization.

Indeed, AI powers a formidable arsenal of analytic capabilities to measure the health of companies. Consider how organizational leaders can now assess team dynamics with newly available data and technologies. Guided team interactions can be recorded and captured in several video formats that can then be analyzed using advanced vision (video content analysis technologies) and natural language processing (NLP) technologies to identify and map group-level attributes to assess the overall quality of team dynamics. Or consider how NLP and text analytics, along with machine learning models, can now be used to build a psychological profile of an entrepreneur or set of employees. According to one study done by Barclays, there are broadly two different types of entrepreneurs: Type A, who are creative, well-organized, highly competitive, emotionally stable, and neither extrovert nor introvert; and Type B, who are traditional, spontaneous, team players, emotional, and neither extrovert nor introvert. These attributes can be analyzed by scraping textual data and parsing images/

videos from social profiles (Facebook, Twitter, LinkedIn). From there, a board or other decision-making team can build out the psychological profile of a particular entrepreneur and assess (using supervised learning functions) how effectively he or she might function in different scenarios. Such psychological profiles can be used to support decision making in deal sourcing, deal selection, deal structure, post-investment value-added, and exit scenarios.[10]

It's important to note, however, that along with the significant value that business and investment leaders stand to gain from using digital advances to assess organizational health, there is also a need for caution. For more on that topic, see the sidebar "Developing and Using Digital Technologies Responsibly."

Developing and Using Digital Technologies Responsibly

New sources of data and technologies, of course, are not without drawbacks. Using AI and other digital resources responsibly means building capabilities to ensure that people's privacy is respected and that data-mining efforts are done for the benefit of all. For example, principles developed by organizations like the Institute for Ethical AI & Machine Learning represent the type of guardrails that companies can adopt. An important first step that leaders can take to protect their own and their employees' data is to embed privacy and risk frameworks in their digital systems. Such software tools make transparent to all stakeholders what data is being captured, held, and used.[11]

There are also ways to mitigate the kinds of ethical problems that can arise in digital programs themselves—specifically, bias concerning race and gender. Particularly with AI, it's important to ensure that bias isn't baked into the algorithms. Over the last decade or so, many instances of such bias have been exposed. Among other things, both facial- and voice-recognition systems sometimes have proven faulty because the AI embedded in them was developed by white men. Both Microsoft and Amazon have had to abandon certain AI programs whose algorithms for doing things like hiring (in Amazon's case) and risk-scoring for loans (in the case of one Microsoft financial services algorithm) were radically skewed toward white males.

But the bias issues go beyond discrimination against individuals; bias in AI also can damage businesses themselves. "The problems are not simply that we're not getting promotions [because of bias in algorithms] . . . but it is also affecting the world beyond," said Meredith Whittaker, a research scientist and cofounder of the AI Now Institute at New York University. "The products that are created in these [less diverse] environments reflect these cultures, and that's having an impact on billions of people."[12]

Apart from training and hiring more diverse populations of technicians to develop AI algorithms in the first place—which would represent a shift toward equity whose time has clearly come—a few other kinds of solutions are emerging in the meantime. According to a 2021 article titled "Fighting Algorithmic Bias in Artificial Intelligence," researchers are employing physics to make the AI programs they use more accurate and reliable. For example, principal researcher Payel Das of IBM's Thomas J. Watson Research Center, says her team is developing machine learning algorithms that increase by a hundredfold the chance that a new scientific discovery will prove viable. She does this by including learning in the programs from both data and physics principles. "We often enhance, guide, or validate the AI models with the help of prior scientific or other forms of knowledge, for example, physics-based principles, in order to make the AI system more robust, efficient, interpretable, and reliable," says Das. By using such physics-driven learning, "one can crosscheck the AI models in terms of accuracy, reliability, and inductive bias."[13]

How Private Equity Firms Are Leading the Charge in Measuring Org Health
Private equity firms today are enjoying what is probably the most exciting era of computing power and technological advances to date. As perhaps few other kinds of organizations do, PE firms understand precisely how critical assessing organizational health is to the success of the companies in which they invest, whether those transactions be leveraged buyouts, venture capital, or growth capital. Accordingly, PE firms use digital tools that can cross pre-deal, portfolio acceleration, and exit phases with both precision and speed.

Thus, PE firms offer many lessons not only for PE-backed hypergrowth companies but also for any organization seeking better ways to measure and manage the seven health conditions we examined in part I. To be sure, organizations of all kinds now have an unprecedented ability to collect more and better data on org health. Analytics and other advances in technology such as AI bring incredible speed. They also increase accuracy and enable professionals seeking to improve org health to do their best with a heightened degree of precision.

For PE firms, however, the stakes are high indeed when it comes to assessing a target organization's health. Whether it is providing financial backing to startups and nonpublic companies or to public companies that are being taken private, PE firms' reputations and financial success depend on increasing the value of their investments. This means that they tend to place greater emphasis on actively managing their assets, relying on evaluating and monitoring the health of the organization to find new ways to boost performance and enrich their internal rate of returns (IRRs). By applying advanced analytics techniques, investors can avoid hidden landmines across the entire value chain and improve investment performance.

Another reason that PE firms are leading the charge in organizational-health checkups is because their typical stance—a data-driven, show-me-the-facts mindset—enables investors to extract more value from the transactions they execute. As Laela Sturdy, general partner at CapitalG, says: "The growth stage business requires data and intuition. To determine the best next step, you need to ask the right questions and interpret data in the right way."

Consider how one company in an established PE firm's portfolio—the chemical industry player Crystal—used data-based insights to achieve its goal of moving faster than its competitors and securing new business while retaining existing clients to maintain its rapid growth.[14] The insights came from a surprising source for a chemical company—social networking analysis—which illustrates how companies across many kinds of industries can do likewise.

Crystal, which serves clients across a distributed team of sales and technical employees in Indonesia, wanted to deepen client loyalty by gaining a better understanding of their needs. The company therefore adopted a relationship-analytics platform called TrustView as a network analysis tool to uncover social business connections of its top performers. This would complement the existing solutions Crystal already had been using—IBM Notes and Domino—to analyze its employees' communication patterns with external clients that would otherwise be hidden. Using these programs, management can now make data-driven decisions based on reports and visualization tools and dashboards like Tableau, which can help leaders see and understand organizational data by the strength, frequency, and speed of communication between internal and external parties. This allows the company to easily identify the top influencers in its social business network. Ultimately, the investment in TrustView resulted in 60 percent faster identification of at-risk client relationships, an increase of 30 percent in client retention, and 75 percent faster onboarding for new client reps.

This type of organizational analytics program can be employed by teams of experts within a private equity firm's portfolio operations group. Such groups are essentially experts in organizational health: it is their job to evaluate targeted assets just as they would any other investment—by linking business results to the essential conditions of org health, which in turn helps to pinpoint and seed change.

Similarly, publicly held companies like Google, Facebook, and numerous others now deploy a much wider range of capabilities to capture value. For example, they are building agile teams of organizational consultants, adding more specialized data science expertise to measure and analyze key intangibles like organizational health.

Next, we'll continue our look at the useful model that PE firms provide and examine how they track organizational health across two critical phases of the investment process.

Private Equity Firms: What to Measure Pre-deal and Post-deal

In one study, 49 percent of private equity professionals believe that digital innovations such as AI and analytics will increase returns in five years, and 22 percent say they are already doing so.[15] Indeed, such innovations enable deal teams to understand the cost, composition, and makeup of their talent, leadership, culture, and organizational design on the front end. For some PE deals, getting the needed information will require an up-front investment in advanced analytic and AI capabilities and reporting tools. If the deal proceeds, a more in-depth review and focus on organizational health will be executed. Given this, let's look at the role of org-health checkups across two aspects of the investment process: pre-deal organizational risk management and post-deal portfolio optimization.

Pre-deal: Organizational Risk Management

In private equity, conducting rigorous organizational due diligence well before the deal is made is considered equally and perhaps even more critical than the legal and financial vetting that target portfolio companies undergo. And private equity firms that utilize advanced analytics to their fullest are reaping the benefits of speed, intelligence, and organizational agility.

Due diligence efforts are typically spent assessing tangible assets such as financial statements, market share, economies of scale, products and services, and the like. Yet efforts such as these miss the mark in applying a critical and rigorous review of less tangible assets such as leadership, talent, organization, culture, well-being, and diversity and inclusion. Because organizational health involves both hard and soft elements, producing a quality organizational audit requires the due diligence completed to cover both qualitative and quantitative analyses of the target investment's organizational health. This includes the "visible," such as structure, governance and physical layouts of an office, executive compensation, and the like. And it has dimensions of the organization's behavior that are less visible, such as mindsets, values, and sentiment that can affect how the company functions.

Most important during due diligence, however, is assessing how effectively the top management team functions (and in the case of startups, the quality of the founding team)—and what kind of culture the organization nurtures. Consider how GV (formerly Google Ventures), the venture arm of Alphabet Inc., uses quantitative algorithms to aid in making investment decisions. Founded in 2009, Google Ventures is the venture capital business of Alphabet that invests in cutting-edge technologies in the areas of healthcare, robotics, transportation, cybersecurity, agriculture, and more. The firm heavily relies on data (indeed, it has access to the world's most extensive data sets) and cloud computing infrastructure to gather and clean data from academic literature, publicly available information about startup companies and their founders (including their past experience), and other data sources to feed into algorithms that help identify what factors are essential in analyzing different kinds of deals.[16]

Similarly, SignalFire, hailing from San Francisco, is the self-described "most quantitative fund in the world," and "the only VC that brings a data platform to its portfolio companies." Core to its operations is its data platform called Beacon, which functions like a Bloomberg terminal for the startup industry. Chris Farmer, CEO of SignalFire, describes it as "a proprietary mini-Google" powering the entire value chain of a venture—from deal origination through identifying and selecting the right investments and from deal agreements between limited partners (LPs) and general partners (GPs) to portfolio operations support. Beacon is capable of tracking the performance of more than 6 million companies in real time by drawing upon millions of data sources including academic publications, patent registries, open-source contributions, regulatory filings, company websites, sales data, app store rankings, and several others. Companies that outperform or do something notable are flagged on a dashboard, effectively allowing SignalFire to see deals earlier than traditional venture firms.[17]

Pre-deal: Spotting Deals Early

Data assessments such as I've just described in the examples of SignalFire and GV, or as reflected in the table titled "What to Measure" in this chapter, can help PE firms find potential investment opportunities early on. As one deal executive put it, "Being first to the deal matters." Consider how one investment firm made a shift from labor-intensive analyses of reams of data associated with mergers and acquisitions to AI-powered analyses that can scan and monitor critical data points at an accelerated pace. Powered by advanced data and analytics, this investment management firm can continuously monitor a portfolio of over 25 acquisition targets by sourcing public data ranging from patent findings and citations to social media that reveals customer feedback, employee engagement, and corporate culture. The benefit: speed and accuracy of analyzing a ton of data, backed by AI-powered recommendations of other companies to consider for the acquisition or comparisons of a peer group.

In one survey of PE firms, respondents said they most wanted to use machine learning in their operations to improve their ability to find and execute deals.[18] Already, organizations like EQT Ventures, the venture arm of EQT Partners, a global private equity firm, is using a proprietary AI algorithm it calls MotherBrain to identify the underappreciated founders others may overlook and back them early. It draws on 40 sources of data, including founders' résumés, to help it find potential target investments. So far, it has directly led to investments in seven startups out of the fifty the firm has made. MotherBrain even helps VC professionals prepare for meetings by generating notifications that include summaries of past interactions with a person.[19]

Hone Capital, the U.S. venture capital arm of Chinese private equity firm CSC Group, also uses proprietary data-driven intelligence platforms to source and select deals. They have created their machine learning models from database records of more than 30,000 deals from the last decade fetched from different sources, such as Crunchbase, PitchBook, and Mattermark. After exploring around 400 characteristics per deal, they identified 20 characteristics for seed deals that are highly predictive of future success, including founding teams' background (diverse universities) and syndicate partners' lead area of expertise.[20]

Venture funds have been experimenting with using sophisticated data and analytics to help them spot deals. Consider how Bloomberg Beta, an early-stage venture firm focused on the future of work capitalized solely by Bloomberg LP, is taking a fascinating approach toward data science. The firm teamed up with Haas Business School, People.co (a talent data company), and AngelList to create algorithms capable of predicting "Future Founders." Future Founders is a list of people working in the tech industry who are likely to launch their own companies in the future, often before they have even begun the actual process. Having identified these potential future game changers, the firm can directly reach out to them and start building relationships months or even years before other venture firms, leading to a massive competitive advantage.[21]

In another instance, Bloomberg Beta partnered with Mattermark, a deal intelligence company, "to build its own database of future founders." Mattermark identified the most likely career paths of successful company founders and created a pool of 1.5 million people who are connected to tech startups but are not founders themselves yet by just one or two degrees of separation. Education, previous companies, seniority, geography, and age were identified as the strongest predictors of an individual starting a company. The project aimed to find insights that were not common on the path to entrepreneurship since if patterns were evident, other firms would already have spotted them. Bloomberg Beta identified a short list of 350 potential founders from the database and invited them to New York and San Francisco events for networking. Eight of the people that the initial study predicted were future founders did indeed start their own companies.[22]

Using data to help evaluate people instead of relying on mere opinion or intuition can help managers look beyond stereotypes and misconceptions. Many of the future entrepreneurs identified by Bloomberg Beta, for example, challenge common stereotypes about entrepreneurs; 40 percent identified were over the age of 40, and some didn't have any technical experience at all.[23]

Post-deal: Ongoing, Continuous Measurement to Gather Trend Line Data
Post-deal, all dimensions of organizational health should be assessed and monitored regularly to get trendline data. Digital advances enable investor leadership and portfolio management teams to accelerate executive decision making, so startup teams can adhere to or beat their timelines. Consider the following company examples of new ways to measure each essential of organizational health post-deal:

- **Strategic direction.** Labx Ventures, a San Diego–based investing firm, has doubled down on a value proposition that places science, algorithms, and rules engines called "Venture Science Capital" at the center. The company describes Venture Science as "a new, multi-disciplinary field that uses valid scientific methodologies to make an objective and independent analysis of business practices and outcomes. This field uses advanced analytics, pattern recognition, predictive algorithms, information science, artificial intelligence and machine learning to uncover evidence and develop theories about business, venture, enterprise, capitalism and how they affect startup and emerging growth companies. Venture Science examines business core strategies and how and why deals are selected, made, qualified, and executed." The firm claims it was among the first companies subjected to double-blind testing, including a published major university study that showed its assessor tool was over 90 percent accurate in predicting successful exits.[24] Not only can the tool assess a company across its strategic direction, core capabilities, risk, and a host of other parameters, but it also can improve and accelerate outcomes in their Venture Lab.
- **Culture.** KeenCorp is a new startup that has an index powered by advanced analytics and AI that helps companies monitor internal emails and chats (aggregated, never at the individual level) to examine what's going on in the workplace and gauge culture, engagement, and flag potential problems. For example, a review of dips in

engagement among women in a particular part of business can unearth possible instances of sexual misconduct by men in that part of the business.[25] Meanwhile, GE's culture application, based on an algorithm built by its team of data scientists and HR leaders, enables the company to zero in on elements of its operating model that affect how fast and nimble the organization can operate to deliver on customer outcomes.[26] Or take Freddie Mac, which uses Microsoft's Workplace Analytics to mine employee Microsoft applications like email, calendar, and social collaboration data to assess culture, and then to drive a cultural transformation across its managerial ranks. By examining time-usage metrics related to engagement and retention, the company uncovered how critical manager behaviors such as 1:1 manager time, level of leadership exposure given to employees, and the degree to which work can be distributed evenly across an organization were influencing employee engagement and retention.[27]

- **Leadership.** Heidrick & Struggles's Agile Leader Potential (ALP) solution is the first AI-driven product of its kind for assessing leadership through video analytics and AI.[28] Supported by technology from HireVue, ALP uses state-of-the-art game and video intelligence to provide a quantitative, scalable, and objective indicator of competencies and traits critical for successful leadership. What Heidrick & Struggles's research reveals is that agile behaviors connect to leadership potential. ALP applies digital technology to psychometric and cognitive measures of leadership potential, creating an engaging experience that measures characteristics that point to agility. The company defines the attributes of leadership potential as:
  - **Thinking dexterity.** The ability to solve complex problems, think logically, and develop effective solutions.
  - **Curiosity.** The tendency to seek new experiences, opportunities to learn, and alternative ways of thinking.

- o **Tenacity.** The tendency to strive for achievement, practice self-discipline, and maintain focus.
- o **Social agility.** The tendency to effectively balance assertiveness and self-confidence with empathy and warmth toward others.
- **Talent.** Sandy Ogg—the former Unilever chief of human resources and Blackstone operating partner—and his firm, CEO.works, have analytics that assess critical roles and the value they should deliver. The approach taken quantifies the specific contribution expected of each critical role, allowing a leader to identify the value hot spots as places in the talent-to-value hierarchy where the roles matter. Once identified, the analytics quantify the specific contribution expected of each of these critical roles. What's relevant for investors and portfolio management teams is that the analytics assign each critical role a number based on the value expected from that role (for example, $50 million in EBITDA times the multiple) to deliver that chunk of value. This offers substantial benefit, as the analytics help prioritize the value-creating roles that should get 100 percent of the value they are aiming to create, and value-enabling roles that should get a percentage based on the value at risk that the leader or group of leaders are seeking to mitigate. Such numbers are handy, as they give investor leadership and portfolio leadership clarity about how much value the company would have at risk.[29]
- **Organizational design.** Klick Health's machine learning technology it calls Genome helps employers manage autonomy. Analyzing every project in the company at every stage, Genome rewards more responsibility to people who have demonstrated consistent performance. The AI tracks every decision made in the company in the context in which it was made. The more an individual proves their competence in judgment, the more flexibility the system grants in making more significant decisions. These factors eliminate bias and politics and reward people according to the evi-

dence of their merit.[30] Another example is OrgMapper, which helps clients see beyond the traditional organizational structure, getting them to see the informal organization, connections, and influence at work across the width and depth of their company, divisions, and geographies, across lines of business and functions, or just within teams.[31]

- **Equity, inclusion, and diversity.** Investment management firms use an AI tool developed by CompIQ to help assess and create fairer gender pay. Instead of relying on job titles to benchmark pay, as is traditionally done, it collects a wide range of data to benchmark pay based on responsibilities and performance, not titles. The goal is to help companies set wage scales that align with other companies in the same sector. Data on such things as location, seniority, and performance reviews are run through various AI algorithms to produce a market pay range for each employee. Categories such as gender, race, and age are not entered into the equation, so the algorithm doesn't "think" about them in making its decisions. And instead of relying on job titles for assessing fair compensation, CompIQ reviews employee responsibilities to identify issues that businesses often miss regarding pay discrepancies.[32] Meanwhile, companies like PepsiCo and L'Oréal use AI technology to help identify biases in their past hiring decisions. By analyzing hiring records, the technology can reveal, for example, if the company has favored candidates with light skin.[33]

- **Well-being.** First Horizon National Corporation, a holding company that operates First Tennessee Bank and other wealth management and capital market subsidiaries, uses an AI-based product from Ultimate Software to measure employee sentiment and identify the firm's top-performing employees. The software uses natural language processing and automatically differentiates among more than 100 emotions, such as confusion, enthusiasm, and frustration. Previously, it would take more than one month to receive employee data from the annual survey, after which the management team would spend months analyzing the results. Now the AI-powered software provides the analysis the day after the survey closes and helps First Horizon make correlations across the data and then align training and management programs accordingly. The AI platform is also being deployed for smaller employee feedback streams, such as exit interviews and performance reviews.[34] Meanwhile, the company Hitachi provides its employees with smart badges loaded with sensors that collect data on them 50 times a second throughout the day—including the time they spend sitting, walking, nodding, typing, and talking. An AI tool then uses all this data to suggest ways to improve their happiness—such as speaking up at meetings or devoting mornings to discussions with other people rather than desk work. By examining fluctuations in happiness levels, Hitachi managers can tweak schedules to increase productivity and staff's well-being. One test company that used data from Hitachi's system learned that call-center workers were the happiest when they had lively conversations during break times. The solution: Let people take breaks at the same time. The result: Productivity soared. In the end, employees in Hitachi departments using AI to a greater degree are happier and post higher sales. In one test, they beat next-quarter order volume targets by 11 percent.[35]

Although these examples reflect mostly what's currently being done in the PE industry with portfolio companies, every organization can learn from these advances and use these newly available data and technologies to measure and monitor the seven critical aspects of a business's health.

Strengthening the Organization with Subject-Matter Data Experts

As discussed earlier, using a mobile health monitor typically reflects a broader commitment to improving one's health. And if the initial data that the monitor gathers isn't optimal, you might hire a personal trainer to improve. Just as the data from your mobile health monitor helps the trainer help you, putting data in the hands of management teams without assisting them to use it is counterproductive. That is why I encourage companies to create a small internal team of deeply skilled human-capital practitioners to help interpret and act on any data gathered about the organization's health. For example, such a team's experience and expertise can help leaders:

- Develop organizational-health scorecards for or against key value drivers
- Identify gaps and opportunities in organizational health and share insights with management or deal teams
- Develop organizational strategies to act on those gaps and opportunities to boost new levels of productivity and strengthen overall business performance and value creation
- Codify standardized and repeatable organizational practices and methods to develop an organizational playbook for how key organizational practices are systematically deployed at the company or across the portfolio in a PE firm
- Hold management teams and deal teams accountable to scorecards for an organization's overall health strategy

Activating a small team of subject-matter experts who are skilled in organizational health—i.e., chief performance officers in a PE firm or a core team of organizational performance experts in a public or private organization—to work in conjunction with company executives or investment professionals can help the business strengthen its operations. Financial investments in organizational health are only as useful as the advisory support (the personal trainers) deployed to help leaders optimize their organization to achieve their promised results.

For example, one Hong Kong–based alternative investment and advisory company has a team of entrepreneurs-in-residence—comprised of former executives and CEOs from different industries—to help with portfolio acceleration. The organization also has functional experts who can help support the portfolio company in areas where it cannot dedicate enough resources, such as human resources and organizational health. All these advisors rely on ongoing assessments and measurement of organizational health to help steer their portfolio investments, identifying tangible actions they can take to help their portfolio organizations unlock growth and performance.

Analytics insights can also help leaders remove bias from their interactions to model and execute organizational and operational improvements. By integrating a broad set of data about an individual C-suite leader or management team, the cultural attributes, written or verbal communications (such as meeting minutes, speeches, or media interviews), organizational performance teams, or chief performance officers can reduce biases, identify drivers of health and behavioral root causes, and flag issues (i.e., management decisions) that fit predefined patterns, before executing a transaction or performance improvement initiative.

Just as holistic health practitioners diagnose the state of one's mind, body, spirit, and emotions to improve the health of their patients, companies that adopt a similar comprehensive approach can answer important questions about the organization's health. By routinely engaging organizational decision makers to address each component of the business's health, leaders will gain insights into important questions, such as: What initiatives drive step-changes in organizational performance? After a merger, restructuring, or sale, what organizational levers need to be leveraged to get the company performing at its peak? Which critical roles in the organization have a disproportionate impact on the business, exposing the business to far greater risk if left unfilled or, far worse, held by poor performers? Which practices will unlock the full potential of the workforce to perform at its best?

Digital advances are radically transforming our ability to measure, monitor, and unleash organizational health. In the PE industry, 90 percent of private equity firms expect AI to have a transformative impact on the industry.[36] For a VC firm, the use of AI tools and techniques will improve a fund's returns and help reduce various risks related to a fund's portfolio management, portfolio companies, and relationships with limited partners. Such tools can also improve VCs' operational efficiency, increase performance incentives, provide clear fund strategy, reduce the average fund's life cycle, and reduce network biases, similarity biases, and gender biases.[37] One of the most transformative aspects of AI in the PE industry will be the ability to assess the health of an organization far more effectively—leading to actionable, real-time insights that can help organizations scale and grow. Although the PE industry is leading the charge, every organization can learn from its advances and gain a step-change in performance by harnessing newly available data and technologies. Moreover, my colleagues and I expect this developing field of measurement tools to grow tremendously in the next five years, requiring a whole new set of data, AI, and analytics capabilities in organizations and PE firms alike.

In the next chapter, we will look at how an organization can evolve from simply capturing and measuring data to transforming into the kind of AI-first company, such as Google, that thinks differently about data in everything it does.

Checklist for Agenda Setting

- Build and share an enterprise-wide framework that defines what good organizational health looks like based on a shared set of principles, practices, and tools and their accompanying measures and metrics.
- Invest in analytical talent and new technologies such as AI to more accurately and quickly assess the organization's health.
- For PE firms in the pre-deal phase, use new sources of data and AI to assess organizational health when finding and screening potential deals and conducting due diligence, paying attention to the quality of top management.
- For all organizations and PE firms in the post-deal phase, use new sources of data and AI to continuously monitor all aspects of org health, identify gaps and opportunities, and prioritize actions.
- Ensure management and deal teams are held accountable to organizational health scorecards.
- For PE firms, develop an organizational playbook for how key organizational practices are systematically deployed at the portfolio company or across the portfolio.

9 ■ To Become AI-First, Put Org Health First

Think Differently about Organizational Matters

Throughout this book, we've seen how artificial intelligence can unleash organizational health and provide us with more effective and real-time ways to monitor it continuously. Rather than simply optimizing what was done in the past, AI is now on the cusp of re-inventing organizations, providing entirely new opportunities to redefine work and the workforce for the future. This demands new ways of thinking about how organizations approach strategy, leadership, talent, culture, organizational design, and more—in short, all of the dimensions of organizational health.

Today's advances in artificial intelligence are redefining business models, transforming the customer experience, and enabling organizations to shapeshift based on changing conditions. But without a healthy organization, the full potential of AI can never be unleashed. Not only is organizational health critical to scaling and realizing the value of AI, but the reverse is also true: AI-first organizations—those that lead with advances in digital technologies such as machine learning to capture and mine data and, ultimately, train algorithms to constantly improve—set themselves up for success by adopting unique approaches to nearly every dimension of organizational health.

Amazon, Google, and Facebook are examples of AI-first companies that quickly scale and manage fast-paced growth. They've done this by decreasing their dependence on "hard assets" such as machinery or facilities, and instead, they focus on the key intangibles of organizational health and use AI to unleash the full power of their impact. Along with rapidly adopting AI technologies in the past few years, these organizations have reshaped their talent and organization practices for an AI world. For example, learning algorithms are used to match prospective employees with job openings, allowing recruiters to sift through applications and fill positions faster.

And it isn't just the Amazons, Googles, and Facebooks of the world that are taking AI-first seriously. Most organizations are now in the early phases of transitioning to AI-first as well, with varying degrees of success. Although 75 percent of business leaders surveyed believe their business will be obsolete in five years if they are unable to leverage how to scale AI, only 8 percent of companies engage in core practices that support widespread AI adoption.[1] Most companies have run only ad hoc pilots or are applying AI in just a single business process.[2]

In this chapter, we'll explore ways that companies can improve those numbers and evolve from simple capture and measurement of data to transform into AI-first organizations that think differently about data in all that they do. Let's start with a look at how one financial institution made the leap to AI-first.

The Case of Saxo Bank

In 2016, Patrick Hunger, then-CEO of Saxo Switzerland, led the bank through a technological overhaul. Not only was Saxo Bank embarking on robotic process automation (RPA) to improve efficiency and free humans to do more value-added work, it also developed a variety of AI and machine learning initiatives to create new value. The effort included three main areas of focus: an AI-based information engine, predictive analysis, and personalized marketing. Collectively, the bank referred to these initiatives as "robotics."

But Patrick Hunger also recognized that success of the bank's digital initiatives would hinge on a handful of first principles, described as follows:[3]

- **Start from the top.** Leaders need to be fluent in robotics so that they can create and advocate a compelling robotics vision and journey for the organization and articulate the strategic importance for the enterprise. In other words, leaders must empower robotics advocates who will become the day-to-day change agents.
- **Break organizational silos.** Many companies have built a cultural gap between their business and IT teams, with the latter focusing on keeping the lights on for the former. Robotics demands that these teams work together as closely as possible to ensure that they keep up with the evolution of the business and foster it. As Patrick Hunger believed, "It was less imperative on how the organizational setup of the company was intellectually designed. What created organizational mindshare and value was 'human transactions'; all guided by a collective and culturally well-anchored business purpose." Prabhu Venkatesh, Saxo's head of data at the time, reinforced this, explaining, "We have a bi-directional, collaborative model, with free flow of ideas and information between tech and business teams. Tech knows what's possible, and business knows what's useful—magical products are born in that intersection." Ongoing dialogue and clear alignment between IT and the business as equal parts of the company were critical to silo smashing efforts—so much so that the machine learning and AI development team were designed to function as an integral part of the business organization to bridge the gap. Christian Busk Hededal, Saxo's head of big data and AI, explained, "We have the

mentality of being a data-driven organization with close alignment between IT and business."

- **Expose data to a wide variety of stakeholders.** Prabhu Venkatesh noted that an important aspect of robotization was the ability to expose data and key performance indicators to a wider group of stakeholders. In other words, helping every employee keep the big picture in mind while becoming more data-driven in decision making was more than just a set of pronouncements, it was a principle put into action. As simple as it sounds, being transparent with execution data creates a common understanding among different teams about what is happening in the company and how everybody's work affects it. The unintended positive consequence is an outcome-based culture where humans act upon visible issues rather than rely on the process itself.

- **Establish a robotics change engine.** By establishing strong governance, Saxo leaders could more effectively manage the delivery of robotics solutions against the expected business value and constantly investigate new ways for the business to benefit from robotics. This required challenging the status quo and overcoming organizational and process boundaries that were rendered obsolete by robotics. Lastly, Saxo needed to enable operational managers with practical methodologies and tools for the daily management of a mixed workforce made of both humans and machines. Saxo developed a plan to balance how managers and staff coped with the anxiety that comes with any change, thereby strengthening the close collaboration with HR early on to provide recommendations on the redeployment of the human workforce.

- **Ensure human-machine inclusion.** The role of leaders is to consciously design organizations as organisms that reach their full potential through inclusion, not separation. Human-machine collaboration meant something more to Saxo than some catchphrase for the day; it was a system of logic where innovation and performance thrive best in a human-machine ecosystem. Patrick Hunger noted, "When we say that we are a tech company at heart, we mean that technology is the primary instrument to put into practice human skills. Technology amplifies our organizational capabilities to the point that size is no longer a limitation." While some see digital advances, particularly AI, as a clash between machines and humans,[4] others see tech as an unprecedented way to bring out our humanity—a way to elevate organizational health. Algorithmic organizations with intelligent operating models at their core will be a mainstay for how companies boost performance at individual and team levels, allowing for new approaches to human and machine collaboration to take hold. Therefore, the greatest opportunity for organizational evolution isn't just to redesign jobs or automate work but to fundamentally rethink the "intelligent operating model's architecture" to create new sources of value for the enterprise, teams, and individuals.[5]

Moreover, during the pandemic, as Saxo's journey toward digitizing customer experiences evolved, the full value of the bank's AI-based tools became clear. This was true particularly regarding the tools' ability to unleash *human potential*. With consumers staying home or at the very least staying away from physical bank branches, it became increasingly clear that the organization's AI-based tools helped employees anticipate and facilitate fast-changing client needs and preferences in ways they could not have predicted. Ultimately, the bank's workforce became adept at learning on the go, which also meant that the bank responded in faster, more agile, and more accurate ways. And it was available to scale and operate on a 24/7/365 basis.

What Makes AI-First Companies Different

In March 2017, Alphabet and Google CEO Sundar Pichai announced that the company was shifting to an AI-first world. A series of announcements focused on how AI would be applied in various ways followed, including the development of specialized chips for optimizing machine learning, or the use of a broader family of machine learning methods based on artificial neural networks—deep learning—in new applications, such as cancer research. It also included placing Google's AI-driven assistant on as many devices as possible. Simply put: Pichai stated the company was transitioning from "searching and organizing the world's information to AI and machine learning." The announcement was a strategic shift in vision. That same month, Microsoft announced its intentions to be "AI-first" and its shift away from both "mobile-first" and "cloud-first."[6]

As already mentioned, many organizations, not just the big three or four, are now transitioning (or attempting to transition) to becoming AI-first as well.[7] Even small and mid-sized businesses no longer can ignore AI. AI-driven software will be used for better decision making, machine learning tools will help to predict outcomes, and the future will witness machines outperforming humans on several tasks more cost-effectively.

But what does AI-first really mean? Being AI-first is not simply a matter of embracing the power of analytics (or decision making) to enhance collaboration between humans and machines; it's about reinventing the future organization based on AI and preventing AI from being used as a tool to optimize the organization. Put another way, it's not just about doing the *same* activities better, cheaper, or faster; it's about doing *new* activities to create more value.

The current global digital economy—referred to sometimes as an "Internet economy"—demands more alignment, agility, and intelligence on the part of the organization than at any other moment in history. It requires embedding AI in all aspects of how the organization functions, such that unleashing a company's full potential effectively becomes part of the organization's DNA. In earlier times and less turbulent environments, it may have been possible to make a CEO and the top management team responsible for understanding the full potential of an organization. Today, however, the essentials of an organization must act in concert and be in sync on behalf of the entire enterprise.

Barriers to Scaling and Deploying AI—and the Key to Knocking Down Obstacles

In earlier chapters, we explored the use of AI to measure organizational health. Here we examine new research that says 84 percent of business executives believe they need to use AI to achieve their growth objectives, but 76 percent of executives say they are struggling with *how* to scale AI across their business.[8]

Similarly, another study shows what different organizations consider significant barriers to AI adoption, nearly half of which are organizational health–related. (See figure "Barriers to AI Adoption.") That study, published in MIT's *Sloan Management Review*, segments the respondents into four specific maturity segments: Pioneers (organizations that understand and have adopted AI), Investigators (organizations that understand AI but are not deploying it beyond the pilot stage), Experimenters (organizations that are experimenting with AI without a deep understanding of the technology), and Passives (organizations that don't understand and are not adopting AI).[9]

The Four Investments

How, then, can companies break down barriers and successfully scale value from AI? Based on the implications of the MIT study, I believe

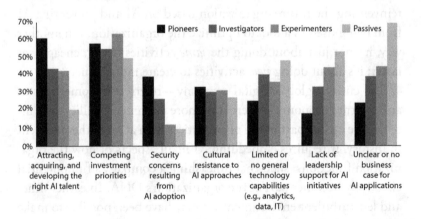

Barriers to AI Adoption

Source: Michael Chui and Bryce Hall, "How High-Performing Companies Develop and Scale AI," *Harvard Business Review*, March 19, 2020, https://hbr.org/2020/03 /how-high-performing-companies-develop-and-scale-ai. Used with permission.

it all comes down to a laser-like focus on four particular essentials for organizational health. Specifically, companies that successfully adopt AI and other digital advances excel across four dimensions—what I think of as the four investments.

- **Investments in strategy and decision making.** A McKinsey study showed that while most survey respondents said their companies had gained value from AI, some attained greater scale, revenue increases, and cost savings than the rest. The research reveals that this is not luck; how companies formulate their business strategy, the capabilities they implement, and the change management employed to tackle AI adoption in the workplace can collectively impact their potential for transformation. Those companies finding more success in scaling AI efforts are more likely than others to apply a core set of practices, including aligning AI and business strategies. Five of the six practices are org-health related. Companies that are more prone to use AI effectively can drive adoption and business value. In another study, 36 percent of respondents from high-performing companies, and only 8 percent of all others, say their front-line employees use AI insights in real time to enable daily decision making.[10]
- **Investments in organizational and work design.** McKinsey found that nearly 90 percent of the companies engaged in successful scaling practices had spent more than half of their analytics budgets on activities that drove adoption, such as workflow redesign, communication, and training. Only 23 percent of the remaining companies had committed similar resources.[11] The companies that were doing best in terms of successfully achieving widespread adoption of AI were spending as much of their money or budget on change and adoption—workflow redesign, communication, training—as they were on the technology itself.[12]
- **Investments in talent.** McKinsey found that companies successfully adopting AI across the organization are

investing as much in people and processes as in technology. In McKinsey's recent survey of 1,000 companies, they found that only 8 percent of firms surveyed engaged in such practices that allowed for widespread adoption of AI.[13] Countless studies echo these findings; joint research between *MIT Sloan Management Review* and Deloitte Digital published in the book *The Technology Fallacy: How People Are the Real Key to Digital Transformation* presents compelling evidence that digital maturity is more about people and organizational change than it is about the specific technologies being used.[14]

- **Investments in risk mitigation and learning.** The way that companies approach how they mitigate risk (i.e., quality-assurance audits or compliance training) largely determines accountability. Similarly, the way organizational learning takes place (through use of knowledge and collaboration platforms) often defines the company culture. When it comes to using AI technology, there is a great risk indeed—namely because AI is often underpinned by large sets of data (things such as search-engine habits or the number of hours logged on video calls), and misuse of such information is illegal. Therefore, no company should risk its future by overstepping on the kinds of data it collects and uses without providing full transparency to its employees about that data usage. Maximum fines under the EU General Data Protection Regulation (GDPR) are now as high as €20 million, or 4 percent of an entity's global turnover. The cost of potential liabilities for breach/misuse can exceed the purchase price on a deal, and if issues are identified, the value of an acquisition will be reduced, as GDPR fixes are expensive to implement. Therefore, deal teams must carefully scrutinize whether AI businesses are compliant or risk assuming significant liabilities. And CEOs and boards must likewise build governance and oversight structures to ensure the responsible use of AI.

A joint MIT and BCG study found that few companies have developed full-scale AI capabilities that are systemic and company-wide. But those that have done so have clear patterns. The study revealed that unleashing the true power of AI requires scaling it across the entire business. Yet just when trying to scale, many companies hit a paradox: it's easy to launch pilots, but hard to scale, because AI systems change constantly as they ingest data and learn from it. Seemingly isolated use cases interact and become entangled. To overcome the challenges and pain points that come with scaling, my observations and the research suggest that organizations must transform their structure, people management practices, and product/technology platform (i.e., machine architecture).[15] They must also transform how the organization learns, making investments in capability building initiatives and programs, helping employees learn how to work with smart machines and develop new skills for the digital era. With 99 percent of organizations saying they wanted to embark on transformation in 2020, and almost all reporting significant skills gaps, the C-suite regards reskilling as the top talent investment capable of driving business success. Workforce capability and lack of skills for competing in the future are seen as primary reasons why transformations—in particular digital transformations—fail.[16]

Now that we've looked at *what* dimensions of org health are important to invest in, let's take a deeper dive into exactly *how* each dimension could be shaped to unleash the potential of AI.

How to Use AI to Invest in Organizational Health

As I've pointed out before, one thing that sets AI-first companies apart is that they are uniquely human (see the table "The AI-First Enterprise Is Inherently Human"). Likewise, these businesses take human-centered approaches to the four investment factors we've just discussed—strategy, organizational and work design, talent, and a culture of ethics, risk mitigation, and learning. Let's look at each of these in turn.

The AI-First Enterprise Is Inherently Human

Traditional, Industrial Era–Inspired Enterprises	AI-First Enterprises
Workers perform most of the work.	AI takes away the "dull, dangerous, and dirty" aspects of work from people, leaving them to focus on their uniquely human capabilities, such as judgment and empathy.
Jobs are composed of narrowly defined, prescribed tasks, with little time or support for human empowerment.	AI enhances and augments people's human capabilities by allowing for more space and time in the day for enabling greater self-reflection, learning, social connections, autonomy, and more.
Work and organizations are stable.	AI enables dynamic problem identification, resolution, and teaming, allowing for more fluid, human-centric work.

Investments in Strategy and Decision Making

Consider why AI. First things first: before company leaders make an investment in AI, they should be able to answer, "Why AI?" To what end, exactly? Is it to reduce cost, improve operational and organizational efficiency, expand and enter into new markets, create greater agility and responsiveness in meeting evolving stakeholder needs? Or is it to create a new customer experience or business model? Or all of these? Whatever the intent, there are countless ways to use AI. How do organizations decide what to focus on?

To scale successfully, start by defining what value means to your business. Then assess and prioritize the various applications of AI against those strategic objectives. Companies that benefit most from AI are two-and-a-half times more likely than others to align their AI strategy with their company's broader strategy. They are also nearly four times more likely than others to have a clear enterprise-level roadmap of use cases across business domains.[17] Take Peloton, the exercise equipment and media company. Peloton uses scores of digital technologies such as analytics and AI to fundamentally shift not only the products the company offers but also the ways Peloton operates.

Use AI to model and uncover multiple strategic futures. We are facing a future in which smart machines will help us model and design new strategies. In their *Harvard Business Review* article "Designing the Machines That Will Design Strategy," authors Martin Reeves and Daichi Ueda argue the merits of what they call an "integrated strategy machine, a collection of resources, both technological and human, that act in concert to develop and execute business strategies." As they explain it:

> [The integrated strategy machine] comprises a range of conceptual and analytical operations, including problem definition, signal processing, pattern recognition, abstraction and conceptualization, analysis, and prediction. One of its critical functions is reframing, which is repeatedly redefining the problem to enable deeper insights. Within this machine, people and technology must each play their particular roles in an integrated fashion.

Already, AI is widely used to model the decision making of governments and corporations.[18] Amazon, for example, represents the state of the art in deploying an integrated strategy machine. It has at least 21 data science systems, including several supply chain optimization systems, forecasting systems for both inventory and sales, a profit optimization system, and a recommendation engine. These systems are closely linked with one another and with human strategists to act as a well-oiled machine. For example, if the sales forecasting system detects that the popularity of an item is increasing, it triggers a series of events across the system:

- The inventory forecast is updated, causing the supply chain system to optimize inventory across its warehouses.
- The recommendation engine pushes the item more, causing sales forecasts to increase.

- The profit optimization system adjusts pricing, again updating the sales forecast.

Additional interactions occur downstream. While many of these operations happen automatically, human beings play a vital role in designing experiments and reviewing data to continue learning and evolving the machine's design.[19]

Investments in Organizational and Work Design

Design an organizational structure for AI. Creating robust human and machine partnerships starts with optimizing organizational structures for humans and machines. Those that have developed full-scale AI have clear patterns, one of which is their organizational structure. In an environment where humans and machines work together, companies' organizational structures must be optimized for both. What does that look like in practice? Expertise should be centralized and harnessed at headquarters for AI technologies, data governance, platform decisions, and cybersecurity. They may also do things like setting standards and practices for AI, recruiting, and training. They must also define what it is to be a data scientist in the hub and the business units. The cross-functional teams and their access to business data pools needed to develop AI use cases should be centralized in the business units. Managed in a decentralized way—at the shop floor, marketplace, and field level—should be any actions supported by AI.[20]

To avoid organizations becoming more and more siloed and potential breakdowns in communication that only widen the division between machine learning experts and the rest of the company, companies should be more deliberate about their organizational and work design practices. Companies with the most success in scaling AI are implementing cross-functional teams where people from the business, people from analytics, IT, and operations all work side by side to achieve particular outcomes. One study found that organizations that scale up AI are twice as likely to set up interdisciplinary teams within the business units. Such teams bring diverse perspectives together and solicit input from front-line staff as they build, deploy, and monitor new AI capabilities.[21]

But companies should have a centralized capability as well; research shows that companies that successfully adopt AI are three times as likely as their peers to have a centralized capability.[22] Indeed, Lucas Persona, the chief digital evangelist of the Brazilian company CI&T, believes the most significant business innovations belong to companies that enable data science teams to work side by side with other employees—meaning data science teams should not be treated like wizards operating behind the scenes.

One Asian Pacific retailer benefited from its AI investments in work design by optimizing storage space and inventory placement. An interdisciplinary execution team helped break down walls between merchandisers who determined how items would be displayed in stores and buyers who chose the range of products. Previously, each group had worked independently, with the buyers altering the AI recommendations as they saw fit. That led to a mismatch between the inventory purchased and the space available. By inviting both groups to collaborate on the further development of the AI tool, the team created a more effective model that provided a range of weighted options to the buyers, who could then choose the best ones with input from the merchandisers. At the end of the process, gross margins on each product category that had applied the tool increased by 4 percent to 7 percent.[23]

Infuse AI into every job and every team. AI has joined the workforce as our new digital teammate. AI-first organizations know that to harness the potential of AI, they will infuse it into the very fabric of work to help people do their jobs in new ways, complementing one another's strengths and balancing any weaknesses. But it's not just about enhancing one's job or performance; some of the most potent benefits of AI can be achieved by infusing AI into teams, both as a teammate that provides input into decision making and as an enhancer of team effectiveness. For example, scheduling and meeting bots or digital assistants can transcribe meeting notes to improve team collaboration and productivity. As more teams work together, they will come to learn and understand the limitations placed on machine learning. For this reason, different businesses across an organization must inform the data science team about the kinds of challenges they encounter when retrieving data or implementing a machine learning model.[24] In short, the entire organization should be encouraged to become AI-literate. Every employee and every team can create greater value through human-machine collaboration and think about ways to tackle the company's biggest problems.

Work *with* employees to infuse AI into organizational design— don't just throw AI *at* them. Similarly, reinvent and reimagine work based on the new possibilities that AI creates, including greater agility, workforce empowerment, and the ability to create greater meaning at work. Organizations that effectively scale AI are changing how they make decisions. There is much less top-down decision making, and instead, there is much more empowerment of front-line teams to make decisions using judgment and algorithms to help improve the way they make decisions.[25] Said another way, empower employees to cocreate and experiment with how and where work gets done. Once an organization has identified the process or workflow where people and AI can work symbiotically, leaders should ensure that all stakeholders work and experiment together from the start. This may mean that teams employ designers and data experts to collaborate as early as possible while also engaging in routines to assess and measure not just productivity but the quality of the teaming experience. Across a different set of team types, such as top management, product management, or engineering teams, for example, companies like Asana, Lattice, and Unu Motors apply an AI time management platform, Clockwise, to optimize the timing of their meetings.[26]

Investments in Talent

The type of talent needed in AI-first organizations. Beyond needing AI and analytics talent, organizations will need to invest in creating new roles to empower and monitor how AI augments human capabilities. As Paul Daugherty and H. James Wilson point out in their book *Human + Machine: Reimagining Work in the Age of AI*, organizations will need *trainers* to teach AI systems how to perform by monitoring and correcting their behavior, *explainers* who explain the inner workings of complex algorithms to nontechnical professionals, and *sustainers*, who ensure that AI systems are operating as intended and that unintended consequences are addressed with the right level of attention urgency.[27] Accordingly, in many companies, new titles are emerging, such as AI ethicist, chief AI officer, AI business analyst, chief data scientist, AI quality assurance manager, and more.

Beyond specific roles, AI-first organizations will need to invest in helping all employees learn how to work effectively with intelligent machines and become data- and AI-literate. But perhaps most importantly, as AI frees workers to focus on what humans do best, our uniquely human capabilities—such as sense-making, creativity, emotional intelligence, adaptability, teaming, and more—will be at a premium. Countless studies show that such human skills will be those that are most needed in AI-first organizations. Few organizations know how to carefully cultivate them—measuring, developing, hiring, and rewarding such capabilities. Yet it is these very human capabilities that will endure and help workers continuously learn and adapt in a world in which the half-life of skills is continuously shrinking—especially in AI-first organizations. (See sidebar "How Anthem Transformed into an AI-First Enterprise.")

New talent practices needed in AI-first organizations. AI-first organizations are characterized by networks of teams, fluid change, an experiment and learn mindset, cross-disciplinary project work, greater autonomy and empowerment, and a focus on human capabilities. Accordingly, such organizations have reinvented their talent practices—discarding standard practices rooted in the industrial era and creating new ones. Instead of hiring on education and experience, companies like Compose, a cloud-storage firm, and One Month, a company that offers coding classes, are hiring based on potential, human capabilities, skills, fit with teams and culture, and accomplishments. Instead of measuring and rewarding people based on individual performance as perceived by a supervisor in an annual cadence, they are measuring and rewarding people far more frequently based on various people's input and on factors such as collaboration,

How Anthem Transformed into an AI-First Enterprise

AI-first organizations make timely, effective, and sustained changes when and where such changes will result in a performance advantage. Consider how Anthem's Rajeev Ronanki, SVP and chief digital officer, led the company's transformation from a traditional health insurance provider to a digital, AI-first enterprise.[28] Under Ronanki's direction, Anthem benefited from a strategic direction anchored in anticipating the future, small wins, engaged leadership, and mobilized talent.

- **Anticipate the future.** Ronanki started with an overarching plan in the form of a mission statement, which laid the groundwork for the structure that would support Anthem's transformation. Ronanki's compelling new vision of healthcare featured the use of advances in digital technologies with an AI-first mindset. As a first step, Anthem set up a platform-based AI engine that enabled the company to evolve from gathering data to mining actionable insights. That meant automating and speeding up processes and working toward continuous improvement.

- **Small wins.** Ronanki studied how AI could impact business outcomes and then connect related, fit-for-purpose use cases to achieve small wins. By approaching AI and machine learning with a process-level view, Anthem has been able to deploy next-generation technology in a way that significantly improves its customers' experiences.

- **Engaged leadership.** To realize AI's full potential requires enterprise-wide support, which means getting stakeholders involved in conceptualizing positive business outcomes. To kick off the digital transformation at Anthem, business partners were asked how the company could use AI to rethink, reimagine, and reimplement its core business processes. Based on that input, the company focused on automating data processing where AI could best impact the business: serving customers more efficiently. Anthem built a proof of concept focused on the applications that provided the most value—and those are where the company targeted its use of agile methods, pushing the process into production.

- **Mobilized talent.** To execute on a company-wide vision for AI, Ronanki knew he had to be rigorous in broadening Anthem's talent base. Anthem therefore created a structured AI training program—Anthem AI—to attract skilled technologists and develop existing internal talent. The unit's mandate is to retain talent by building a culture that promotes innovation of AI solutions.

potential, and skills needed for the future. They are adopting more agile work designs, using internal talent markets to match people to short-term projects and roles—rather than jobs—on an ongoing basis. And they are developing new ways to help employees continuously learn, designing learning into work itself rather than porting employees out of work for training.

Of course, AI itself can help organizations reinvent talent practices better suited for the AI era. Seventy-three percent of U.S. CEOs and chief human resources officers (CHROs) plan to improve talent management in the next three years.[29] AI will provide the insights needed for CHROs to retain and grow their best talent, according to Jared Lucas, chief people officer at MobileIron. He explains, "I predict that AI will drive better internal mobility and internal candidate identification as companies are better able to mine their internal talent to fill critical roles," and "I predict that AI will become a requirement for companies in the screening of candidates due to the pervasive need to find higher-quality candidates at a faster pace."[30]

Adopting AI also means helping people learn how to effectively "friend a machine," and arm them all with AI coaches to unlock their potential. Consider one telecom provider that was launching a new AI-driven customer-retention program in its call center. The company invested simultaneously in AI model development and in helping the center's employees transition to the new approach. Instead of just reacting to calls canceling service, they would proactively reach out to customers at risk of defection, giving them AI-generated recommendations on new offers they'd be likely to accept. The employees got training and on-the-job coaching in the sales skills needed to close the business. Coaches and managers listened in on their calls, gave them individualized feedback, and continually updated the training materials and call scripts. Thanks to those coordinated efforts, the new program reduced customer attrition by 10 percent.[31]

Investments in Risk Mitigation and Learning

Compliance is table stakes. The standards and rules of conduct that companies adopt to promote ethical behavior when it comes to use of AI are just a start. Beyond such basic compliance, AI-first organizations place AI ethics and responsibility at the forefront, making it everyone's job, as well as creating new roles to coordinate it across the workforce. Companies committed to using AI to scale are more likely than others to have a clear data strategy for AI, protections around data privacy, and well-defined governance processes for key data-related decisions. Oilfield services company Schlumberger, for example, has clear data privacy rules in its use of AI algorithms and advanced analytics to improve operations and work processes, including video analysis of people working. The company anonymizes and aggregates video data for general trend analysis and gives individuals the choice to opt in to privately see their own productivity data so that they can improve their performance.[32] Successful companies also have a clear data ownership structure, with business units owning business-relevant data and accountability for the quality of the data they generate.[33] From a governance perspective (think "G" in ESG), companies should put risk frameworks and contingency plans in place in the event of a problem. Companies should set up clear decision rights to establish who is accountable for the decisions made by AI systems, and define the management approach to help escalate problems when necessary.

In short, the governance of responsible AI depends on the entire C-suite and board. Explains Alex Badenoch, group executive for transformation and people at Telstra, "Technology is changing so fast and can have so many unintended consequences that we need to take the time to educate the C-suite and the board on the issues, possibilities, and risks."[34] Many organizations have created ethics review boards that not only harness the coalition's diverse insights but also collaborate with external experts, ethicists, and other specialists to proactively address any of AI's unintended consequences.

Don't just "learn AI"; learn *with* it. As mentioned earlier, successfully scaling AI also means adopting a learning culture and shifting the organizational mindset. Organizations that effectively scale AI have evolved mindsets. They move from being risk-averse and only acting when they have the perfect answer to being much more agile, willing to experiment, fail and learn fast, and get programs and products out quickly.[35] AI-first organizations don't just rely on the algorithm to make decisions; they continue to value human judgment, using AI as an input into decision making and the ability to learn rapidly. To speed adoption, leaders often align AI initiatives with the very cultural values that may seem at first like obstacles. For example, at one financial institution with a strong emphasis on relationship banking, leaders highlighted AI's ability to enhance ties with customers. The bank created a booklet for relationship managers that showed how combining their expertise and skills with AI's tailored product recommendations could improve customers' experiences and increase revenue and profit. The AI adoption program also included an employee contest for sales conversions driven by using the new tool. The CEO's monthly newsletter to employees was used to spotlight the winners' achievements.[36]

Leadership, EID, and well-being also have a role to play when it comes to scaling AI. Studies show that personal traits such as curiosity, extraversion, and emotional stability are twice as important as IQ in predicting how effectively a leader will perform. Research consistently suggests that companies need to rethink what successful leadership means in a digital age where the adoption of AI will become more prominent in how companies operate. Qualities like decisiveness, authority, expertise in one's domain, and focus on tasks are becoming less important. Meanwhile, traits such as humility, adaptability, vision, and engagement will increasingly define agile leadership.[37]

When it comes to diversity and EID issues, again, AI can play an important role. In fact, research shows that people in organizations can even begin to think of AI programs and devices as additional "diverse" members of teams.[38] In organizational psychology, improved outcomes or what Scott Page calls a "diversity bonus" result from forming teams composed of different kinds of thinkers, meaning that heterogeneous teams outperform homogeneous ones at solving problems, making predictions, and developing solutions. Other research shows that organizations with above-average diversity produced a greater proportion of revenue from innovation (45 percent of total) than those with below-average diversity (26 percent), which translated into stronger overall financial performance.[39] With AI bringing its own style of "thinking" to a team, the mix of human and machine intelligence can yield diversity bonuses that exceed those produced by teams composed of only humans, however diverse.[40]

So, while big data and machine learning are providing exciting opportunities for businesses and their workforces, the risk of failure increases if companies and the leaders who head them do not handle the potential bias that surrounds them. In other words, diversity and all its forms are the best way to ensure companies get the best business value out of AI.

Meanwhile, everyone, everywhere, is writing about the value of human and machine collaboration. But a lack of attention has been given to how to develop productive, satisfying, healthy relationships with our new digital coworkers. This is where a key condition of the organization's health—employee well-being—comes into play. In a world of human and machine collaboration, we must rethink well-being to account for the new dynamics of work in the digital era. Workers around the world are working more hours, companies have invested more heavily in tech, GDP is going up, but productivity is almost flat. The problem is that digital technologies are not yet optimized for humans or the ability to get work done. Leaders will have to find ways to engage and retain their best talent, act responsibly to avoid digital overload that can harm employee well-being, and maximize the business potential of our tech investments. One way to begin is by crafting an AI-first strategy that takes an integrated approach in which every part of an operating model, every individual within it, is inspired and encouraged to foster the health of the organization through the adoption of digital advances.

Steering the AI-first enterprise is hard work. As this chapter highlights, today's companies operate more like platforms and ecosystems than the brick-and-mortar institutions of old. We can think of them as part human and part machine. The same is true of the health of the organization. As CEOs from rapidly expanding fast-growth companies repeatedly show the markets, today's AI-first enterprise needs to reshape the organizational essentials in new ways and be agile to unleash organizational health with artificial intelligence. In other words, AI redefines what constitutes organizational health and simultaneously changes how organizational health can be achieved. These are highly challenging tasks. But accomplishing them also means that AI has enabled a company like Spanish bank BBVA to transform itself from a traditional storefront bank into one of the most successful financial services organizations of the digital era.[41]

As companies rethink their competitive strategy and organizational edge toward becoming AI-first, business leaders are finding that they have to be adept at overseeing and managing tensions: between creating space for experimentation and habitual routines, between automation and physical work, between analytics and judgment, between users (or customers) and shareholders, between a challenger mindset and a fixed one, and between a gig-like, remote workforce and a physical one. And as the paradigm for an organization's effectiveness shifts to an AI-first model, managing the multiple tensions that result will depend heavily on the state of the company's health.

Companies such as Amazon, Facebook, and Google have proven that they can scale new businesses while operating with speed. But for non-digital-born organizations to shift from analog, they must harness the power of AI to unleash organizational health. That will allow them to adapt during times of intense change, volatility, and industry disruption amid the aftershock of a global pandemic.

Ultimately, to unleash organizational health with advances in AI, leaders should focus on investing in all four dimensions of health discussed in this chapter—strategy, organizational and work design, talent, and culture—while also noting their implications on leadership, EID, and employee well-being. Effective AI-first organizational leaders adapt and help the entire company be agile; ultimately, they know how to unleash their company's full potential, which hinges on its health.

The chapter that follows begins part 3 of this book: a focus on the priorities—in digital and in key elements of the organization—leaders need to cultivate for investment and growth.

Checklist for Agenda Setting

- Use AI to not only optimize what was done in the past but to reinvent the organization to become more human-centric and create entirely new sources of value for the enterprise, teams, and individuals.
- Commit to spending as much of the AI budget on change and adoption as on the technologies themselves.
- Reshape organizational essentials to be fit for purpose in AI-first organizations while simultaneously using AI to unleash organizational health and redefining how it can be achieved.
- Invest in reshaping strategy and decision making—including aligning AI with business strategy, empowering front-line employees to use AI insights in daily decision making, and using AI to model and uncover multiple strategic futures.
- Invest in responsible AI, not just compliance, and hold the entire C-suite and board accountable for responsible AI governance.

- Create both a centralized team of deep expertise in AI and cross-disciplinary teams in the business units to develop AI use cases to achieve particular outcomes.
- Infuse AI into every job and every team, empowering employees to cocreate and experiment with how and where work gets done, and helping employees not just "learn AI," but "learn *with* AI."
- Invest in talent—not just AI and analytics talent and new roles to empower and monitor how AI augments human capabilities, but also in workforce capability and skill-building for everyone.
- Redefine talent practices for the new world of work characterized by networks of teams, fluid change, an experiment and learn mindset, cross-disciplinary project work, greater autonomy and empowerment, and a focus on human capabilities.
- Redefine the scope of well-being and EID to include AI—helping employees develop productive, satisfying, healthy relationships with their new digital coworkers, and using AI to add diverse perspectives and reduce bias.

PART III

LEAD A BETTER ORGANIZATION

Top Priorities for Leaders Seeking

Investment Optimization

10 ■ Investors and Boards

Set Priorities for Companies Backed by Private Equity and Venture Capital

> Boards and investors ultimately share the same goal: to provide oversight and guidance to help an organization and its stakeholders thrive and grow. No longer are boards just focused on regulatory compliance, and no longer are investors relegated to being mere passive providers of capital. Today, the real focus of both is elevating the organization's health as a key lever for optimal performance.

Throughout part 1 and part 2 of this book, we've examined why organizational matters matter and how leaders can fast-track growth with the right organizational setup: through the use of artificial intelligence to measure and improve the health of the business. As we turn the page to the final part of this book—part 3—we explore our third building block: the partnership required across key leadership categories in order to design and build better organizations and answer a vital question: What will it take to harness digital technologies and the conditions that foster an organization to reach its full potential?

Accordingly, we begin by examining in this chapter the perspectives of investors and boards. In the next chapter, we introduce the concept of the chief performance officer and provide a deeper exploration into the mandate of this new leadership role in cultivating the organization's health. Lastly, we conclude part 3 with a call to action for CEOs to become more fluent in the language of change.

Let's launch into this chapter's theme with a story that illustrates how boards and investors no longer see corporate governance as simply providing oversight on issues of conduct and compliance. Rather, today's governing bodies have become, by necessity, more deeply involved in monitoring and improving the health of organizations they oversee—and enlisting digital to enable that process.

The Case of InsurCo: How One Governing Board Spurred Fast Growth

When a chief strategy officer (CSO) took on her role at a fast-growth insurance technology company, which we will call InsurCo, it had recently received a $250M investment to help it scale for its next stage of growth. Although InsurCo considered itself strong in the areas of responsible growth, innovation, and its ability to capitalize on market disruption, the new CSO saw plenty of opportunities to make the business more competitive. One of her first actions, therefore, was to undertake a review of the company's organizational health, which she did with the full support of the board and CEO. The review involved interviews with executives as well as an examination of existing strategy documents and data on employee engagement and customers.

Among the review's key findings: InsurCo lacked a clear understanding of its purpose and its overall value to customers and employees. Upon further exploration, some underlying flaws in the company's leadership and communications/HR functions came to light, as did a distinct lack of diversity in the workforce. These problems reinforced a sense of the company as insular in its vision and lacking in close employee collaboration.

With those findings in mind, the new CSO met with the board, the company's investors, and InsurCo's founder/CEO to articulate the company's vision for the future. What, they wondered, did they want InsurCo to look like in five years? What did they need to do now or soon to achieve that five-year ambition? They all acknowledged that change would be a constant: the last five years had been wrought with a seismic shift across the insurance industry in product lines, customer expectations, and new entrants like InsurCo itself. Yet the group also knew the opportunity was ripe for growth, efficiency, and impact, and InsurCo was determined to embrace disruptive change in an AI-first context.

Ultimately, the board agreed on four principles. First, the founder/CEO and investors would need to engage in a profound shift in the way they thought about the business model. InsurCo would need to establish itself as a player in all segments of the insurance technology industry, expanding beyond the few segments in which it had been operating, and boost revenue by growing in new areas. It would need to sharpen price competitiveness in all segments and establish an ecosystem of partnerships to grow. Second, InsurCo would need to be seen by customers and shareholders as a leading insurance technology company in the digital era, setting the bar for innovation. Third, it would need to compete on speed and agility, responding to new market shifts faster than competitors. And finally, it would need to move from the startup phase to a new era of organizational growth and scale, led by the business but guided by the board.

All of those shifts, agreed the board and top management, would entail a laser-like focus on the health of the organization. They knew that to become a magnet for talent and innovation, InsurCo would need a more diverse workforce. Empowerment, simplification, and decentralization of decision making would be critical to achieving speed and agility. All this required InsurCo to significantly elevate its organizational health, placing it at the heart of its ability to execute the new strategy and scale for growth.

The board approved a new strategy, including key actions that company leaders would undertake. First, they clearly articulated a new vision for InsurCo, including its purpose and value to customers and employees, with a document outlining its five-year ambition for growth. Second, they raised the bar on the HR structure and systems required to drive the new vision, including changes in the culture, leadership, employee experience, HR operating model, and workforce diversity. And third, to ensure a strong focus on the new vision, the CSO engaged her peers in top management to identify current initiatives and behaviors that did *not* align with InsurCo's stated strategic direction. (For example, the "stop" list would include eliminating ways of working that reinforced silos and hand-offs rather than close collaboration.)

As a result of the new strategy, InsurCo's commercial and product lines grew nearly 32 percent year on year. Moreover, the board created a committee to provide direct oversight over people and organizational initiatives. This became key for helping InsurCo shift from operating like a startup to working as a growth-stage company that remained agile and nimble. Finally, the CSO, backed by the board, crafted a prospectus to convince a new round of investors to provide additional financing that would modernize InsurCo's platform and enable enterprise-wide digital innovation.

What's Changing in Corporate Governance and Why It Matters

The things that once were considered sustainable competitive advantages for companies—such as a breakthrough product or innovation, or a distinct customer or user experience—now provide little assurance for growth. As the case of InsurCo illustrates, no longer can companies compete effectively without a central focus on the organizational dimensions needed to sustain the long-term health of the organization and all its stakeholders. And digital and AI are the keys for measuring and improving those organizational dimensions. Successful operating models are increasingly designed and built on AI and digital assets to absorb the necessary tasks to scale and operate quickly.

That is why the way boards govern is changing across industries in both public and private, sponsor-owned markets. As the AI era dawns and advances in digital technologies are redefining everything, governing boards today are focused on approving capital to fund digital transformations. Yet it's important that they do so while not overlooking the organizational requirements necessary for scaling, things such as a clear operating model and structure and recruiting engine to source and onboard the best talent quickly.

Likewise, both boards and investors need to recognize that ESG criteria and compliance will be critical to their organizations' scaling and growth plans. In other words, they must consider: How does the organization affect and interact with the environment, society, and government bodies at the local, state, and federal levels? As companies grapple with ongoing disruption and the need to create value for all stakeholders, businesses must become more transparent in all ESG areas.

Just as significant, in the next three to five years, new regulations will redefine the role of startup and private-equity-backed company boards and investors. The U.S. Securities and Exchange Commission (SEC) will expect a new level of disclosure of material organizational health matters of companies, not unlike the level of disclosure it has long required regarding financial and legal matters. This will take many forms, including reporting on metrics related to engagement, succession, executive compensation and incentives, actions to protect human rights, and the composition, skills and capabilities, health and safety, and productivity of the workforce. And yet, today most boards don't report on such metrics; even Fortune 100 companies don't report much beyond diversity and compensation.[1]

All of which is to say that the demands on corporate governance are transforming, and board members will need to develop much greater comfort with disruptive change and agility—and increase their ability to monitor and influence strategies around improving the organization's health.

The Crucial Roles of Governance and Oversight

Hypergrowth and scaling have a direct effect on all aspects of executive leadership, and corporate governance and investor oversight are no exceptions. At such times of change and growth, good governance, investor oversight, and a focused board can provide key value—by helping to shape the ethics or culture of the organization and offering insights gained from the tried-and-true experiences of other companies. Conversely, the absence of good governance can also destroy an organization's value (see sidebar "Bad Governance Can Lead to Bad Health").

Bad Governance Can Lead to Bad Health

It's improbable that a company can maneuver around the ebbs and flows of the private markets—much less capitalize on them—if its board and investors are ill-prepared or worse. A few tales of the consequences of poor governance shed a stark light on the importance of good governance.

In a digital world, board directors must be capable of active oversight. In other words, AI is not a risk-free pursuit. From biased algorithms to breaches of data privacy to poor decisions made by AI without enough human input or oversight, the risks of AI are many. Consider the Facebook–Cambridge Analytica data scandal. Millions of Facebook users' data was collected and used without their consent by British consulting firm Cambridge Analytica, predominantly used for political advertising. Or consider how JPMorgan Chase ousted its special operations head after learning that his insider security group had started spying on the bank's top executives. Although the bank had sanctioned the original surveillance as a means to keep tabs on potentially dishonest traders, the data collection went rogue, collecting data on the bank's senior executives and sparking an internal scandal.

Promoting ethical and responsible uses of advanced data and analytics (and avoiding the dark side of AI) requires boards to direct management teams to leverage their organizational health to address the risks of AI and ensure AI creates value for everyone from an ESG and stakeholder capitalism perspective. What that means concretely is that directors are in a position to ensure security protocols are put in place to minimize algorithmic bias, technologies that unlawfully or unnecessarily create job destruction, and develop protections when it comes to data privacy, especially sensitive data.

With the rise of the "unicorns"—private tech companies valued at over $1 billion—the evolution of the private tech market has focused its governance attention on private venture–backed companies. There have been a series of governance failures and setbacks in some of the most prominent private venture–backed companies in this context. Hypergrowth health tech Theranos is one such company that fell from grace when founder Elizabeth Holmes engaged in illegal and destructive behavior that led to fraud and severe failures of culture and ethics. With the help of whistleblowers, John Carreyrou, a *Wall Street Journal* investigative reporter, broke the story.[2] Besides illegal acts, Carreyrou's sources describe a set of management and leadership practices that would hinder the health of any organization. For example, collaboration between teams and functions wasn't encouraged, which effectively walled off innovation. Meanwhile, board members remained uninformed about the technology the company produced. The U.S. Securities and Exchange Commission settled fraud charges against Holmes. In addition to being barred from serving as an officer or director of any public company for 10 years, she agreed to pay a penalty of half a million dollars and return millions of her shares. She also relinquished her voting control in the company. Holmes and the company's former chief operating officer, Ramesh "Sunny" Balwani, are under indictment for alleged wire fraud schemes that ultimately plummeted the company from its status as a tech unicorn ($9 billion valuations at the high) to one that was struggling for survival. Where were the investors? They were absent and, as one reporter notes, failed to ask for audited income statements, balance sheets, and cash-flow statements signed by a qualified public accounting firm.

In short, good governance (and ethical leadership) pays. This is true for both public and private companies, and especially for the governance of private equity–backed companies. Why? Because the reputation and governance of a corporation translate into higher price/earnings multiples and other improved metrics.[3] A report by the Organisation for Economic Co-operation and Development (OECD) confirms this, concluding that adherence to good corporate governance practices helps improve investors' confidence, may reduce the cost of capital, and may induce more stable investment sources of capital.[4] Boards boost their company's chances of successful outcomes when they consider the interplay between the essentials of an organization and its overall performance as they oversee strategies for growth and scale.

What makes the boards of private equity–backed companies different from publicly listed boards is that they are far less passive; they truly operate like a supra-executive management team. (See the sidebar "The PE-Backed Board Advantage.") A study conducted by McKinsey & Company documented the benefits reaped by PE firms being actively involved in guiding the business. The study found that "although three-quarters of private equity firms perform no better than the stock market over time, the top 25 percent outperform the stock market considerably and continually." The secret to their success? It wasn't purchasing assets for less than the market price, nor was it riding a rising market or sector. Instead, the real source of value was the outperformance of the company itself due to the active input of PE firms in the business, spending time to make the board more effective, and ensuring a more direct and engaged form of corporate governance compared to public companies and rivals in the PE industry itself.[5] For example, companies with boards active in oversight over organizational matters exhibited 10 percent better performance in innovation and revenue growth over the last three years than peers with low involvement in an organization's health. These same worse-performing companies saw a revenue decline of at least 5 percent during COVID-19.[6]

In other words, companies with strong organizational performance have better financial performance. Boards of directors and

The PE-Backed Board Advantage

Although boards are crucial to creating value in all companies, it is essential to note the significant differences between public and private boards compared to private equity–backed boards. This isn't the place for an exhaustive breakdown, but let's look at a few distinct differences. To begin with, PE-backed portfolio company boards look and behave differently than public-company boards. For example, there are fewer onerous compliance obligations for the board due to private ownership. PE boards are typically smaller, often a mix of external members (often former managers in similar companies) and professionals from the PE firm's fund for the investment in a portfolio company (always including and led by the fund manager, i.e., "deal partner or captain"). Unlike directors serving on public-company boards, directors of private equity portfolio companies face very high economic stakes.[7]

Let's explore further. The PE style of corporate governance relies heavily on a model in which owners' incentives and portfolio company management are tightly aligned. What does that mean, practically? First, PE ownership leads to greater operational efficiency, in part because of the short, intense "pressure cooker" holding period requiring active governance. Second, smaller and better incentivized PE-backed boards are more likely to make better decisions concerning strategic endeavors such as an M&A or the approval of a new product line. Third, PE-backed boards are more likely than management to make difficult decisions that improve operational performance, such as approving layoffs, spinning off underperforming divisions, and even replacing top executives.[8]

Significant incentives linked to aggressive targets are often used to stay true to the key performance indicators as defined by a value-creation plan "written in blood." Take PE partners,

(continued)

for example: to assert their claim to an investor premium, PE partners argue that their companies enjoy success not because of improved strategic positioning and increased operational efficiencies but because of superior governance. Private equity ownership, they maintain, improves governance, whereas public companies' weak governance and oversight undermine the company's value. Together, this may prompt boards and all other parties involved to work toward a favorable exit of a portfolio company. In a startup context, the portfolio company's board, typically established during the raising of a round of financing, operates as an active or managerial board—helping that company's founder/CEO and management team with the connections and expertise needed to launch its innovative product or service to the market.

We also know that with an early-stage company betting on the founders, their vision and product will become ever more critical, and strategic direction and purpose, leadership, and talent will have to become a key board focus. That's particularly true in venture capital–backed companies. Why? Because founders often won't have developed managerial muscle; early-stage startups, therefore, may select board directors to fill in experience gaps. Indeed, in an AI-first era, the issue of board expertise will become more important to portfolio management teams in their fight for top talent.

In a pre-exit stage (be it IPO, acquisition, or buyout), in which a newly incorporated company purchases the target company (or, sometimes, its assets), all the essentials of the organization matter. Even at this later stage, the board is an integral part of the company's governance. Its decisions on organizational matters amount to recommendations to the shareholders of the PE fund and some members of the portfolio management team.

PE-backed boards tend to be very hands-on with company operations. And they are often also very involved with the investors as they work together to steer the company toward growth. As PE-backed boards consider what organizational dimensions they may need to help management actively evolve toward—based on the company's stage of development, geographical footprint, shareholder mix, and other pressures related to the investment or holding period—directors also recognize that there can never be a one-size-fits-all model of governance. In other words, what works for a late-stage unicorn in Asia won't be the same as what's needed in a fast-growth ride-sharing startup in Dublin, Ireland.

investors know that having a "healthy" or "effective" organization is critical. What once may have taken up a small fraction of their time and energy is now a core focus of their agenda as they approve capital and initiatives to improve their organization's effectiveness. Boards today are likely to balance their attention between intangible matters (such as talent and culture) and tangible matters (such as operations and finances). In fact, intangible assets now comprise an estimated 52 percent of a company's value.[9] That, along with mounting pressure from industry leaders and governing bodies to disclose ESG metrics, is propelling boards to make organizational health a top priority for the long-term future.

Moreover, ESG performance can no longer be separated from financial performance, as board directors and investors know. By extension, organizational health, including ESG factors, must be considered in all board oversight and risk management decisions related to scaling, growth, and diversity. What once was a sideline affair is now increasingly mainstream and a vital part of the board's agenda. Yet most board directors—both in public and PE-backed companies—are only now starting to think about what this means for them, how to lead effectively to build better organizations, and how to work with each other, their investors, and the company's management team to address these essentials.

As a start, boards and investors need to ask:

- How should the health of the organization be assessed to understand where and how it can deliver new value to the company?
- How can that value be translated into practical and achievable objectives and key results and then simply and effectively communicated for all key stakeholders?
- What quantifiable metrics will increasingly matter most when it comes to determining the best way to execute oversight over organizational health?
- How can board directors seamlessly integrate ESG into their organizational health and compensation strategies?
- What are the best governance practices to juggle in balancing long-term health with short-term financial pressures, particularly in a condensed period of investment or ownership?
- How can the board check the pulse on what's going on so they can sense and respond to weak signals in the internal and external marketplace?

Note that when it comes to PE-owned companies, their governance often has a distinct built-in advantage—namely, that the "companies are the servants of only one master," as noted by one leading academic in the field.[10] In other words, the hands-on and active engagement model of the board with the management team insulates them from multiple shareholder demands: there is only one primary stakeholder to engage and that is the PE firm, where typically several of the firm's deal partners will hold board seats or might even serve as board chair. This helps reinforce the direct relationship with the PE sponsor and ensures speed to impact and immediate course correction when needed. Perhaps because of that advantage, many public companies today are going private with the help of PE companies who seek to buy, transform, and incorporate them into their portfolios.[11]

What do these developments and others portend for the role of the board and for investors in providing oversight over organizational health and what matters most? Let's begin with a look at the implications for boards before moving on to investors.

Boards: What Matters Most

Although traditionally boards have focused on overseeing compensation and succession, today there is no question that the board must operate as the "apex of the firm's decision control system"[12] by building and sustaining the controls essential for effective oversight of the organization's *human* capital—that is, the seven elements of organizational health that we've looked at in this book: a clear strategic direction; a performance-driven culture; agile leadership; top talent; nimble organizational design; a diverse workforce supported by equitable and inclusive practices; and employee well-being. These topics are shifting from being a time-boxed agenda item to a more robust set of discussion topics—all intended to drive strategic and investment decisions about the velocity and acceleration of innovation, scale, and the ability to grow and outperform peers.

Ideally, then, boards and investors who back founders, CEOs, and management teams work together to elevate and unleash the health of the organization and improve its odds of winning. Specifically, the real value-add of a PE-backed board will be characterized by the board's active engagement and ability to do several things:

- Review material organizational topics during due diligence to reduce risks or create value
- Invest in AI to guide business strategy and operations so that returns in line with the investment thesis are in ample supply
- Help CEOs establish a new kind of management discipline—one that works actively to monitor and engage ESG risk
- Oversee talent and culture, identifying opportunities to create value and reduce risk such as failing to align the best talent with the most tremendous value potential
- Oversee the responsible and ethical use of customer and workforce data and AI

The Board Talks Health and Organizes to Oversee It

Increasingly, boards place far greater emphasis on organizational health and use new metrics to discuss it. As it rises in importance, boards are also organizing new ways to oversee it.

Some public companies have already articulated board responsibilities for oversight of organizational health–related matters. Consider an August 2019 study by Willis Towers Watson that found that nearly 40 percent of S&P 500 companies have renamed the committee responsible for compensation to reflect its broadened scope better, to include matters not historically overseen at the board level, such as organizational culture, EID, engagement, talent management, and succession planning below the C-suite.[13] One multinational recently expanded its nominating/governance committee's charge to include additional oversight on human capital issues. In line with this expanded remit, the multinational's board renamed the "nominating, governance and management development committee." As part of its expanded focus, the committee proactively seeks out and expects regular updates at board meetings by the company's chief people officer on talent and organization issues, including metrics around succession planning and equity, inclusion, and diversity for the company's most critical roles.

Similarly, consumer goods company Newell Brands renamed and broadened the responsibilities of their compensation committees to reflect this expanded focus. The company's organizational development and compensation committee, whose board demonstrates the shift toward greater responsibility for business functions that are part of human capital management, optimizes organizational essentials, including diversity initiatives, talent management strategies, leadership succession, and culture. Other companies have moved to place oversight of organizational health within the nominating or governance committees—extending succession planning to include oversight of issues like employee engagement, development, and diversity and inclusion.

This evolution in organizational health oversight has led some companies to consider the role of chief human resources officer (CHRO) on par with the CFO. Progressive companies expect the

CEO, CFO, and CHRO (or what some leading practitioners call the golden triangle or G-3[14]) to work closely together, aligning strategy, financial capital, and human capital. This is consistent with a KPMG Board Leadership study, where some Russell 3000 Growth Index companies added directors with significant HR expertise. Of the 169 current or former CHROs serving on 198 boards, almost half were added in the last three years.[15] Another finding from Spencer Stuart reveals that of all surveyed board members, a full 24 percent said they brought human capital management expertise to the board.[16]

Similarly, today's boards are more likely to proactively engage the CHRO, interacting with him or her individually, and many (86 percent) engage the CHRO to provide actionable feedback at least quarterly. Moreover, the CHRO has an active and strategic voice that helps inform board oversight with transparent metrics beyond executive compensation. Despite these progressive shifts, I contend that in an AI-first world that now places humans front and center in an organization's growth strategy, board oversight of org health should be a full board responsibility, not just that of a committee. It is time to give organizational health a seat in the boardroom.

In a PE context, governance goes well beyond being just a fiduciary responsibility. It is the main job. And it is one that is deeply connected to the other side of the coin necessary for driving growth—the investor context—as we will see in the next section.

Investors: What Matters Most

To maximize the potential of organizational health to unlock growth and scale, boards that are backed by private equity can work with those investors to provide oversight and guidance. In fact, venture capital and private equity–backed companies have a distinct advantage that other firms do not. Because there is a well-defined holding period to achieve the internal rate of return or profitability of the investment in the company, the private equity–backed board and its investors must double down on how the organization thinks about essentials like talent or equity, inclusion, and diversity or issues related to ESG criteria. They must be able to translate digital advances into an advantage to create company value, including greater operational efficiency.

Although boards and investors ultimately share the same goal, there are a few differences in perspective that are unique to investors. For example, in the case of growth equity and leveraged buyout, there is always the possibility of an investment eventually going public. Hence, establishing healthy organizational and ESG practices early on will prove to be helpful pre–initial public offering or buyout. What makes the growth stage unique? Here's how Laela Sturdy, general partner for CapitalG, describes it: "Early-stage businesses work exhaustively to land on something that works. Mature businesses know what works and turn the dials to make it work better. The growth stage sits right in the middle."[17]

To find out more about how the focus on organizational health in the minds of general partners (GPs) is evolving, I interviewed several GPs and operating partners of leading companies. While operating partners go into the portfolio companies and make strategic and operational decisions, GPs are investment professionals who make investment decisions. They are responsible for ensuring the deal is profitable for all involved, including the limited partners (LPs) that invest for a short period and are not involved in the day-to-day maintenance of the fund or company.

What GPs and operating partners told me about their experience in organizational health–related themes was consistent with the trendlines in the market and academic studies. Most GPs would agree that if they picked one thing to get right, organizational health is it. It starts with the founders. "What startups do is very hard. So, the ones that survive to get growth capital and ultimately grow to become big companies must do a lot of things right, and organizational health is at the absolute top of the list," one general partner I talked to noted. For example, GPs and limited partners recognize that investments in companies are about investing in the people, starting with the founders. What does this mean, concretely?

First, founders/entrepreneurs are more likely to receive funding if they can demonstrate outstanding leadership, a clear vision, and the ability to communicate well. These are more than just admirable qualities; they are essential attributes to the company's performance and ability to raise money for future rounds of investment. Second, investors are more likely to back companies that have a solid and thriving culture. With the amount of organizational data that is accessible, investors tend to examine various aspects and metrics vital to corporate culture, especially when it can have an impact on elevating the employee experience and driving talent attraction, development, and retention. These organizational insights are more commonly used to inform discussions that affect how capital is deployed to build high-performing, inclusive teams and help the founders shape a compelling value proposition and culture.

Third, investors need to be ruthless in how they prioritize. Depending on the investor type (for example, angel investor, pension fund, or venture capitalist), investors must put capital up to focus on the right things for a potential portfolio company to work on. Regarding differences across investor types, research shows that family offices, growth equity funds, and leveraged buyout funds place a higher value on profitability than business angels and venture capital funds. Venture capital funds, in turn, pay more attention to companies' revenue growth and business models.[18] Building a great product and creating a differentiated sales and go-to-market strategy requires prioritization and an excellent organizational health strategy in a highly competitive environment.

Lastly, part of the added value of investors comes from improving governance and active monitoring. This often means replacing entrepreneurs or CEOs if they are not up to growing their companies and providing oversight of human capital strategy. Investors will want to back companies whose boards can provide the necessary direction and hold management accountable for delivering on the value-creation plan.

Priorities of Private Equity and Institutional Investors
Venture capital and private equity–backed companies are not immune to any of the forces hammering public companies—or every board for that matter. But as already mentioned, VC and PE-backed companies do have a distinct advantage over public companies: they

must by necessity begin with a laser focus on the organization's health. Along with a mandate to instill greater operational efficiency, they must be able to translate digital advances into creating company value across areas like talent, culture, EID, and ESG concerns. Let's explore in more depth how governance by investors enhances firm value.

First, VC and PE-backed companies have the power to find and place top talent in their portfolio companies (although VCs can't hire or fire in the same way that a PE firm can). And as we've explored throughout the book, acquiring and retaining top talent—especially diverse top talent—pays. Today and heading into the future, executive leadership—that is, who runs your company and who sits on your board—is a competitive advantage. But finding the right people takes work, especially when it comes to the board's composition. Investor leadership and portfolio management teams need to use the same vigor to recruit and place their talent at the top, most notably their board directors, the same way big college football teams recruit talent out of high schools to build teams. Among the advantages that PEs and VCs wield is their wealth of networks and connections from which they can draw to spot, recruit, and place diverse top talent. Through its ownership and practices, private equity can create a lasting impact because they are reshaping policies, top management, and the board. Even if a portfolio company is held by a PE firm for only three to five years, some of those changes, particularly when it comes to instilling diversity and equitable practices, can last beyond that period. As Kara Helander, inclusion and diversity chief at the Carlyle Group, shared with me recently, "Analysis of our U.S. portfolio companies' past three years of data of average earnings growth reveals that companies with diverse boards deliver growth five times faster, and that with each diverse board member, you get a 5 percent increase."

Second, compliance and other issues related to environment, social, and government concerns are here to stay. For starters, 34 percent of assets under management from 2016 to 2018 were ESG related, encompassing more than $30 trillion. Therefore, business leaders, investment managers, and boards will engage more and more in ESG integration—the systematic and explicit inclusion of ESG factors into financial analysis. Strong ESG governance and transparency will be essential to the investment process as boards need to ensure investors are aligned on social mission and values, especially as the legitimacy of the tech enterprise (i.e., "techlash") comes under immense scrutiny throughout society. Institutional investors will prefer to fund companies with compelling employee and corporate responsibility initiatives that allow employees to contribute positively to society and their own well-being, at the same time as they execute against their enterprise goals. According to Anna Grotberg, associate partner at EY-Parthenon, there is a real PE governance advantage relative to ESG. She suggests that "purpose, responsibility, and transparency have been on the private equity agenda for years, but the trend is accelerating during the COVID-19 pandemic."[19]

As more and more companies are being called upon to navigate climate risks, the question becomes: Will this compel asset managers and investors, and by default, boards, to provide oversight on those issues? The answer is yes. Or consider how the new regulatory guidelines that make climate-risk reporting in the U.K. mandatory by 2025 will potentially start a similar trend for reporting on human capital/organizational topics, thereby prompting companies to step up ESG disclosures.[20] Doing so will likely boost investor confidence as they review a company's management of organizational and ESG issues, especially when it comes to checking the health of the organization and ESG ratings of an acquisition target when evaluating a potential transaction.

Investors Talk Health and Organize to Oversee It

My observations and research confirmed the growing importance of investor confidence in organizational health. Indeed, investors are increasingly demanding greater transparency regarding organizational matters. The number of company proxies disclosing organizational health–related information, for example, continues to rise. Many companies, more and more, are now disclosing their talent and organization-related policies and initiatives in their securities law filings and other publications. This is evidenced by enhanced disclosures to shareholders and others about their policies and efforts. These disclosures are included in a company proxy statement as part of public disclosure on employees, as seen by big tech companies like Salesforce,[21] or as part of an expanded section on CEO pay ratio, as seen by CVS Health,[22] or in some cases as supplemental disclosures on company websites, as seen by Boston Scientific.[23]

Also, innovative analytic methods that harness the diverse insights of newly available organizational data are on the rise. Not only can this help organizations report information to investors, but also investors and boards must be careful to attend to the business opportunities (and the potential ethical risks) that organizational data, analytics, and AI reveal in identifying and transforming portfolio companies.

In recent years, major institutional investors such as BlackRock and State Street Global Advisors have prioritized organizational health and amended voting guidelines, calling companies to pay more attention to organizational health and disclose how they are incorporating it into governance practices. Some investor leaders are already speaking eloquently about the importance of organizational health, including ESG issues. Larry Fink is one of them. In January 2019, BlackRock's CEO sent his annual letter to CEOs, titled "Purpose & Profit," arguing that companies should focus on long-term profitability over short-term results and focus on stagnant wages, worker retirement, and the effect of technology on jobs.[24] Fink's January 2020 annual letter to CEOs and BlackRock's January 2020 client letter both focus on sustainability, especially concerning climate risk, emphasizing that "we believe that sustainability should be our new standard for investing."

Meanwhile, State Street's president and CEO, Cyrus Taraporevala, is on record in a letter sent to independent chairs and lead directors advising board members to oversee and articulate corporate culture as a critical directive. In particular, Taraporevala emphasized that corporate culture and corporate strategy should be aligned and, as a starting point, companies should improve reporting so that directors can discuss their role in influencing and monitoring corporate culture.

As I will discuss in the next chapter—which concerns the new role of chief performance officer—PE and VC investors' commitment to organizational health is reflected in how many are now creating new ways to incorporate org health into their own operations and structures. The trend is rooted in the rise of "operations" groups in PE firms that have emerged in the past decade. These are founded on the belief that financial engineering alone does not maximize return and that operational transformation across a fund's portfolio companies is essential to success. The deal teams, the thinking goes, can then focus on what they have long done best: buying and selling, with input from the operations teams. Moreover, the mandate for organizational health in PE firms typically falls under the charge of "operations"—sometimes also known as an asset management group, portfolio support group, resources group, or strategic portfolio services. Likewise, "operating partners" may also have titles such as "global head of portfolio transformation." Indeed, the operating partner role is relatively new; recent estimates show that the total number of full-time operating partners in PE is about 500. Not surprisingly, the number of operations professionals scales with the fund size.

Simple Principles to Get Governance Right

Organizational health is vital to the success of all companies, but it is essential for the success of hypergrowth companies pursuing risky investment strategies. It has become one of the critical concepts in founder and investor circles, and by extension, boardrooms. When investors and boards approach their value-creation efforts with an organizational health mentality, superior results ensue. Good governance is not just an approach to be applied in times of distress; it's a hallmark of vigilant boards in PE, which can preempt failure and recognize opportunity in times of significant change. As investors and directors alike think about aligning their board effectiveness to the times, a few first principles will point in the right direction. Let's look more closely at what principles they can adopt:

- **Focus on providing active oversight.** Boards and actively involved investors alike need to engage in dialogues that enable them to learn from experience. How? They can exploit organizational hacking methods that leverage AI to capture formal and informal insights prepared by management teams to prepare boards to make the experience of learning from real-time sentiment more accessible and agile. Boards and investors that understand their company's organizational health will have a better pulse on what the prognosis is and, from there, determine what is suitable for where the company needs to go.

- **Create and land clear governance practices.** Rather than anchor in a set of standard operating procedures, create a statement of purpose, a simple definition of roles, and a set of operating principles (simple rules) that will guide the board in shaping its domain of responsibility and in selecting its most crucial agenda topics and metrics that balance the interests of investors with the needs of portfolio management.
- **Create shared board, investor, and management accountability and build the strategy.** Directors should shape a governance and accountability framework to engage founders or portfolio CEOs and their management teams in clarifying and evolving the organization's truly game-changing investments. That is, they need to be able to school the portfolio's top management in the power of AI by helping them access platforms that deepen their ability to make better decisions.
- **Engage in a robust process of continuous board improvement.** The board should establish practices for self-examination to take advantage of otherwise hidden or untapped board member expertise and allocate and/or match each board director to key committees or opportunities. Doing this requires boards to set up a cadence of postmortems based on real, tangible board actions, formulating a small number of simple rules to define what topics belong on the board's agenda, and/or engaging a governance expert in board structure/process to lead a capability-building experiences workshop on

the state-of-the-art practices and technologies for
boards. Likewise, actively involved investors should tap
their networks for expertise to guide portfolio companies and engage in continuous self-reflection and improvement on how best to work with the board and
management team.

- **Get the right types of people.** Board composition should
look different than it traditionally has—meaning more
diverse and with a different set of perspectives and experiences. This kind of diversity is important for those from
PE firms working with a portfolio company. Equally
important is getting the right expertise. Research on PE
firms shows that deals generate the greatest value when the
lead partner's skills are directly relevant to the strategy of
the portfolio companies and related boards (one or two
investor-directors or deal partners) to which they are
assigned.[25] Venture capitalists spend 25 percent of their
time serving as directors and mentors.[26] In a leveraged
buyout situation, board directors often have a track record
of being hands-on and well versed in operational details
given their previous operating experience.

- **Look ahead to build an AI-ready board.** The investment
in digital technologies and AI now requires organizations
to consciously create a change muscle allowing organizations to scale and adjust fluently (i.e., anticipating and
adjusting to market demands at scale). Therefore, a
digitally savvy board leverages advances in digital
technologies—from the use of AI and analytics to the
Internet of Things—to act on insights that will not only
frame the right discussions and priorities with top management across a variety of business topics and social issues
for their organization and investors but will also enable
growth and the achievement of the investment thesis.

To operate at the peak levels of governance, accountability, and transparency that today's hypergrowth contexts demand, companies need

board directors to engage at two levels: oversight on the organization's effectiveness for both the short and long term, and investments in digital improvements to the way portfolio management teams run the business day to day. To achieve this, boards should proactively communicate organizational and ESG performance to investors and gain their confidence and trust by demonstrating effective oversight of organizational health. Whether it is to provide leadership over a culture of ethics and responsible AI initiatives; navigating the web of legislators, regulators, and business watchdogs; approving a company's strategic direction; signing off on an M&A transaction; or simply to complement the knowledge and perspective of the management team, an effective board can add real value to help companies scale and grow. Because boards in professionally sponsored buyout firms are more informed and hands-on and have more investment at risk than boards of public companies, they are more likely to spot problems and intervene before the problems become crises.[27] Therefore, better governance of portfolio companies helps PE firms enhance value creation, reduce risk, and build trust with investors.

Boards will need to self-assess and then devise an action plan against three factors: its clarity of purpose and structure, its commitments, and its ability to steer the company forward. In other words, first there needs to be clear agreement with management about what defines the board's highest value-adding contributions to the company. Second, individual directors must clearly articulate their commitments to each other and their preferred ways of working (including decision-making styles) to make the board as a whole most effective in their thinking and actions. And third, boards will need to call upon their collective intelligence to act as stewards for the company's assets and provide direction for the future.

Investor leaders realize that helping to sharpen the board's clarity of focus, cultivating its commitment, and shaping the composition is not just the responsible thing to do, it's essential for a real competitive edge—as well as for directing, guiding, and monitoring high-value yields. The very idea of "value" will give way to something more like "temporal value," which may involve periods of evolution punctuated by moments of challenge. These will be critical inflection points requiring investors to compose, place, and refresh boards at every stage of a company's critical moments of growth. This holds especially true for startups where each round of additional financing generally brings shifts in the company's governance structure (such as the size and composition of the board and the potential dilution of the investors' ownership percentage in the company), prompting VC investors to negotiate (or renegotiate) for designated board seats and specific exit rights.

Checklist for Agenda Setting

- Ensure active and ongoing governance and oversight of organizational health at both the board and investor levels, with transparent governance practices and a view toward continual improvement.
- Organize to incorporate organizational health into governance for boards.
- Expand the remit of the compensation and succession committee or nominating and governance committee to include oversight of workforce and org health issues (including the responsible use of workforce data and AI).
- Create chief performance officer roles in PE firms' portfolio operations groups and engage with outside experts to advise on org health issues.
- Make organizational-health metrics transparent to the investor community through disclosing or reporting on ESG and human capital metrics.
- Hold the CEO, CFO, and CHRO (the "G-3") accountable for working closely together to align strategy, financial capital, and human capital, and make org health a shared board, investor, and management responsibility.
- Build a diverse, digital-savvy board with the right expertise.

11 ■ Chief Performance Officers

Create a New Leadership Role to Oversee the Health
of an Organization

> We know that the elements of healthy organizations are para-
> mount to success for today's investment and portfolio leaders.
> But making step-change improvements in areas such as strategic
> direction, talent, diversity, organizational design, and the like can
> be a tall order. Having a trusted counselor in place to support a
> portfolio company's CEO and management team is vital. Enter the
> chief performance officer.

As seasoned executives like Sandy Ogg and academics like Dave
Ulrich point out, today's investors and portfolio companies will
need to focus more on a broader set of organizational dimensions
than they have in the past if they hope to optimize the value of
their investments.[1] And as we've learned throughout this book, research reveals that more and more portfolio companies are competing specifically on a more holistic business agenda: the health of
the organization.[2]

That is why today's private equity and institutional investors increasingly rely on a relatively new position in the executive ranks of their portfolio operations: the chief performance officer (CPO).[3] As the executive charged with ensuring the organization performs at its best, the CPO can also serve the portfolio company's CEO as a trusted advisor. Moreover, the best CPOs are experts in conducting organizational due diligence, and once they have assessed a company's health, they then can lead initiatives to boost value growth by improving on any areas where the company is found lacking.

The fact is that almost every dealmaker and CEO today could benefit from the help of a CPO or someone in a similar role—sometimes called head of talent or portfolio talent lead—given the expanding range of skills needed to deliver on an investment in an AI-first, increasingly volatile world. Having such an executive on the top-management team gives investment firms and their portfolio companies an edge over firms whose portfolio optimization groups haven't yet evolved to include such a role.

Consider the many challenges that make it even more difficult for value creators or operating partners to successfully execute the performance initiatives needed to grow and scale. They must deal with complex executive compensation structures, rigorously assess and align top talent for management teams, and shape a compelling yet cost-effective employee value proposition, including total rewards. They must create new organizational designs, shift mindsets and behaviors, or set up transformation offices for strategy execution. The challenges value creators or operating partners face are simply too many and too complex not to bring in a specialist to help.

In this chapter, we will examine the four different but related roles that CPOs simultaneously fulfill in their jobs assisting investors and portfolio companies. We will also explore what kinds of shifts the CPO role undergoes as a company grows and matures. To deepen and broaden this chapter, I gathered perspectives from people who hold CPO and CPO-related roles in several high-profile private equity firms (including buyout, growth equity, and venture capital firms). In a series of conversations with private equity and venture capital insiders, backed by research (including a review of LinkedIn profiles and articles in the business press by the operating partners at investment firms), I examined the complexities inherent in the role of the CPO and the significant challenges they face.

Defining the Job: Four Roles of the CPO

In PE and venture capital–backed companies, finding and hiring a CPO begins with the general partners creating a portfolio operations group. (See the sidebar "What Is a Portfolio Operations Group?") Whomever the GPs appoint as the portfolio talent lead or human capital partner effectively becomes the chief performance officer.

But the relatively recent rise of the CPO role in top-management teams raises a number of questions, such as: How deeply involved should CPOs be with strategies and implementation to do with employees and the organization of a portfolio company? Which performance metrics address both short- and long-term expectations?

The CPO's particular role and focus, of course, will vary based on the investment philosophy of the firm with which they are affiliated, or type of firm (i.e., venture capital, growth equity, or leveraged buyout). But in general, CPOs assist investors and portfolio companies by simultaneously fulfilling four different but related roles:

- Due diligence advisor—laying the groundwork for a better deal and decisions for investors
- Talent shaper—assessing, selecting, and coaching the right leader and top team to drive rapid returns
- CEO whisperer—providing strategic, independent counsel to senior executives in the portfolio in the first 100 days
- Transformation architect—defining and orchestrating talent and organizational change to increase company value

In their goal to assess and nurture the health of an organization, CPOs often play one or more of these four roles. The first two roles are focused on the two critical phases of the deal life cycle. The last two focus on portfolio company transformation in preparation for premium valuation for sale or exit. Essentially, CPOs act as partners

What Is a Portfolio Operations Group?

Portfolio operations groups or growth teams typically work with investment and portfolio company management teams to improve portfolio companies' strategic, financial, organizational, and operational performance. They are responsible for driving value creation and performance improvement initiatives across the portfolio. They accomplish this by working closely with both deal and portfolio management teams in the diligence, post-close planning, and value-creation planning and execution phases of the portfolio company's life cycle. They also develop the tools to do so while managing an internal and external network of operating partners (e.g., former chief experience officers and business operators) and functional experts (e.g., finance, procurement, sales and marketing, and organizational health) to meet portfolio companies' needs.

The private equity practice of the global executive search firm Lancor identified three general models for portfolio operations. The first and most highly evolved model is "centralized and core to the firm," with a sophisticated, dedicated operations team driven by creating portfolio transformation. These funds take majority or complete ownership and believe they can find new ways to get EBITDA and cut costs. These operating partners may have generalist expertise that includes organizational health. Or they may organize operations into subteams of functional experts, such as pricing, bankruptcy, process improvement, and, of course, organizational health or human capital management.

But even firms without the dedicated support of CPOs are finding a way to bring in the expertise needed to elevate the organizational health of their portfolio companies. In a second model, what Lancor calls the "virtual individual contributors—ops light" model, the PE firm will hire a few senior operations executives and then engage strategy consulting firms for the specific expertise needed for areas such as organizational health.

(continued)

> The third, most common model is to affiliate and enter into a quid pro quo agreement with outside advisors—typically retired executives who will often also sit on the boards of the companies in the PE firm's portfolio. Although these are generally former CEOs, one can envision a growing position for former talent executives to play such a role as well. What's important here is not so much how investors bring in expertise on organizational matters but that they are increasingly doing so at a rapid pace as a critical part of their ability to execute their investment theses.

with the CEOs, boards, and deal teams to identify, frame, and tackle issues—functioning in a consultative way as they independently evaluate the health of the organization and its top management.

To understand the value that these four related roles can have across the life of an investment, consider the following scenarios. As you read through them, note what each of the scenarios have in common: CEOs are under pressure to accelerate individual, team, and organizational performance in a tight time frame during the holding period to realize the full potential of the value to be realized by the growth opportunity. Likewise, in all scenarios, investment leaders—mindful of the complexity of a deal and the prohibitive cost of the deal not delivering its full potential—frequently turn to trusted advisors to help guide them through the velocity of change as they help a company scale and grow.

Scenario 1: Conducting Due Diligence

A midmarket investor seeks to conduct organizational due diligence on an Asia-based target in the education technology or "EdTech" sector. The investor is looking at taking a minority stake in the business, with a fivefold return valuation stemming from the monetization of the platform and targeted M&A activity. As part of the diligence, the investor brings in a CPO to assess the leadership and culture. What the CPO learns results in the investor shifting, midway through the deal, the way it interacts with the organization's cofounders, with a goal to shape the growth strategy to deliver on the investment thesis and transform the organization. Although the investor team doesn't want to impose unnecessary controls on the founders and management team, they aren't confident that they have the leadership required to maintain the performance culture that has led to the company's success thus far. More to the point, the investors are worried the company won't be able to ensure profitable growth of the investment through exit (by taking the company public or selling it to another owner).

As was the case in this example, investment firms increasingly are calling on CPOs to conduct an intensive organizational review of the leadership plan of the organizations they seek to invest in or buy. This assessment, which occurs during due diligence and the first 100 days of a private equity deal, identifies costs to take out, new markets and profit pools to pursue, and portfolio company changes to make. The CPO's role is to help produce the outcome: a believable value-creation plan to all involved (including management) because of the intensity of preparation.

What's unique about a CPO's role in this stage is that the CPO delivers a good sense of the significant people and organizational risks and opportunities. This may entail looking at how effective the organization is at decision making and its ways of working, and often, how effective the management team is. Publicly traded companies engage in similar activities in their strategic planning processes, but they typically lack the same intensity. What holds for both contexts is this: the CPO needs a high degree of skill in trust-building with the target company.

Based on this scenario, a CPO advising on due diligence can take the following actions:

- **Lead the creation of an organizational-health strategy that has full buy-in of the portfolio management team.** From day one of deal selection and due diligence, the CPO becomes the go-to person who can provide immediate answers to important questions about the risk and reward of pursuing a deal and what it will take to execute against the value-creation plan in the first 100 days and throughout the holding or investment period. After a deal closes, CPOs must work with deal teams and senior management to facilitate and support the cocreation of a comprehensive organizational-health strategy that aligns with the portfolio company's strategic priorities and value-creation plan (VCP). This requires CPOs to provide guidance on where, when, and how to leverage deal teams and third-party support for the strategy and value-creation plan.

- **Start by focusing on key value-creating roles and an analysis of the other big factors in org health.** In shaping the value-creation plan, CPOs commonly start by identifying the key value-creating roles and then hiring the best possible players for those roles. As Annmarie Neal, Hellman & Friedman's partner and chief talent officer, shared with me, "My work is focused on getting three roles right. The CEO, CHRO, and CFO and any other major value-creation roles that we assessed in diligence that we feel we need to pay attention to. For instance, in tech this may be a head of product or chief revenue officer if there is not a good head of sales." Key is setting up that leadership team from the start. For some CPOs, most of their work in this phase is to ensure that there is a strong management team before their firm makes the investment. "It's hard for my partners to want to make an investment if there isn't a strong management team in the beginning," Neal continued. "Our view is that we don't want to be a rip and flip firm. If I have to rip and flip a management team, then that means I didn't do my work during due diligence."

- **Act as a coach from acquisition to exit.** Value creation doesn't end after the first 100 days; it's a long-term process that starts at acquisition and ends at the sale. During the private equity firm's period of ownership, the CPO can work to leverage and strengthen the relationship with the CEO and portfolio management team and perform organizational-health checks to identify opportunities for realizing value. In some instances, a CPO may work through the CEO and head of HR versus doing the work themselves. This helps the organization's leadership team retain the feeling that it is their company. In this case, the role of CPOs is to use their deep expertise to guide the leadership team on the organizational health work to ensure quality standards.

Scenario 2: Finding the Right Leaders to Drive a Growth Transformation
By 2013, Dunkin' Brands had transitioned from a regionally focused group of brands to a global franchiser of quick-service restaurants. The successful transformation began with a partnership formed in 2006 between Dunkin' Brands Group and the Carlyle Group, Bain Capital, and Thomas H. Lee. As a result, Dunkin' achieved operational improvement and growth, which was ultimately driven by a top-notch leadership team of senior managers with deep experience in retail food service and franchise company expertise, among other areas.[4]

Based on this scenario, a CPO could take the following actions as a talent shaper:

- **Provide important judgment and insight on the quality of talent and develop scorecards for senior leaders against key value drivers. These can be used for performance evaluation, hiring, or off-boarding decisions at the portfolio companies.** CPOs often play a role in managing a rigorous but efficient process for placing top-tier talent while leveraging their internal and external networks to do so. It is perhaps one of the reasons why sometimes CPOs are sourced from executive search firms. In that regard, CPOs recruit A-player talent to management teams across the portfolio. They will cultivate and manage top talent pipelines for typical roles across the portfolio, including CEO, COO, and CFO (and chief product officer and revenue officer for software companies) in partnership with other operating leaders in these functional areas.

- **Extend the CPO role to identify gaps and opportunities in talent within the portfolio companies and craft a clear talent management strategy for raising the skill levels as needed to support the portfolio companies in achieving strategic priorities.** Perhaps the most critical role of the CPO, a role that ought to be institutionalized and not treated as temporary, is to ensure that succession planning processes are in place for key portfolio company leaders. CPOs may at times help define C-level job descriptions to support the investment thesis, and then rigorously evaluate leadership candidates against those job descriptions. In some cases, the CPO will perform the search for those candidates in order to expand their scope, quality, and diversity. AI-based systems for identifying and sourcing talent, such as Beacon Talent, help CPOs augment their human capabilities with emerging technologies—directly addressing one of the most significant friction points in recruiting: research, which typically consumes half of the total time of a candidate search. With such technology, CPOs can leverage intelligence across nearly the entire talent ecosystem of the tech industry—from engineers and data scientists to product managers and designers. Such systems can rank each person across dozens of quality dimensions, provide real-time predictions on how likely they are to switch jobs, and deliberately identify potential new candidates as they become available to help portfolio companies recruit rising stars.

Scenario 3: Providing Trusted Counsel in the First 100 Days
Ten weeks after a private equity firm took ownership of a software company, the investment leaders wanted to replace the CEO and build a high-performing management team that could kick-start growth and deliver on their aggressive growth strategy. The investors had three viable candidates who all looked good on paper. They were all qualified for the CEO position and had substantial experience with M&A, which would be required to scale the business and

deliver on the investment thesis. Once a CEO was picked, a CPO entered the picture to provide the new CEO with counsel in the first 100 days. That meant that the CPO had to deeply understand the organizational health of the company. But more, the CPO would need to partner with the CEO, management team, and deal team to optimize ways of working while building strong relationships and planning for succession.

Based on this scenario, the CPO could make the following no-regret moves as a "CEO whisperer."

- **Be a credible advisor on organizational issues for deal teams and portfolio management teams.** CPOs are increasingly being called upon to advise deal teams and portfolio company leadership on both urgent and strategic human capital issues within the portfolio. As trusted advisors, CPOs work with portfolio management teams to execute organizational health initiatives and to monitor progress against plans. To achieve this requires that they develop strong partnerships with CEOs and senior leadership teams within the portfolio company. Sometimes that means providing coaching and counseling to the CEO and other senior executives on organizational matters, as appropriate. In short, CPOs must build collaborative relationships with management teams while maintaining strong antennae for potential organizational risks or other performance-related situations.
- **Create an ambitious 100-day program.** In my experience, the first 100 days after a private equity firm takes ownership of a company are critical to value creation. During those early months, CPOs can take several steps to kick-start growth and support operational improvement and profitable growth, especially considering that delivering profitable growth is the most critical driver to generate attractive equity returns. Beginning on day one after the deal closes, the CPO can work with top management to create an organizational design and governance approach

that reduces uncertainty felt by the broader organization. A 100-day plan can describe the critical value-creation levers (i.e., pricing, product, or sales) or cost-management levers (such as procurement or general and administrative), or people and organizational levers (such as the elements key for health noted in part 1). Thus, the firm has at its disposal an action list to make step-change improvements after the close of the purchase of a company. As the Carlyle Group's chief performance officer, Mindy Mackenzie, told me: "When doing work with portfolio companies, we identify the value-creation drivers that support our investment thesis and then align the financial and human capital to deliver on that plan. We may double down on certain areas of strength to help us accelerate performance. And then we look at the one or two capability gaps or weaknesses in the organization that we absolutely have to buy, build, or intervene in to rapidly get better than where we are today. It's about knowing the critical few things that will yield the greatest financial performance, so we deliver beyond the 2.0X MOIC returns for our investors. Our business is to build better businesses."

- **Continue to coach the CEO on building world-class organizational health capabilities during the scale and growth period.** As the portfolio company scales and grows, CPOs tackle whatever challenges are required to build world-class organizational health capabilities, while also ensuring the portfolio company stays current with next practices and thought leadership. To do this, the CPO will need to craft an internal team or external network of outside consultants who are experts and practitioners, with the goal of elevating the investor's ability to assess, develop, and exit a healthy organization.

Scenario 4: Architecting Large-Scale Growth of a Portfolio Company
The management team of a $10 billion financial-technology operation backed by a large PE firm aspired to double the business's size

in three years. The management team was initially comfortable with the value-creation plan based on an aggressive acquisition strategy that they had planned with the fund managers. But nine months later, the CEO wondered whether her company could pull it all off. The company had just acquired one large target and was now pursuing a second. The CEO was concerned that focusing on the second acquisition might dilute the performance of the first acquisition.

In addition, a problem had cropped up in the company's human resources function. Despite having planned the right combination of acquisitions and organic growth to hit the company's goals, the chief HR officer was struggling to build his department and hire the people to meet the needs of the growing company. In short, to establish credibility with the management team, the HR chief needed to show that his department was adding value beyond just managing transactional activities.

Although the early presence and guidance of a CPO would have been beneficial, now a CPO would be key to any forward movement. If the fund managers and portfolio company's management team wanted to continue with their aggressive value-creation plan, they would need to understand what organizational investments would be required, considering the current structure, processes, and people capabilities.

Based on this scenario, the CPO can make the following no-regret moves as a transformation architect:

- **Provide guidance on architecting and executing changes where needed.** CPOs must demonstrate the ability to provide sound strategic guidance based on data and analytics while being able to roll up their sleeves to push performance improvement and change initiatives forward. In other words, they must not only use rigorous and proven approaches for managing a large transformation, they also must show that they have the courage and experience to lead change management efforts to make the tough calls and shape action plans and approaches. As one CPO shared with me, "We look at whether the portfolio company has demonstrated evidence of doing change well. Then we look ahead at the three-to-five-year time frame, at what organizational capabilities the company is competitively capable of winning in a compressed time frame. Have they done it, can they do it, and what will be required?" CPOs must help create roadmaps with clearly defined measures and targets so that the portfolio company's CEO and others have concrete goals to ensure success.

- **Develop executional muscle.** The only way the value-creation plan can be executed properly is if change readiness and capability are in the muscle and DNA of a portfolio company. In other words, an organization that can adapt to a quickly changing external or internal environment, combined with a mindset of willingness, will improve its odds of success. CPOs must be able to identify and prioritize opportunities to boost operational performance. By focusing on health-related improvements in supply chain, R&D pipelines, or sales and marketing overhauls, CPOs can identify initiatives for short-term cash generation and achieve some immediate returns to fund long-term transformation journeys.

- **Create an organizational playbook by drawing on best practices and a network of resources across the investment company's portfolio.** In some cases, CPOs will bring the organization a playbook of best organizational practices drawn from their experience in working across multiple portfolio companies and then help the organization implement and manage these practices. This enables the company's management team—most notably, the chief HR officer—to ensure that best practices are used. That is one of the reasons CPOs maintain a network of potential chief HR officers for current and future portfolio companies. The playbook can also help accelerate certain critical organizational capabilities, such as workforce planning or resource allocation and prioritization. That way, the CPO can hold management teams and deal teams accountable to scorecards for organization building at the portfolio company, in areas such as compensation, performance management, succession planning, and organizational structures, and act on those gaps and opportunities as appropriate, making the hard decisions when needed.

Each of these scenarios is real and representative of the issues facing CPOs who are advising private equity and publicly held companies of various sizes and across a range of industries. Beyond the essential step of identifying the right value-creation plan, these scenarios demonstrate that growth requires something more: an examination of the organization's health; the shaping of the executive management team and, in some cases, the board; the ability to provide independent counsel untainted by ambition; and the design and implementation of the right portfolio of organizational and operational initiatives to execute change and support growth. Moreover, to make growth a less risky proposition, CPOs need to align the organizational-health strategies they pursue with the stage of organizational maturity and the private equity continuum (i.e., venture capital, growth equity, buyout, or IPO).

The CPO's Shifting Role in a Growing and Maturing Organization

The role of the CPO varies across the stages of organizational maturity: startup (the focus of venture capital firms), growth (the focus of growth equity firms), scaling (pre-exit stage, when companies move beyond growth into unicorn phase), and maturity/stability (the focus of leveraged buyout funds). For example, if the investor is affiliated with a VC, generally, they are betting on the founder. As one CPO who is an operating partner in a growth equity firm notes, "In VC, you are probably not going to be in the business of changing out the founder or CEO that often. And you are hoping that out of your 100 investments, one hits, which is very different from what we do in the growth equity or buyout space."

Consider the following stages of organizational maturity, what matters most at each stage, and the role of the CPO in driving speed to impact.

Stage 1: Startup—the Launch and Early Stages
These companies likely have an idea or a prototype for a product/ service and are in proof-of-concept mode, aggressively trying to land their first customers. They likely have funding from incubators, accelerators, angel investors, and/or early-stage VCs. The founders are running the show; most of the company's employees have probably been around since launch.

The CPO will need to keep an eye on the seven elements of an organization's health, as well as on an eighth key consideration: the digital technology that will support the business's health and overall success. (See the table "Focus for CPOs: Organizational Conditions in the Startup Stage.") Although all elements of organizational health matter, at this stage the most important focus for the CPO will be on the following:

- **Leadership.** Investors are betting on the founders—there's not enough information anywhere else to make a judgment. They hope that these founders will someday be leaders of a scaled and profitable organization, and the investors need to make sure they're supported and empowered to build the business.
- **Talent.** It's critical that any new employee at this stage is the right person in the right role. The CPO needs to make sure that those individuals have the skills, support, and structures to do their jobs in helping the business take shape.

Stage 2: Growth—Moving from Startup to Expansion
At this stage, there is a clear product/service with an obvious value proposition. Now it's about expanding it: testing new markets, new features, and maybe even a new product line. The organization is taking shape. There's likely a basic operating model/organizational

Focus for CPOs: Organizational Conditions in the Startup Stage

Purpose	• Clearly articulate the company's purpose (connected to broader strategic/product management work that's being done in this stage).
Culture	• Begin identifying the values that will set this organization apart.
Leadership	• Provide mentorship opportunities for the founders. • Empower them to be the leaders the business will need as it grows.
Talent	• Work with the right recruitment partners to begin sourcing needed talent into the organization. • Establish recruiting practices that can mature with the organization. • Create the structures for goal setting and conducting honest 360 reviews throughout the organization.
Org design	• Start thinking about what the org design will need to be in the future, and consider how the early hires might fit into those leadership roles.
EID	• Make sure there's diversity among the founding team and early hires.
Well-being	• Encourage a work-life balance among the early hires. • Identify any bad habits and keep them from becoming embedded into the culture. • Be on the lookout for signs of burnout and mitigate.
Technology	• Help choose various tech platforms to enable HR delivery at the early stage (out-of-the-box solutions for things like payroll, vacation time, benefits management, etc.).

chart and some light structures and procedures—all of which are constantly growing and evolving as the company shifts from a viable business into a thriving enterprise.

Again, the CPO will need to mind the seven elements of an organization's health, as well as the digital technology that will support the business's health and overall success. (See the table "Focus for CPOs: Organizational Conditions in the Growth Stage.") Although

Focus for CPOs: Organizational Conditions in the Growth Stage

Purpose	• Refine the company's purpose to be in line with how the company has grown and is planning to grow. • Consider a communication campaign to make sure the purpose is clear to all employees (and customers) and that everyone's bought in.
Culture	• Formally articulate the values that are most important and define the relevant behaviors that are unique to the organization. • Work with leaders and the early employees to embed the culture into the organization.
Leadership	• Start thinking about succession planning and pathways to leadership within the organization. • Encourage and empower decision making throughout the organization, allowing the founding team/C-suite to focus on the most important areas. • Extend mentoring support to nonfounder leaders; make sure they are in a position to lead future departments. • Formalize board practices and establish clear governance structures.
Talent	• Create an initial job architecture that can grow and adapt with the organization; define competencies for different talent segments/levels and identify which ones are critical for the future. • Articulate an initial employee value proposition to encourage employees to stick it out through the growing pains of the organization. • Encourage role-specific learning and development and offer time and opportunities to develop. • Formalize performance management throughout the organization.
Org design	• Formalize reporting structures, including managers and direct reports. • Start creating business or market units as needed.

EID	• Weave EID into the purpose, culture, and talent practices of the organization (e.g., examine recruiting for any sources of bias; train leaders on unconscious bias, create learning programs on allyship, etc.).
Well-being	• Identify ways to promote well-being in compensation and benefits packages (e.g., paid time off, mental health support, fitness support, etc.).
	• Foster a culture that encourages work-life balance, makes wellness a priority, and integrates well-being into the design of work.
Technology	• Use the appropriate tech platforms for the stage of business (i.e., the enterprise human capital software company Workday may be more than you need at this stage, but recruitment can likely be automated in some form).
	• Begin gathering workforce metrics that will enable analysis and understanding as the organization grows.

all elements of organizational health matter, at this stage the most important focus for the CPO will be on the following:

- **Culture and purpose.** No longer is the organization made up of people who've been with the company since the beginning. Therefore, it's imperative that new employees familiarize themselves with the purpose and culture of the organization. This will be especially important as the company begins to grow—any new areas need to align with the purpose, and the culture needs to be refined to help deliver the new ambitious goals.
- **EID.** As the company grows, leaders need to make sure that EID is woven deeply into the organization itself. It's best to begin as they intend to go on.

Stage 3: Scale—Pre-exit Stage
This is a mature organization with a clear exit path for early investors (be it IPO, acquisition, etc.). There are clear product and service

lines and defined organizational structures to deliver them. The company is deciding whether to maintain its growth at this stage or invest in scaling the business.

At this stage, the top priority for leaders and investors is ensuring that the company is in the healthiest possible position for a successful exit and future growth. Therefore, the CPO's focus needs to be on *all* seven elements of organizational health, along with the business's range of supporting technology. (See the table "Focus for CPOs: Organizational Conditions in the Scale Stage.")

Stage 4: Stability—the Mature, Well-Established Business
The products and services are well known, there are clear and loyal customers, and solid and effective processes and operations deliver the products and services to the customers. The early investors have likely exited, and the organization now likely has a diverse range of shareholders. Growth has slowed down, and the company has (hopefully) reached a phase of stability.

The CPO will continue to focus on the seven elements of an organization's health, as well as the state of the company's technological capabilities. (See the table "Focus for CPOs: Organizational Conditions in the Stability Stage.") In particular, CPOs will need to ensure the company doesn't stagnate. Mature organizations have to find ways to keep innovating, and the answer is usually to focus on people.

What to Look for in a CPO
As one CPO for a large PE firm shared with me, "My role is getting the right leader into the right role and then getting the team behind that leader." As I learned, helping leaders and top teams perform at their peak is core to the CPO's job.

Although the potential benefits are clear, bringing on a CPO is not without its challenges. Finding someone with the track record of driving transformation in organizational health, who also has the business and financial acumen to act as a trusted advisor to C-suite leaders and investment professionals across a multi-sectoral portfolio can be a tall order. Executive recruiters confirm that searching

Focus for CPOs: Organizational Conditions in the Scale Stage

Purpose	• Examine the company's purpose and work with the business to adjust for this new phase. • Put the purpose front and center, make sure that all business decisions link back to the purpose.
Culture	• Help new employees understand the culture and how they can live out the values. • Hold leadership accountable for modeling the company's culture. • Tie performance decisions to the company's culture, making sure that it's more than "corporate wallpaper."
Leadership	• Take succession planning seriously and ensure a bench of potential leaders (both inside and outside the organization). • Examine the leaders who are in place and make the necessary changes to ensure the right leaders with the right competencies are in the right roles.
Talent	• Integrate the job architecture and competencies into all talent practices (e.g., workforce planning, learning and development, performance management, etc.). • Refine the employee value proposition and create a strong talent brand. • Examine compensation and other rewards to make sure they're in line with and competitive with industry standards. • Build out a learning and development program that defines clear learning paths throughout the organization. • Make sure that performance management results clearly tie into career advancement opportunities.
Org design	• Examine the org design and make sure that the company is structured in the best possible way to meet its current goals and growth plans. • Align talent practices to the new org design (e.g., team-specific learning plans, competencies defined by business unit, compensation standardized across geographies, etc.).

(continued)

EID	• Set ambitious goals for EID and make it a priority for the organization.
	• Use data to understand the makeup of the organization and identify gaps within any EID goals.
	• Map the employee experience and look for bias along the moments that matter and address them.
	• Establish employee resource groups.
	• Consider ways to engage customers into the EID conversations.
	• Fiercely defend EID as a core element of the organization's purpose and culture.
Well-being	• Provide benefits that promote employee well-being.
	• Encourage leadership to set the right example on prioritizing employee and team well-being.
	• Look for signs of burnout and mitigate accordingly.
Technology	• Measure employee satisfaction and take a data-driven approach to improving the employee experience.
	• Invest in the right HR platform (e.g., Workday) that will enable a tech-first approach to HR delivery.

for the right candidate is incredibly important: ideally, the person should have the functional experience to advise on and be accountable for a company's talent, organization, and culture.

That means candidates should have deep knowledge of organizational design and effectiveness—including the use of assessments geared toward understanding the health of an organization, a track record of working with CEOs to improve organization performance, and the financial, commercial, and industry insight necessary to be an analytical, data-driven problem solver with the intellectual horsepower required to advise deal professionals. What's more, a potential CPO should have firsthand, practical experience in driving change—academic or theoretical experience isn't enough.

Therefore, a search for this kind of professional can sometimes take longer than expected—a fact that is particularly frustrating for those investment leaders looking to drive a growth or turnaround

Focus for CPOs: Organizational Conditions in the Stability Stage

Purpose	• Put the purpose front and center, making sure that all business decisions link back to the purpose.
Culture	• Continue to find ways to highlight the culture as a clear differentiator for the organization.
	• Encourage leaders and employees to make the culture real rather than an HR artifact.
Leadership	• Formalize leadership development programs throughout the organization.
	• Define a differentiated leadership profile so that employees at all levels have something to work toward.
	• Formalize succession planning and ensure that there's a deep bench for all leadership positions.
Talent	• Formalize job architectures and competency management.
	• Examine and improve recruiting practices.
	• Map the employee experience and look for ways to improve it.
	• Create a learning and development organization and make it a priority.
	• Standardize an approach to performance management.
	• Review compensation, benefits, and rewards and make sure they're competitive.
	• Engage in workforce planning.
Org design	• Regularly review the org design and op model and transform them as needed.
EID	• Set ambitious goals for EID and make it a priority for the organization.
	• Use data to understand the makeup of the organization and identify gaps within any EID goals (e.g., promotions, compensation, etc.).
	• Map the employee experience and look for bias along the moments that matter and address them.
	• Establish employee resource groups.
	• Consider ways to engage customers into the EID conversations.

(continued)

Well-being	• Fiercely defend EID as a core element of the organization's purpose and culture. • Provide benefits that promote employee well-being. • Encourage leadership to set the right example on prioritizing employee and team well-being. • Train leaders to look for signs of burnout in their teams and give them the well-being tools they need to support their employees. • Emphasize the importance of well-being in the culture and encourage positive actions like taking time off and talking about mental health.
Technology	• Measure employee satisfaction and take a data-driven approach to improving the employee experience. • Invest in the right HR platform (e.g., Workday) that will enable a tech-first approach to HR delivery. • Automate HR processes. • Review the data that HR is collecting, and update as needed.

agenda quickly. Nevertheless, investment professionals or executive recruiters can often find people from one of three backgrounds to fill the CPO role. First, qualified candidates tend to be organizational psychologists who do assessment and coaching work. Second, they might be former HR professionals (i.e., chief HR officers) or people who have worked in executive search. Third, they sometimes come from top-tier strategic consulting or private equity firms that have truly invested in this capability.

But regardless of the path by which a candidate arrives, recruiters should look for five essential attributes necessary to effectively operate as a chief performance officer:

- First and perhaps foremost, the very commercial nature of the role means they must possess an investor mindset in approaching organizational health work. In other words, it requires substantial commercial financial acumen and a ruthless focus on key drivers of business performance and

investor returns. As one CPO shared with me, to be
effective in her role "requires an investment mindset. In
other words, would you put your own money in this
company and back this?"

- Second, they should be able to act as an influential and
pragmatic advisor to deal teams and senior management
teams. Simply put: they need to understand the implications of engaging in a web of complicated and sensitive
relationships as a strategic advisor, leadership coach, key
business decision influencer, and thought partner to multiple CEOs, management teams, and the investment team.

- Third, they must effectively deal with the high sense of
urgency and speed this role requires. To operate successfully requires a hands-on consultative approach with a bias
toward coaching and "speed to impact" with the ability to
drive decisive decision making. In other words, they have
to be able to work with investment leaders in assessing
prospective investments, translate investment theses into
value-creation plans, and assist in due diligence to help
identify areas of weakness, risk, and opportunity before an
investment is made.

- Fourth, they will need to act as a good confidante, which
often involves managing many leaders' confidences
responsibly. Therefore, they must be a highly strategic
leader themselves, one who builds credibility by demonstrating balanced business judgment, low ego, and exceptional interpersonal and communication skills. This is
especially important for identifying and recommending
optimal approaches to deal with highly complex transformations covering critical strategic, operational, and
organizational areas. It will take an enterprise mindset to
deploy systematic rigor in determining the right resources,
processes, and data to gather and the experience and
judgment to remain flexible.

- Fifth, potential CPOs will need the overarching attribute
of high emotional and ethical intelligence—or what I call

"E2Q." To advise competently, they must possess a strong sense of humility, the ability to read complex human and organizational dynamics, and the discernment to perceive and overcome barriers and obstacles. As one CPO told me: "Being a good CPO requires you to make the CEO happy, keep the deal partner informed, and be an expert, all while engaging your sense of diplomacy rather than offering critiques." Indeed, CPOs need to know when to raise red flags and when to deliver tough messages—such as saying what the investor or portfolio CEO needs to hear, rather than what they might *want* to hear. But again, it's all in the delivery. Diplomacy is the watchword.

Despite the challenges of finding an executive with these attributes and with the necessary range of expertise, more and more private equity firms are exploring the CPO option. For those striving for greater returns, adding a seasoned, energetic chief performance officer is often akin to a professional sports team coach who seeks to develop a championship team through the addition of "A" players. It simply doubles the odds, especially when the stakes are high.

To be sure, CPOs will need to "invest time cultivating relationships as they build empathy to develop a higher level of trust," as one CPO puts it. Doing so enables the bonds forged with the CEO and management team to endure when the pressure of operating under a well-defined holding period hits, no matter what the circumstances of the situation might be.

Often, the relationships a CPO must engage in are complicated and require careful navigation (see the sidebar "Complicated Role, Complicated Relationships"). The fact that those relationships are based on trust is what allows CPOs to make the decisions needed, for example, to place a C-suite leader in a portfolio company or bring in further specialist expertise to help solve difficult problems. This enables them to better deliver impact in ways that improve the organizational health of the portfolio company. The Carlyle Group's Mindy Mackenzie summarizes a CPO's value this way: "Everything we, at Carlyle, do in the talent and organization space is about speed

Complicated Role, Complicated Relationships

In looking at the role of CPOs who become trusted advisors to investor teams, portfolio management teams, and the board, most CPOs I talked to pointed to a clear pattern of tensions they often have to manage. One tension set focuses on the nuanced web of relationships encompassing loyalties and structural dynamics. A second set focuses on the relationship dynamics with the portfolio company's HR chief's.

The Tension Surrounding Loyalty

Who am I professionally obligated to? This is a question that can sometimes complicate the nature of the relationship. Consider, for example, when an HR chief may have to go to the lead investor PE firm partner about issues requiring mediation regarding CEO compensation. Or consider a situation in which a CEO transition is required, and a dialogue and trusting relationship with the head of HR and the board is needed to know what exactly is happening in the company and the future leadership required.

The tension between CPOs and other key leaders across the portfolio or fund is likely to become more complicated as more companies add CPOs to the mix of experts and operating partners. Investor leaders need to ensure that bringing on a CPO to help advise a CEO, HR chief, or portfolio management team works in favor of the value-creation plan and overall organizational health of a company. That means, first of all, recognizing that inherent in the CPO role is a contradiction: the CPO both is and is not a "CEO whisperer." CPOs do play such a role in one sense because they provide independent counsel on organizational related matters. But in another sense, the loyalties of CPOs (unlike those of the HR chief) must ultimately lie with the investor partners rather than the CEO. It is a tricky line to walk. Having to manage

(*continued*)

confidentiality across a multitude of situations is one of the hardest parts of the job. Being an ally to the CEO while staying loyal to the partner group is not for the faint of heart. As one CPO put it, "There is a tension I experience to make sure I hold the line and don't cross it to maintain integrity and loyalty to the partners. It is what makes pure coaching very difficult and why I've stopped coaching CEOs in the classical sense of the term because there is way too much conflict of interest."

Allyship at Its Best

Some HR chiefs note that, when it comes to discussing people and organizational topics, the CPO can be a helpful ally and partner. To be sure, effective CPOs can add great value in creating a network and community of all HR leaders in the portfolio companies to share best practices. CPOs can also support HR chiefs when it comes to leveraging purchasing power for their portfolio companies.

For example, if all of a CPO's portfolio clients decide to buy Workday software, that might put the portfolio companies in a position to cut a deal on the software. The CPO can be a real ally and champion for this effort, as one HR head for a PE-backed software company helped me to understand. In other instances, the partnership between the CPO and HR can help deliver speed to value. When PE firms look at potential investment companies, they want someone to help them independently evaluate the talent. And then if there are gaps, they want someone to help them hire the most senior leader. A CPO with a strong executive search background and digital rolodex of high-caliber talent can be a huge value-add. Similarly, someone who has been a talent leader and operator inside a company can bring a broad perspective regarding landmines to avoid and ways to deliver impact.

to impact. It's about fast insight, disciplined process, and data gathering so that we can get a faster start in our investment and yield greater returns quicker."

Private equity firms are recognizing the ever-growing value of having a trusted organizational expert as a member of the operations team. CPOs serve as executives who can look at an underperforming business through the lens of the organizational drivers. They can identify the culture and capabilities that are lacking, analyze C-suite dynamics, and align the seven dimensions of organizational health (as described in part I of this book) to one another and the investment thesis to create value.

In the next and final main chapter of this book, we'll explore another crucial role in today's companies when it comes to the organization's health: CEOs, especially those in publicly listed companies and private equity–backed portfolio companies, which operate in a more high pressure environment than peer CEOs. Running companies in today's increasingly AI-first world requires CEOs who can quickly develop new skills. A focus on leading change is, therefore, a critical part of building better organizations. And it is undoubtedly connected to a crucial requirement necessary for a CEO to fast-track growth and agility: becoming fluent in the language of change.

Checklist for Agenda Setting

- Add a chief performance officer (CPO) to the PE's portfolio operations team to be responsible for assessing organizational health and leading organizational and operational initiatives to improve portfolio company value growth and exit support.
- Hire CPOs who have practical experience driving change with a track record of working with CEOs to improve organizational performance, an analytical "investor mindset," strong emotional and ethical intelligence, exceptional interpersonal and communication skills, and the ability to operate and execute (or scale) with speed.

(continued)

- Adjust the role of the CPO based on phase of the deal life cycle—conducting due diligence when deciding whether to invest in or buy an asset, shaping talent with a focus on leadership and talent in the early stages of an organization, providing strategic counsel to the CEO and focusing on culture and purpose in the growth phase, architecting organizational transformation in preparation for sale or exit, and creating continuous innovation for mature organizations.
- Arm the CPO with intelligent digital systems to help identify top talent in the entire talent ecosystem, and assess and identify the critical improvements needed for the organization's health.
- As CPO, create an organizational health playbook by drawing on best practices and a network of resources across the investment company's portfolio, create a strong allyship with portfolio company HR chiefs, and carefully balance the tensions surrounding loyalty.

12 ■ The Change-Fluent CEO

Become Adept in the Language of Change

As investors fund emerging technologies that fuel radical approaches to the design and leadership of organizations, how does the CEO adapt to navigate this new environment? By doing what only a CEO can do: ensuring the value placed on robots, machines, and algorithms doesn't compete with the interests of the company's strategy and its people.

Although every CEO's job is unique, some of the more common challenges associated with being a CEO are not what they used to be. Disruption and change are constant nowadays, creating instability and uncertainty. Just as in any competitive sport where players anticipate their opponent's next move, CEOs must marry adaptive strategies, analytics, and design thinking with intuition and judgment to decide which way to lean while remaining ready for anything. They must prepare for many possible futures if they hope to pivot swiftly, innovate, or rethink their business and operating models completely, let alone keep pace with shifting language around things such as gender and ethnic designations.

In short, today's CEO must prepare to be fluent in change. A new and different set of expectations for leadership has emerged against a backdrop of economic volatility, a shifting geopolitical landscape, and technology developments that are constantly in flux. What's more, public distrust of leaders and institutions, including government, has reached epic proportions[1]—just at a time when leaders are being asked to accommodate employees with increasingly diverse backgrounds and designations. In other words, CEOs can no longer categorize their organizations into singular frames or structures with discrete boundaries. Between life in the digital world and technological advances altering how executives lead, CEOs and their teams must move away from the mechanistic, industrial models of the past.

Indeed, how very different is today's digital-era enterprise, compared with the era during most of the last century when a few industrial enterprises called all the shots. (See the table "The Shift from the Industrial to the Digital Enterprise.") Consider this: a CEO facing a challenge today may very well be solving the challenge faced

The Shift from the Industrial to the Digital Enterprise

Industrial	Digital
Structures are static.	Structures are fluid.
Technology dehumanizes work.	Technology humanizes work.
Leaders and managers direct and delegate.	Leaders and managers coach, convene, and orchestrate.
Leaders and managers manage one-on-one (and sometimes in teams) while seeking a kind of conformity.	Leaders and managers manage systemically while drawing out individual talents and unique contributions of small teams.
Companies serve shareholders.	Companies serve stakeholders.
Companies are part of a larger industry.	Companies become ecosystems that span industries.

by another CEO in a whole different industry. In that way, organizations not only leapfrog ahead of competitors but also are propelled into dominating a particular business landscape. For example, iTunes solved Napster's problem (piracy). What might initially have been a fatal blow to the music industry turned out to be a catalyst for a whole new way of consuming music through streaming—legally, ethically, and most of all equitably for the artists. The 2001 release of iTunes was a leap forward for Apple. Similarly, Amazon Web Services solved the scale problem (limits to IT infrastructure). In short, it enabled Amazon's customers to outsource their computing (i.e., storage, servers, or networking) needs.

Confronted with such a set of facts, CEOs today who feel the pressure to change fast might do well to consider this question: What is the biggest problem faced today by the world's most valuable and important companies, and who is going to solve it?

All of which is to say that the future will require leaders who are much more dynamic, agile, and self-adapting. In an AI-first world, disruptive competitors will appear from many corners, and CEOs will need the capacity to learn from disruption and beat competitors to the punch. They will need to ask generative questions to spot opportunities and learn from any quarter: from an ecosystem of partners, customers, competitors, employees, and the communities in which they operate. To ensure a sustainable path forward for their teams and the whole organization, CEOs must learn to change, fail, and recover, and discover new things (while letting go of outdated assumptions about how things should work). They must do this at clock speed.

In this chapter, we will explore what such a shift will mean for CEOs and their organizations, including three specific challenges they face; what is needed from CEOs to meet those challenges; what is being asked of leadership teams specifically in the digital era; and how CEOs can hope to master growth and agility.

Three Challenges for Today's CEO

As both a strategist and executive counselor, I have observed three behaviors that are hindering CEOs in their ability to navigate today's tsunami of challenges. Consider the already tumultuous environment marked not only by the global pandemic but also by a set of pre-pandemic conditions—for example, the move from prioritizing real estate and physical assets to cultivate and maintain in-person work and norms, to prioritizing tech and digital infrastructure investments that support sustained remote work and new ways of working. In the face of such challenges, many leaders now find themselves wholly unprepared. Here is why.

First, when faced with a new set of organizational tensions, some CEOs hinder their own ability to consider multiple valuable perspectives by defaulting to limited either/or thinking. Even though a certain mindset has worked for them in the past, today's environment demands that CEOs try flexing different muscles. One important muscle practices intentional—versus accidental—learning. In other words, leaders need to engage in continual reflection throughout any decision-making process, questioning their thinking and then learning as they go. To be effective, the CEO must engage in ongoing introspection, pausing regularly to reflect and contemplate a set of questions focused on purpose, the enterprise, the workforce, and the community in which it operates and does business. (See the box "Key Reflective Questions for CEOs.") Such constant reflection ultimately costs far less than accidental learning, which sometimes carries a high price indeed. CEOs who are unable to let go of outdated assumptions and playbooks or to adopt the mindsets and strategies for navigating new and important trends hurt themselves in both the short and long term—and the organization with them. For example, hybrid working models that span generational preferences could present talent acquisition opportunities.

The reflective questions I've outlined in the box demand the attention of every CEO, investor, and board director in the new, "never normal" era. To tackle such questions, leaders at every level must understand and embrace changes in technology, society, and the economy. They need to match customers' needs with the kinds of innovation that will delight them and enrich their lives. And they need to understand the essence of how to scale and grow the AI-first

Key Reflective Questions for CEOs	
Key Question	**Focus**
What am I being called to do?	Purpose: Shaping or resetting the CEO's personal purpose, as well as the company's purpose and strategic direction.
What kind of organization is it time for now?	Organization: Continually molding the frame of the organization while breaking it when conditions call for it.
What's the right thing to do?	Workforce: Valuing differences and a workforce based on EID.
What time, energy, and resources will be required of me to bring the new ecosystem into the room?	Trust: Integrating and unleashing capabilities within and beyond the organization based on trust and relationships rather than just transactions. In other words, arm's-length transactional relationships are phasing out in favor of closer and more authentic relationships based on trust.

enterprise: by seeing where the organization is headed strategically, how work will be organized, what kinds of work the company leaders (and employees) will be expected to do, how they'll be expected to behave ethically, and how the company can earn the trust of their multiple stakeholders.

Consider Airbnb, where 80 percent of its business was wiped out after the initial shock of the global pandemic. Despite this massive setback, cofounder and CEO Brian Chesky turned demise into opportunity, learning some valuable lessons along the way that are relevant for other CEOs. How, you might ask, did he manage to steer the company in a direction that helped it go public and come out of the pandemic in better shape than most travel businesses? Three lessons provide guidance. First, he focused on doing the right thing as he saw it. He refunded customers and accepted loans provided by his investors to soften the blow for many hosts. By doing the right thing for customers and listening to the hosts who created the guest experience, he managed to get off on the right foot. Second, he used data to drive his decision making, based on patterns recognized in local stays. In his own words, "the pandemic was a reset for us with cities, in a good way." Focusing on strengthening partnerships with cities and communities, Airbnb set a course to get back on track, all the while converting antagonists to trusted partners. Lastly, he went back to basics—meaning he set expansion plans aside to focus on the core business. In the end, the company's valuation passed the $100 billion threshold and is preparing for its second act, stronger than before.[2]

Second, somewhat paradoxically and contrary to some beliefs, the advent of intelligent machines does not threaten to replace humans. In fact, technology, ranging from artificial intelligence to automation and robotics, places humanity at the pinnacle of how an organization operates and makes money. As organizations continue to be much more reliant and interdependent on such technologies, a new paradigm of human-centric organizations is required. This change will demand an advanced breed of dynamic leadership capabilities that can integrate intelligent and quantum computing. More and more, CEOs will need to become adept at elevating sense-making when it comes to recognizing patterns based on large sets of data that come in quickly, thereby seizing and ultimately transforming capabilities.

Such sense-making and agility gained via human-machine collaboration is part of what Rich Lesser, former CEO and current global chair of Boston Consulting Group, identified as the means for success in today's turbulent times. Especially since the start of the pandemic, he said, CEOs who managed to do well were able to combine four things in their leadership: "The ability to learn very rapidly, and not just consumer knowledge, but to translate that into experimentation and action. A purpose-driven, authentic style. Empathy, for sure. And a high orientation to adaptiveness and agility."[3]

Third, with so many issues vying for leaders' attention today, many CEOs run the risk of developing a kind of attention deficit. This is antithetical to the notion of learning—and it definitely slows down decision making, which can be deadly for both the organization and the CEO's career. Thus, CEOs must learn to look both inside and outside the organization for the information they need to make timely decisions.

CEOs will make fewer mistakes by choosing to act, versus waiting to act. Why? Because they will learn from the action. CEOs who make decisions swiftly help generate new data to make more informed decisions on how to progress.

Fear of failure cannot be part of the CEO's mindset, especially in companies that optimize organizational health. From top management all the way down to a company's entry-level ranks, healthy organizations do not punish failure. Instead, they focus on and reward learning and growth. Consider General Motors CEO Mary Barra. Barra has shown her resilience by not letting fear of failure get in her way, whether investing in new technologies and partnerships or divesting old businesses while pursuing new ones in areas such as ridesharing, autonomous vehicles, and electric cars—none of which come without their share of risk. Barra's focus and decisiveness have led her to drive impact faster, learn from missteps, and swiftly correct course along the way.

Consider too Dr. Steven Corwin, CEO of New York-Presbyterian Hospital, who, amid the burgeoning global pandemic, had to face down initial mistakes and keep moving forward. "Our assumptions around pandemic preparation were flawed," he said in one interview. He went on to describe several missteps that needed course correction early on, including a belief that the hospital's supply of personal protective equipment would be sufficient during the first wave of COVID-19. "That turned out to be completely false," Corwin said. "We went from using 4,000 masks a day . . . to 90,000 masks a day at the peak of the crisis, and we did not have the stockpiles to make up for that." Neither, of course, did the rest of the country. In the end, he said, "We were able to secure some supplies from China . . . [and] we were very careful about how many masks we were using."[4]

Help Wanted: AI-Era CEOs Who Do the Right Thing

As the late Warren Bennis put it, organizations need leaders who cannot just "do things right" but who can also "do the right thing." In fact, Bennis's message serves as an apt encapsulation of what this entire book has pointed to: building better organizations, especially in a digital environment, means minding all of the aspects of the health of the business.

But what sorts of CEOs can be counted on to do the right thing—to lead with purpose, trust, and empathy while mastering the organizational essentials to effectively execute their company's business strategy? And, of course, those things must be accomplished today in the most challenging of environments, where all the familiar assumptions about business and operating models are changing before our very eyes. As the post-pandemic world ferrets out the companies who win from the ones who lose, the CEOs who win will be those who have recommitted to a holistic approach to learning and mastering the art of continual, disruptive change.

Take Chip Bergh, president and CEO of Levi Strauss, who believes that as consumers become more conscious of quality and sustainability, "Levi's will be well-positioned to meet their needs and continue its 167-year success story." Why? Because part of that long history, Bergh says, is "doing the right thing."

Bergh's plan includes several of the seven conditions, starting with establishing clarity about Levi's culture, then assessing what is right for the business, the company, and stakeholders by targeting purpose and broader strategic direction. He focused on gaining the public's trust. As a CEO activist, he embraced ESG issues linking it to the brand's advocacy for stronger gun laws. "After Levi's took a stand on gun violence," Bergh notes, "business started to grow." He concludes: "The pandemic and recession is further separating the winners from the losers, and we're determined to come out of this as a winner."[5]

Riding the waves of change today, for companies of all kinds and all sizes, will be like mastering a new kind of language. Change isn't static, and neither is language. In today's digital context, change is often more important than strategy. To be competitive, large and small companies need to understand when and how to change and adapt at near startup speed. They require a fresh perspective to break the old paradigm of the past's traditional, top-down change methods entirely, so that a new paradigm for change and organizational learning can emerge.

Specific Learnings and Challenges from COVID-19

The global COVID-19 pandemic revealed some significant limitations in organizations across various industries and sectors, exposing the need for CEOs to be more concerned about learning and pivoting under conditions of deep and exponential uncertainty.

Specifically, CEOs find themselves leading across an increasingly volatile array of different contexts: remote workforces, the need to rapidly redeploy talent and skills, organizational capabilities that vary widely from one company to the next, and unique local market forces, to name just a few. The challenge is only magnified by recent and often sizable new developments, such as distressed global supply chains like food production, healthcare, travel, or capital markets. All of this amounts to an enormous strain on a CEO's ability to keep the pieces of an increasingly virtual, digital, and fragmented business connected.

To answer the question of how CEOs can hope to meet those challenges and more, we first must consider several things revealed by the pandemic that many CEOs may not have wanted to examine, let alone talk about.

First, consider that many CEOs are highly uncomfortable with uncertainty and tend to want to project an image of sureness, strength, and confidence in the face of an unstable environment.[6] CEOs who have steered their organizations through COVID have learned (on the fly) to get better at dealing with the unpredictable. Not many CEOs will publicly admit their mistakes, let alone courageously examine and talk about how to break the mold of the modern organization, reinventing it based on entirely new principles and practices.

And yet, this is not the first time that leaders have encountered an unknown future that produced a different modern business paradigm—most notably in the United States. John Whiteclay Chambers II's book *The Tyranny of Change: America in the Progressive Era* aptly captures this sentiment. As Chambers describes it, the industrialization of the nineteenth century did much more than transform the economy; it fundamentally altered the way organizations were designed and led. In other words, revolutionary forms of work predate the current era and reach back as far as the first and second industrial revolution—everything from means of production being exported to (or "appropriated" by) preindustrial nations to the rise of railroads that transformed the concept of speed and introduced the idea of complex, interlocking businesses. The lessons learned: make mistakes early and learn from them earlier. And don't be afraid to pioneer a new model of business for a new era.[7]

Second, consider that most CEOs have not wanted to examine or talk about the issues of structural, systemic inequality—at least until recently. COVID-19 has harshly exposed structural inequality. For example, people of color have suffered disproportionate health and economic impacts from the pandemic. Moreover, for many women, decades of progress in their financial gains were wiped out as they left the workforce to care for children at home, who were suddenly learning remotely. Consider the substantial educational rift between children whose families can afford Internet access, tutors, or private schools compared with those who cannot and therefore fall increasingly behind with prolonged school closures.

Again, we can use history as a guide to consider how disastrous events expose structural inequality. For example, the disastrously inadequate recovery response provided in Louisiana following Hurricane Katrina left poor people, especially people of color, without resources to fall back on: tens of thousands of African Americans left New Orleans and have never returned. In fact, almost every instance of natural disaster exposes the inequity of the societal structures that we have in place, especially in the United States.

Similarly, COVID-19 has revealed the extent to which our societies have largely ignored environmental, social, and governance (ESG) problems. And within each of those issues lies a fundamental crisis in equality, inclusion, and diversity. Although, as we've seen throughout this book, some governments and some companies have indeed acknowledged the deeply entrenched inequalities in our systems and institutions, the responses to the pandemic have largely been calibrated according to familiar crises. The problem is that the global pandemic was something new that demanded much more innovative solutions than we have seen.

Why this failure? Organizations, and many of their leaders, continue to use fear and avoidance of change as a typical management practice. On the whole, top management is still too short-term focused and not optimized to make progress, neither on ESG criteria nor EID issues. The unfortunate truth that today's CEOs must face: disruptive global events like COVID-19 have exposed just how short-sighted their organizations and leadership have been—and how uncomfortable leaders are with uncertainty. The call to action for CEOs today, then, is to strike the right balance between short- and long-term focus and make ESG part of the top management agenda. CEOs should embrace the unfortunate truth that disruptive global events like COVID-19 won't be the last unforeseen and uncontrollable events that expose organizational shortcomings; instead, they should lean into their discomfort with uncertainty and prepare for mastering change to build better organizations. Read on.

Rethinking What It Takes to Be a CEO in the Age of AI

Today's challenges require swift decision making on the part of CEOs. Their aim should be crafting better organizations built on agile but stable structures, processes, systems, and people. That means CEOs and their teams will need to use all of the digital tools at their disposal to gather the needed data—from every edge of the organization—to make such decisions. While there are no easy solutions, the seven vital organizational conditions, when present at various stages of a business's maturity, have important implications for the organization's success and offer a critical lever to help CEOs focus their change initiatives.

To understand exactly what must evolve, let's review a main point I have argued throughout this book: that in recent years, ideas about the relationship between organizational health and the business's agility and growth have progressed. Tending to the health of the organization is no longer a "nice to have" mandate from on high, unattached to quantified business value. Instead, it has evolved into something that both leaders and investors understand can genuinely help the business to scale and grow.

Yet, inherent in that truth is a contradiction that makes the path forward for CEOs less clear.

On the one hand, the thinking goes, given the uncertainty of the future, CEOs and top management should be engaged in scenario planning and modeling—not just to preserve business continuity but also to plan for multiple, simultaneous disruptive business environments. But on the other hand, scenario planning and modeling generally miss the mark when the top managers and investors charged with governing organizations are under duress. In other words, because most leaders are not at all comfortable with true worst-case scenarios, their fear prevents them from doing the needed work to expand their minds and brainstorm possible solutions.

Take the COVID-19 pandemic, for example. What we've seen is that many CEOs did not come close to foreseeing the consequences of that humanitarian and economic disaster. Instead, they viewed their enterprises through a very limited mindset—what futurist Bob Johansen describes as "rigid categorical thinking that freezes people and organizations in neatly defined boxes that often are inaccurate or obsolete."[8] This thinking is rooted mainly in the industrial, mechanized models of the past.

After the onset of the pandemic, I observed a number of CEOs hit major stumbling blocks as a result of harboring outdated mental models. Namely, many were unable to consider multiple points of view and realities simultaneously. While each point of view may have seemed logical when considered alone, when taken together, one or more of the viewpoints suddenly would appear as irrational. That phenomenon ultimately blinded some CEOs to a combination of potential futures that they in fact soon encountered and were thus unprepared to face.

Yet other CEOs managed to quickly integrate facts and viewpoints to address problems head-on. At the height of the pandemic, the biggest challenge in the New York hospital run by CEO Dr. Steven Corwin was having enough intensive-care beds. "We had to create ICUs out of operating rooms . . . ICUs out of conference areas." Then came the ventilator shortage. "Thanks to the ingenuity of our respiratory therapists, we were able to create ventilators out of anesthesia machines. We were able to split ventilators to be able to ventilate two patients simultaneously."[9]

Without doubt, the challenge for CEOs in the digital era will be to confront and resolve paradoxes that will appear with increasing regularity. This calls for their ability to balance issues that often seem at odds. When companies succeed or fail, CEOs typically receive praise or blame. It's understood that the strategic bets and decisions of the CEO and their direct reports can make or break a company. But today, given the rise of employee and multi-stakeholder activism, a company's fate—and its organizational health—extends far into the outer edges of the rank and file.

CEOs who are paying close attention know the importance of recognizing an organization's operating cadence. Approaches to transformation that don't respect a unit's or company's work rhythm are more likely to fail—employees feel change is being done to them rather than in partnership with them. However, change happens quickly when the process reflects the organization's natural learning and operating rhythms. In other words, CEOs of fast-moving or hypergrowth organizations don't organize or transform for success and then wait and do it again. Rather, they think in terms of working with the energy and culture of the organization, not against it.

Consider the insights of Zambian economist Dambisa Moyo, a member of several high-profile corporate boards. She believes it's possible for companies to grow in ways that are equitable while also being environmentally and socially nondestructive. "The manner in which we have created growth has been the problem," she said in an interview. "The reality is public policymakers have been using shortcuts to fuel growth, such as debt, such as a society that rewards capital more than it does labor, such as a lack of appreciation of the global picture. We are too focused on the short term, not just policymakers, businesses too."[10]

Timelines today are obsolete as soon as they are published, technology advances faster than we can document, and watchdog groups catch every misstep, intended or not. CEOs seeking to build resilient or agile organizations need their companies to be made more for speed and elasticity, not just efficiency. They need to be deeply self-aware of their circumstances, assess their organization's ability to take concerted action, stay in motion, and keep on high alert for change, while continuously adapting to the shifting market needs to execute current strategies.

Where do we go from here? Will the current trend toward designing organizations to scale and grow across a wide range of digital priorities pay off? (See the sidebar "Considerations for CEOs as They Cultivate Their Organizational Edge.") Will these efforts magnify the premium put on the CEO's ability to take decisive action amid the organizational shifts required in this digital context? Yet another factor to consider is that these days, decisions that were once

---

Considerations for CEOs as They Cultivate Their Organizational Edge

As CEOs seek to scale and fast-track growth and agility, they should consider the following key actions. They cover each of the seven elements of organizational health, in addition to ways to move forward with digital advances and the counsel of a chief performance officer.

- **Strategic direction.** Ensure that the way your organization generates its competitive advantage is based on the health of the enterprise overall, by making it integral to your business strategy rather than a functional sideline strategy.
- **Culture.** Make a public, ongoing commitment to shape and reshape the culture linked to creating value. Without this, change won't stick. It is about building

an adaptive mindset. Create opportunities for people to enact new, more collaborative ways of working.

- **Leadership.** Make sure the key leaders in your top management team, your board, and your investors understand that organizational health is an enterprise-wide priority.
  - o **Top management.** Link their incentives to performance on specific organizational-health metrics. Ideally, these should be set over a multiyear period to force a longer-term view.
  - o **Board directors.** Create board-level responsibility for organizational health, rather than trying to parcel it off as simply a management task.
  - o **Investors.** Balance the long-term view for the organization with near-term wins that can practically demonstrate the value creation strategies underway.
- **Talent.** Take stock of which workforces and workspaces make sense for the future of your business, whether they are remote or not. Be creative; new employment models and location strategies may need to be invented here to win the war for talent.
- **Organizational design.** Assume that agility and ESG/sustainability (and stakeholder capitalism more broadly) will be the norm in the decade ahead. Map out possible organizational designs against various environmental and economic scenarios to prepare for uncertainties.
- **Equity, inclusion, and diversity.** Translate your EID goals into quantifiable metrics that multiple stakeholders, including financial analysts, shareholders, activist groups, and regulators, can assess in their economic models, employer rankings, and SEC filings.
- **Well-being.** Assess how personally important well-being is for you and, more importantly, your workforce.

(*continued*)

> Stakeholders will recognize committed change aimed at employee engagement versus vague platitudes.
> - **Unleash org health with AI.** Get the org health metrics right by setting targets, ensuring commitment, and focusing your top management team on meeting those. Invest in emerging technologies that can elevate the process of measuring and improving org health. Develop algorithms that map out possible outcomes to help the organization adapt rapidly.
> - **Chief performance officers.** Seek the counsel of trusted advisors who can offer valuable insight into the health of the organization. The CPO can map out strategy execution by helping to align your own role and responsibilities as CEO with those of the company's key players.

made in the hallways of corporate centers now are often carried out at a distance, asynchronously, or through a virtual meeting space. Such elements and questions surrounding today's business landscape affect companies' ability to launch fundamental transformation.

All of which is to say that today even the most successful methods and frameworks that have historically been used to enable transformational change are proving inadequate. Speed, magnitude, and the complexities of digital AI-first enterprises change everything. A new capability is needed: change fluency.[11]

Change Fluency: How CEOs Master Growth and Agility for Today and Tomorrow

Change fluency is a management philosophy for orchestrating a purpose-infused strategy, design of a healthy organization, and change in service of sustainable effectiveness—achieving consistent, above-average economic and ESG outcomes. Born out of a collaboration between Chris Worley and me at Pepperdine and USC's Center for Effective Organizations, the idea of change fluency developed as we launched and took part in Google's Change and Design Forum. Using a systematic approach, we looked specifically at Google's agility before and during the pandemic, reviewing tools, cases, processes, and other business tactics used by Google to change and grow over time.

The concept of change fluency—which Worley and I define as the process organizations must integrate to become agile—builds on organization agility research and employs the metaphor of language fluency. To be fluent implies mastery of a variety of skills but not native capability. Similar to language fluency, change fluency is practiced in steps. In the context of becoming a change-fluent CEO, it means that building fluency isn't achieved in a vacuum but instead takes practice in the flow of work. Fluency needs immersion and requires engagement with others and real-world experiences to learn from. In other words, CEOs can learn from a mode of deliberation that employs thought exercises to focus ideas and actions better and to learn from those actions once taken. The goal is to design change-fluent organizations and, by extension, change-fluent top management teams, based on the shift from "single-loop learning"—a term coined by Chris Argyris and Donald Schön that means actions taken purely in response to unquestioned assumptions—to "double-loop learning"—what Argyris and Schön define as the ability to reframe questions and better understand the underlying variables as part of making decisions.[12]

All of which is to say that the concept of change fluency can be applied quite well to our thinking about organizational health. Today's CEOs increasingly recognize that traditional models of competitiveness no longer apply. They must string together a series of momentary advantages that create business value over time. The implication: they must master the essentials of leading and managing change, build capacity to apply it, and embed a learning mindset. By combining extraordinary clarity of purpose with the ability to excite and engage large groups of people, change-fluent CEOs will be better able to steer enterprise transformation (and, for some, recovery). They can evolve their business and operating models to align more with outcomes that weigh value over volume, effectiveness over efficiency. To achieve this, change-fluent CEOs model three core operating principles:

- **They acknowledge discontinuity.** They understand, better than most, that the job of leading organizations in the past was much easier than today, let alone in the foreseeable future. Technological disruption, changing user demands, competitive shifts, unexpected events like the pandemic, and geopolitical upheaval will not stop. Such things will require the occasional large-scale transformation as well as multiple, continuous, and orchestrated changes. Within such a context, a strategic advantage is fleeting; any current strategy has a limited shelf life. Change-fluent CEOs know this lesson well and, because of it, maintain a strong predisposition toward the future and the capacity to lead through constant and complex ambiguity and respond to the next discontinuity.
- **They confront the undiscussable.** In today's climate, "undiscussables" more often than not begin with the facts around racial inequity, social justice, and the reforms and/ or radical transformations required to shift from outdated mindsets and structures to more equitable and inclusive workplaces for all. Change-fluent CEOs recognize that to carry a license to do business means that they no longer can afford to ignore what makes them uncomfortable. They are attuned to their emotional self-awareness and often challenge the safe and long-held assumptions that have driven their organizational decisions, moving away from policies, management practices, and systems that reward single-minded, short-term ways of working. They design organizations that are dynamic, adaptive, and efficient in delivering on current customer and social demands and organizational priorities needed for long-term success.

- **They cultivate stakeholder trust.** In modern society, what is considered truth can become a moving target. But today's CEOs are learning the hard lesson that stakeholder trust can either accelerate their strategy or kill it. Just consider the collapse of Ozy Media, a digital media company that came under fire for its business practices; it had investors pull out and all but one board member quit. The solution is to confront the tough issues head-on, with integrity and transparency. That means when it comes to the organization's responsibilities to the environment, society, and government, CEOs must learn to empower and build trust by, paradoxically, letting go of power and relying on and trusting the front line. As companies scale and grow in a digital context, creating a culture founded on the highest standards of ethics and responsibility—one that goes far beyond mere compliance on ESG issues—will be paramount. Only then can CEOs hope to establish elevated levels of organizational health to deliver the kinds of outcomes that balance ethics with business value. Achieving such a balance will be among the defining issues of the coming decade.

As with language fluency, change fluency becomes most meaningful and apparent as an almost unconscious mindset for the CEO. Armed with better signals to align the enterprise around a clear, strategic direction and operating model, CEOs can strategically coordinate hubs that create business value and provide meaningful work. They can practice the unique leadership behaviors necessary to navigate a difficult change journey and build digital organizations that can scale and grow with integrity: an attribute that sets the stage for most, if not all, the critical judgment calls.

Consider advice given by former Steelcase chairman Bob Pew to his successor, Jim Hackett, when he took over as the company's new CEO: "If you want to lead others, you've got to have their trust, and you can't have their trust without integrity." In short, change-fluent CEOs are responsible stewards who engage their people forthrightly, especially around change. They are adept at applying sensing routines and maintaining vigilant attention to market shifts and trends, enabling them to anticipate and prepare for disruption, design and adjust their operations to changing conditions, and monitor how the organization learns—all at the same time. To be a CEO in an AI-first business environment, you need to sense and prepare for what might be ahead—the ability to continuously shift your focus back and forth from near-term needs to preparing for multiple, strategic futures. In practice, change-fluent CEOs:

- Shape their enterprise to embrace a common language for change, strategy, and design
- Commit to a learning journey and know how the organization learns
- Employ a zero-base mindset to shape fast and agile structures, systems, and processes
- Integrate ESG goals into the business and operating model

Importantly, a change-fluent CEO has the humility to learn continually. That way, they will be much more likely to tackle hurdles head-on compared with those who are convinced that they have the least to learn. Change fluency has to be intuitive, not just to the CEO but to the scores of leaders, managers, and employees spread throughout the organization. And because change-fluent CEOs are plugged into and aware of the current environment, they are therefore much more likely to ride out an environmental jolt—not because they can react quickly, but because they are prepared to act quickly, have the resilience to bounce back, and have the foresight to see organizational health as a means to outmaneuver competitors.

Ultimately, the most successful CEOs will be those who own and engage in the process of learning a new language for change. Change-articulate CEOs know when to collaborate, coordinate, or cooperate, as a convener of productive conversations to understand different stakeholder needs and wants, and then organize the collective for action.

Many pundits today have pronounced our post-pandemic business environment the "new normal." But a more sobering reality is that nothing will ever be normal again. Operating in today's business environment is far better characterized as the "never normal." Today, effective CEO leadership calls for a deeper comprehension of the factors that will shape the organization, the workforce, and the workplace far into the future. It requires heightened self-awareness to make frequent, calibrated adjustments to an organization's business and operating model. And it demands the conviction to prioritize ethics and responsibility—as well as the character to stay the course so that the vision and enthusiasm of transforming into an AI-first enterprise can be fully realized in the minds, hearts, and souls of everyone. Only by embedding the seven essentials of organizational health deeply into the organization's fabric, to its very edges, can CEOs capture the energy and potential of their people to make the AI-first enterprise a reality.

Checklist for Agenda Setting

To successfully guide their organizations to scale, grow, and realize their potential, tomorrow's CEOs will have to adopt seven mindset shifts to ensure the ongoing health of the business and lead the digital, AI-first enterprise effectively:

- Prioritize purpose over profit
- Create a shared but adaptive organizational identity
- Employ agile and human-centric ways of leading
- Unlock the full potential of the organization's talent
- Design operating models for agility and sustainability
- Adopt a bias for radical transparency and belonging
- Embrace well-being as a vital sign of the organization's health

Conclusion

Looking Back, Looking Ahead

Business leaders everywhere understand that it's one thing to start up an organization and another thing entirely to scale it to achieve its true potential. With growth, complications as well as innovations multiply, sometimes in equal measure. This book has looked at what can be learned about building better organizations from publicly listed tech companies like Alphabet and Amazon, nondigital native companies such as Unilever and Patagonia, and private companies across the portfolios of firms like the Carlyle Group and Vista Equity Partners. What the leaders at those companies found is that the organization's health often determines its success or failure. By applying a digital lens, this book revisits classic organizational topics that, individually and in combination, have demonstrated their value in elevating the health of an organization and its economic value.

Building better organizations is not a sideline project or initiative across top management's agenda. Building better organizations *is* the agenda. The conditions for the health and effectiveness of the organization, the overall advances in digital technologies leveraging AI, and the capital and investor mindset supporting those endeavors all play fundamental roles in how to get from good to better. There is no blueprint, but the three building blocks explored in this book offer wisdom that's at once simple and profound: Start with a better foundation. Grow into a better organization. And lead to be a better organization still.

So, where might you go from here? At its core, the book's perspectives point to at least three possibilities.

First, set an ambitious direction and stick with it. For companies to achieve their full potential, they need to claim health as a critical organizational asset and use artificial intelligence to mine and leverage the breadth of insight available inside and outside businesses—all with the guidance of the kind of investor mindset found most often in VC-backed or PE-owned companies.

Second, be mindful of the level of energy and dedication required to build a better organization. Such an ambition forces leaders to design the conditions that help the organization run effectively and adjust as it scales. No leader can do that alone. But when the board, investors, and top management team work together to adopt a more holistic view, they will find they can balance a healthy risk tolerance with an investor mindset to create the conditions that enable organizations to achieve their full potential.

Third, recognize that mastering change requires practice. This book props up the importance of speed and acceleration in companies seeking to scale and grow. It also emphasizes the importance of an organization's change fluency as a metaphor to guide the growth of a company's agility practices, suggesting that just as with language fluency, learning to master change takes practice, and so does the ability to look beyond the near-term horizon.

We are on the edge of a paradigm shift in the way businesses operate, and the way organizations work must likewise shift if they hope to fuel growth into the future. Meanwhile, leaders across public and private markets who aren't historically known for focusing on a business's "soft" side—people and organizational matters—will need to try on perspectives they might not have tried before. They will need to take actions that build the organization's health to fuel growth and lead in the digital era. By no means is this done in isolation. It requires close collaboration among CEOs, chief performance officers, and board members, including the investors who hold board seats, to map out and chart a course.

Ideally, this book will inspire more research about organizational health in digital, AI-first organizations. Above all, my fervent hope is that the study and discussion of this book will continue to help leaders identify their company's most critical organizational levers, take stock of them, and make them more effective from start to finish as they scale to create more valuable companies in a new era of business that is already with us: the era of AI.

Notes

Preface

1. Aran Ali, "The Soaring Value of Intangible Assets in the S&P 500," *Visual Capitalist*, November 12, 2020, https://www.visualcapitalist.com/the-soaring-value-of-intangible -assets-in-the-sp-500/. Other studies reveal that the value of intangible assets can now comprise an estimated 52 percent of a company's value. Global Intangible Finance Tracker (GIFT) 2018, Brand Finance, October 2018, https://brandfinance.com /knowledge-centre/market-research/global-intangible-finance-tracker-gift-2018/.

Introduction

1. CBInsights study cited in Denise Lee Yohn, "Why Startups Fail," *Forbes*, May 1, 2019, https://www.forbes.com/sites/deniselyohn/2019/05/01/why-start-ups-fail/. See also Noam Wasserman, *The Founder's Dilemmas: Anticipating and Avoiding the Pitfalls That Can Sink a Startup* (Princeton, NJ: Princeton University Press, 2012).

2. Noa Dagan, Lee Baz-Sanchez, and Brooke Weddle, "Thriving during a Pandemic: What Moves the Needle on Organizational Health," *McKinsey Quarterly* blog, July 30, 2020.

3. Robert J. Thomas, Claudy Jules, and Joshua Bellin, "Leaders Coaching Leaders: Cascading Leadership Development through the Organization," in *Experience-Driven Leader Development*, ed. Cynthia D. McCauley, D. Scott DeRue, Paul R. Yost, and Sylvester Taylor (San Francisco: Wiley, 2014).

4. Robert J. Thomas, Claudy Jules, and David Light, "Making Leadership Development Stick," *Organizational Dynamics* 1, no. 41 (2012): 72–77.

5. Aaron De Smet, Bill Schaninger, and Matthew Smith, "The Hidden Value of Organizational Health—and How to Capture It," *McKinsey Quarterly*, April 1, 2014; Chris Gagnon, Elizabeth John, and Rob Theunissen, "Organizational Health:

A Fast Track to Performance Improvement," *McKinsey Quarterly*, September 7, 2017, https://www.mckinsey.com/business-functions/organization/our-insights/organi zational-health-a-fast-track-to-performance-improvement. This is based on ten years of monitoring the health of more than 1,500 companies across 100 countries, and over 4 million aggregated views of employees and managers.

6. Noa Dagan, Lee Baz-Sanchez, and Brooke Weddle, "Thriving during a Pandemic: What Moves the Needle on Organizational Health," *McKinsey Quarterly* blog, July 30, 2020.

7. Wouter Aghina, Aaron De Smet, and Kirsten Weerda, "Agility: It Rhymes with Stability," *McKinsey Quarterly*, December 1, 2015.

8. Rita Gunter McGrath, *The End of Competitive Advantage: How to Keep Your Strategy Moving as Fast as Your Business* (Boston: Harvard Business Review Press, 2013).

9. Scott A. Scanlon, Dale M. Zupsansky, and Stephen Sawicki, "Achieving Diversity in Private Equity," Hunt Scanlon Media, February 5, 2021, https://huntscanlon .com/achieving-diversity-in-private-equity/.

10. Scanlon, Zupsansky, and Sawicki, "Achieving Diversity in Private Equity."

11. Kevin Kelly, *The Inevitable: Understanding the 12 Technological Forces That Will Shape Our Future* (New York: Viking, 2016).

12. Tim Fountaine, Brian McCarthy, and Tamim Saleh, "Building the AI-Powered Organization," *Harvard Business Review* (July–August 2019), https://hbr.org/2019/07 /building-the-ai-powered-organization.

13. As cited in Tom Evans et al., "Is Artificial Intelligence Set to Transform Private Equity Dealmaking?" Latham and Watkins LLP, June 24, 2019, https://www.latham .london/2019/06/is-artificial-intelligence-set-to-transform-private-equity-dealmaking/.

14. Steve Ranger, "Microsoft CEO Satya Nadella: The Whole World Is Now a Computer," *ZDNet*, May 22, 2018, https://www.zdnet.com/article/microsoft-ceo -nadella-the-whole-world-is-now-a-computer/.

15. Marco Insanti and Karim Ikhani, *Competing in the Age of AI: Strategy and Leadership When Algorithms and Networks Run the World* (Boston: Harvard Business Review Press, 2020).

16. Fountaine, McCarthy, and Saleh, "Building the AI-Powered Organization."

17. Sandra Sucher and Shalene Gupta, *The Power of Trust: How Companies Build It, Lose It, Regain It* (New York: PublicAffairs, 2021); Rob Cross, Amy Edmondson, and Wendy Murphy, "A Noble Purpose Alone Won't Transform Your Company," *MIT Sloan Management Review*, December 2019; Robert Hurley, "Trust Me," *Wall Street Journal*, October 24, 2011, https://www.wsj.com/articles/SB1000142405297020 4138204576603031565507232.

18. Christopher Handscomb et al., "An Operating Model for the Next Normal: Lessons from Agile Organizations in the Crisis," McKinsey, June 2020, https://www .mckinsey.com/business-functions/organization/our-insights/an-operating-model-for -the-next-normal-lessons-from-agile-organizations-in-the-crisis.

19. Warren Bennis, "Towards a 'Truly' Scientific Management: The Concept of Organization Health," *General Systems Yearbook* 7 (1962): 269–282.

20. Marcia Blenko, Michael Mankins, and Paul Rogers, *Decide and Deliver: Five Steps to Breakthrough Performance in Your Organization* (Boston: Harvard Business Review Press, 2010); Scott Keller and Colin Price, *Beyond Performance: How Great Organizations Build Ultimate Competitive Advantage* (Hoboken, NJ: Wiley, 2011); Colin Price and Sharon Toye, *Accelerating Performance: How Organizations Can Mobilize, Execute, and Transform with Agility* (Hoboken, NJ: Wiley, 2017); Scott Keller and Bill Schaninger, *Beyond Performance 2.0* (Hoboken, NJ: Wiley, 2019); Patrick Lencioni, *The Advantage: Why Organizational Health Trumps Everything Else in Business* (San Francisco: Jossey-Bass, 2012).

21. Bryce Klempner, Bill Schaninger, and Elizabeth Skovira, "Why Healthy Institutional Investors Outperform," McKinsey, September 2, 2020, https://www.mckinsey.com/industries/private-equity-and-principal-investors/our-insights/why-healthy-institutional-investors-outperform.

Chapter 1

1. See Andrew Ross Sorkin and Nikole Hannah-Jones, "Race and the Role of Business," *New York Times*, Aug 23, 2020; and "6 Brands Keeping Their Promises to Become More Diverse and Inclusive," YPulse, February 9, 2021, https://www.ypulse.com/article/2021/02/09/6-brands-keeping-their-promises-to-become-more-diverse-inclusive/.

2. Dana Givens, "Netflix Doubles Its Black Workforce in New Inclusion and Diversity Report," Black Enterprise, January 15, 2021, https://www.blackenterprise.com/netflix-doubles-its-black-workforce-in-new-inclusion-and-diversity-report/.

3. YPulse, "6 Brands Keeping Their Promises."

4. Peter Eavis, "Why Not Treat Diversity Like a Profit?" *New York Times*, July 15, 2020.

5. Jeffrey Pfeffer, *The Human Equation: Building Profits by Putting People First* (Boston: Harvard Business Review Press, 1998).

6. James Allen, "The Changing Nature of Strategy: Reflections on Thirty Years," Bain and Company, Founder's Mentality Blog, February 7, 2019, https://www.bain.com/insights/the-changing-nature-of-strategy-reflections-on-thirty-years-fm-blog/.

7. Kip Krumwiede, Raef Lawson, and Lucy Luo, "Haier's Win-Win Value Added Approach," *Strategic Finance*, February 1, 2019, https://sfmagazine.com/post-entry/february-2019-haiers-win-win-value-added-approach/.

8. David Gelles and David Yaffe-Bellany, "Shareholder Value Is No Longer Everything, Top C.E.O.s Say," *New York Times*, August 19, 2019. This article describes how Business Roundtable CEOs, including companies such as Apple and JPMorgan Chase, argue that companies must also invest in employees and deliver value to customers, https://www.nytimes.com/2019/08/19/business/business-roundtable-ceos-corporations.html.

9. Alan Murray and David Meyer, "The Pandemic Widens Rifts; Businesses Need to Help Heal Them," *Fortune*, May 11, 2020.

10. 2015 Nielsen Global Corporate Sustainability Report, https://nielseniq.com /global/en/insights/analysis/2015/the-sustainability-imperative-2/.

11. According to Gallup's 2016 report *How Millennials Want to Work and Live*, millennials are an exceptionally purpose-driven generation.

12. Adele Peters, "Most Millennials Would Take a Pay Cut to Work at an Environmentally Responsible Company," *Fast Company*, February 14, 2019, https://www .fastcompany.com/90306556/most-millennials-would-take-a-pay-cut-to-work-at-a -sustainable-company.

13. Claudine Gartenberg, Andrea Prat, and George Serafeim, "Corporate Purpose and Financial Performance," Harvard Business School Working Paper, No. 17-023, September 2016, http://nrs.harvard.edu/urn-3:HUL.InstRepos:30903237.

14. "Two researchers, Millward Brown and Jim Stengel, developed a list of the world's 50 fastest-growing brands (FedEx, Coca-Cola, and Starbucks, for example) based on 10 years of empirical research involving 50,000 companies. Known as the Stengel 50, it was found that these purpose-driven companies saw 400 percent more returns on the stock market than the S&P 500." Jen Lim, "A Study Says Your Company's 'Purpose' Can Increase Returns by 400 Percent," *Inc.*, https://www.inc.com /jenn-lim/a-study-says-your-companys-purpose-can-increase-returns-by-400 -percent-heres-how-to-create-one-that-works.html.

15. Cross, Edmondson, and Murphy, "A Noble Purpose Alone Won't Transform Your Company."

16. Dan Schawbel, "Jerry Stritzke: How He Leads REI, a Purpose-Driven Organization," *Forbes*, April 12, 2017, https://www.forbes.com/sites/danschawbel/2017/04/12 /jerry-stritzke-how-he-made-rei-a-purpose-driven-organization/#6ed67d101fac.

17. Arne Gast et al., "Purpose: Shifting from Why to How," *McKinsey Quarterly*, April 22, 2020, https://www.mckinsey.com/business-functions/organization/our-insights /purpose-shifting-from-why-to-how.

18. Personal communication, Joe Bonito, SVP, Bank of America, March 7, 2021.

19. Larry Fink, "A Sense of Purpose," January 17, 2018, https://corpgov.law .harvard.edu/2018/01/17/a-sense-of-purpose/.

20. Eric Leininger and Andrea Brimmer, "When Building Your Brand, First Find Your Purpose," April 3, 2020, https://insight.kellogg.northwestern.edu/article/when -building-your-brand-first-find-your-purpose. A conversation with the CMO of online bank Ally about staying committed to your company's purpose as the organization grows.

21. Case adapted from personal communication with Robert J. Thomas, one of the lead architects for UL2020's Purpose to Impact leadership development program, May 2021; Milan Samani and Robert J. Thomas, "Your Leadership Development

Program Needs an Overhaul," *Harvard Business Review*, December 5, 2016; Nick Craig, *Leading from Purpose* (New York: Hachette, 2018).

22. Donald Sull, Stefano Turconi, and Charles Sull, "When It Comes to Culture, Does Your Company Walk the Talk?" *MIT Sloan Management Review*, July 21, 2020, https://sloanreview.mit.edu/article/when-it-comes-to-culture-does-your-company -walk-the-talk/.

23. Case adapted from personal communication with Thomas; Samani and Thomas, "Your Leadership Development Program"; and Craig, *Leading from Purpose*.

24. Carol A. Masser, "Unilever CEO Sees Purpose-Led Businesses Only Gaining Relevance," *Bloomberg Businessweek*, May 11, 2020.

25. Sull, Turconi, and Sull, "When It Comes to Culture."

26. Joe Devanesan, "WeChat—How Open, Agile Culture Built the World's First Superapp," *Techwire Asia*, July 16, 2020, https://techwireasia.com/2020/07/wechat -how-open-agile-culture-built-the-worlds-first-superapp/.

27. Rob Wile, "A Venture Capital Firm Just Named an Algorithm to Its Board of Directors—Here's What It Actually Does," Insider, May 13, 2014, https://www .businessinsider.com/vital-named-to-board-2014-5.

28. Akkinapally Yugendhar and Syed Mahamood Ali, "Evaluation of Implement-ing Holacracy: A Comprehensive Study on Zappos," *International Journal of Engi-neering and Management Research* 7, no. 5 (September–October 2017): 163–171, https://www.ijemr.net/DOC/EvaluationOfImplementingHolacracyAComprehensive StudyOnZappos.pdf.

Chapter 2

1. Edgar Schein, *Organizational Culture and Leadership* (San Francisco: Jossey-Bass, 1985). Schein argues that organizational culture is essentially "the accumulated shared learning of a given group" and "its pattern of shared, taken-for-granted basic assumptions."

2. *2019 Governance Outlook: Projections on Emerging Board Matters*, a publication of the National Association of Corporate Directors and Partners.

3. "Update on Talent Conversations in Earnings Calls in 2017," *Investor Talent Monitor*, CEB Corporate Leadership Council.

4. Steve Klemash, Bridget M. Neill, and Jamie C. Smith, "How and Why Human Capital Disclosures Are Evolving," EY Center for Board Matters, Novem-ber 15, 2019, https://corpgov.law.harvard.edu/2019/11/15/how-and-why-human-capital -disclosures-are-evolving/#1.

5. "Update on Talent Conversations."

6. "How to Drive a Digital Transformation: Culture Is Key," BCG, https://www .bcg.com/capabilities/digital-technology-data/digital-transformation/how-to-drive -digital-culture (accessed December 2021).

7. Fons Wijnhoven, "Acquiring Organizational Learning Norms: A Contingency Approach for Understanding Deutero Learning," *Management Learning* 32, no. 2 (2001): 181–200.

8. John P. Kotter and James L. Heskett, *Corporate Culture and Performance* (New York: Free Press, 1992).

9. Eric Loveday, "How and Why the BMW Project i Team Grew from 7 Individuals in 2007 to Several Hundred Today," *InsideEVs*, May 31, 2013, https://insideevs .com/news/317964/how-and-why-the-bmw-project-i-team-grew-from-7-individuals -in-2007-to-several-hundred-today/; "BMW i's Ulrich Kranz Talks about How BMW i Started," Electric BMW i3 blog, May 31, 2013, http://bmwi3.blogspot.com /2013/05/bmw-is-ulrich-kranz-talks-about-how-bmw.html; Claire Ballentine and Giles Turner, "Faraday Makes a High-Profile Hire from BMW to Get the FF 91 on the Road," Bloomberg, July 17, 2017, https://www.bloomberg.com/news/articles/2017-07 -17/bmw-lifer-brings-steady-hand-to-shaky-electric-car-maker-faraday.

10. Claudine Ogilvie, CIO Jetstar, interviewed by Byron Connolly, Australian Editor, CIO, April 19, 2017, https://www.cio.com/article/206424/interview-claudine-ogilvie-cio -jetstar.html.

11. J. R. Lowry, interviewed by Renee Boucher Ferguson, "A New, Analytics-Based Era of Banking Dawns at State Street," *MIT Sloan Management Review*, May 27, 2014.

12. Douglas Ready et al., "The New Leadership Playbook for the Digital Age," *MIT Sloan School of Management Review*, January 21, 2020.

13. Schein, *Organizational Culture and Leadership*, 2.

14. "How to Cope with Middle Age: Google Has Outgrown Its Corporate Culture," *Economist*, July 30, 2020.

15. "HR4.0: Shaping People Strategies in the Fourth Industrial Revolution," World Economic Forum, 2019.

16. Adapted from Larry Greiner, "Evolution and Revolution as Organizations Grow," *Harvard Business Review* (May–June 1998).

17. General Stanley McChrystal, with Tantum Collins, David Silverman, and Chris Fussell, *Team of Teams: New Rules of Engagement for a Complex World* (New York: Portfolio/Penguin, 2015).

18. "The Story of One of the Most Memorable Marketing Blunders Ever: The History of New Coke," Coca-Cola, https://www.coca-colacompany.com/company /history/the-story-of-one-of-the-most-memorable-marketing-blunders-ever.

19. Keller and Schaninger, *Beyond Performance 2.0.*

Chapter 3

1. Sandy Ogg, *Move: The CEO's Playbook for Capturing Value* (Charleston, SC: Advantage Media Group).

2. Noel M. Tichy and Warren G. Bennis, *Judgment: How Winning Leaders Make Great Calls* (New York: Portfolio/Penguin, 2007).

3. Sonali Basak, "Carlyle Group CEO Lee on Creating Inclusive Culture," Bloomberg, September 23, 2020, https://www.bloomberg.com/news/videos/2020-09 -23/carlyle-group-ceo-lee-on-creating-inclusive-culture-video.

4. Rosalind Picard, *Affective Computing* (Cambridge, MA: MIT Press, 1997).

5. Claudy Jules, Robert J. Thomas, and Nandani Lynton, "Leadership Ensembles Disrupt Traditional Management," *Talent Management*, March 2014; Robert J. Thomas, Joshua Bellin, Claudy Jules, and Nandani Lynton, "How Global Companies Are Really Led," *Leader to Leader* 71 (Winter 2014): 38–44; Robert J. Thomas, Joshua Bellin, Claudy Jules, and Nandani Lynton, "Global Leadership Teams: Diagnosing Three Essential Qualities," *Strategy & Leadership* 40, no. 3 (2012): 25–29.

6. Howard Gardner, *Five Minds for the Future* (Boston: Harvard Business Review Press, 2009).

7. Gardner, *Five Minds for the Future.*

8. Thomas W. Malone, *Superminds: The Surprising Power of People and Computers Thinking Together* (New York: Little, Brown, 2018).

9. Ben Horowitz, *The Hard Thing about Hard Things: Building a Business When There Are No Easy Answers* (New York: HarperCollins, 2014). The cofounder of Andreessen Horowitz and one of Silicon Valley's most respected and experienced entrepreneurs offers essential advice on building and running a startup—practical wisdom for managing the toughest problems business school doesn't cover.

10. Douglas A. Ready, Carol Cohen, David Kiron, and Benjamin Pring, "The New Leadership Playbook for the Digital Age: Reimagining What It Takes to Lead," *MIT Sloan Management Review*, January 21, 2020; Robert J. Thomas, "Leading the Digital Enterprise," Accenture Report, 2016.

11. Richard E. Boyatzis, "A Behavioral Approach to Emotional Intelligence," *Journal of Management Development* 28 (2009): 749–770, doi: 10.1108/02621710910987647. Behavioral EI was defined as follows: "(a) an emotional intelligence competency is an ability to recognize, understand, and use emotional information about oneself that leads to or causes effective or superior performance; and (b) a social intelligence competency is the ability to recognize, understand and use emotional information about others that leads to or causes effective or superior performance."

Chapter 4

1. See, for example, "Winning with Your Talent-Management Strategy," McKinsey, August 7, 2018; and "The Financial Impact of a Positive Employee Experience," IBM Smarter Workforce Institute and Workhuman Analytics and Research Institute, 2018.

2. "Discussing Corporate Culture with the Street," Gartner, 2019, https://www .gartner.com/en/human-resources/trends/discussing-corporate-culture-with-the -street.

3. Eva Sage-Gavin, Yaarit Silverstone, and Barbara Spitzer, "Modern Boards," Accenture, October 20, 2020.

4. Bryce Klempner, Bill Schaninger, and Elizabeth Skovira, "Why Healthy Institutional Investors Outperform," McKinsey & Company, 2020. Research reveals that across all twenty-three institutions surveyed, there were statistically significant positive correlations between investment returns and talent acquisition, talent development, and use of outsourced expertise. In that same study, talent development proved to be a more significant contributor to organizational health than financial incentives, suggesting that a focus on talent management may be at least as important as compensation, if not more so.

5. Klempner, Schaninger, and Skovira, "Why Healthy Institutional Investors Outperform."

6. Reid Hoffman, Ben Casnocha, and Chris Yeh, "Tours of Duty: The New Employer-Employee Compact," *Harvard Business Review* (June 2013), https://hbr.org /2013/06/tours-of-duty-the-new-employer-employee-compact.

7. Sandy Ogg, "Understand the Value Agenda, Part 1," CEO.works, September 19, 2018, https://www.ceoworks.com/blog/connecting-talent-to-value.

8. Mike Barriere, Miriam Owens, and Sarah Pobereskin, "Linking Talent to Value," McKinsey, April 12, 2018.

9. Will Douglas Heaven, "This Startup Is Using AI to Give Workers a 'Productivity Score,'" *MIT Technology Review*, June 4, 2020, https://www.technologyreview.com /2020/06/04/1002671/startup-ai-workers-productivity-score-bias-machine-learning -business-covid/.

10. "Investigation of Competition in Digital Markets," House Subcommittee on Antitrust, Commercial, and Administrative Law, 2020, https://judiciary.house.gov /uploadedfiles/competition_in_digital_markets.pdf; Brian Fung, "Congress' Big Tech Investigation Finds Companies Wield 'Monopoly Power,'" CNN Business, October 6, 2020, https://www.cnn.com/2020/10/06/tech/congress-big-tech-antitrust -report/.

11. Cecilia Kang and David McCabe, "House Lawmakers Condemn Big Tech's 'Monopoly Power' and Urge Their Breakups," *New York Times*, October 6, 2020.

12. Julian Birkinshaw, "Kraft Heinz vs. Unilever: A Contest Between Two Models of Capitalism," *Forbes*, February 20, 2017, https://www.forbes.com/sites /lbsbusinessstrategyreview/2017/02/20/kraft-heinz-versus-unilever-a-contest -between-two-models-of-capitalism/.

13. Gary Leff, "Delta CEO Calls 17,000 Departing Employees 'Heroes,'" View from the Wing, July 30, 2020, https://viewfromthewing.com/delta-ceo-calls-17000 -departing-employees-heroes/.

14. Tom Spiggle, "What Does a Worker Want? What the Labor Shortage Really Tells Us," *Forbes,* July 8, 2021, https://www.forbes.com/sites/tomspiggle/2021/07/08 /what-does-a-worker-want-what-the-labor-shortage-really-tells-us/.

15. Cade Metz, "AI Gains, but It Still Needs People," *New York Times*, September 16, 2021.

16. Tomas Chamorro-Premuzic, Michael Wade, and Jennifer Jordan, "As AI Makes More Decisions, the Nature of Leadership Will Change," *Harvard Business Review*, January 22, 2018.

17. Patricia A. Gallagan, "GM's Internal Disruption Engine," ATD, December 17, 2018, https://www.td.org/magazines/ctdo-magazine/gms-internal-disruption-engine; Michael J. Arena, *Adaptive Space: How GM and Other Companies Are Positively Disrupting Themselves and Transforming into Agile Organizations* (New York: McGraw-Hill, 2018).

18. Sheila Simsarian Webber et al., "Team Challenges: Is Artificial Intelligence the Solution?" *Business Horizons* 62, no. 6 (September 2019).

19. H. James Wilson and Paul R. Daugherty, "Collaborative Intelligence: Humans and AI Are Joining Forces," *Harvard Business Review* (July–August 2018), https://hbr.org/2018/07/collaborative-intelligence-humans-and-ai-are-joining-forces.

20. Basak, "Carlyle Group CEO Lee."

21. Robyn Reilly, "5 Ways to Improve Employee Engagement Now," Gallup, January 7, 2014. https://www.gallup.com/workplace/231581/five-ways-improve-employee-engagement.aspx.

22. Jazmine Hughes, "The Young and the Restless," *New York Times Magazine*, February 23, 2020, 26.

23. Reilly, "5 Ways to Improve Employee Engagement Now."

Chapter 5

1. Mary Baker, "Nine Future of Work Trends Post-Covid-19," webinar with Brian Kropp, Gartner, April 29, 2020, https://www.gartner.com/smarterwithgartner/9-future-of-work-trends-post-covid-19.

2. Alfred D. Chandler Jr., *Strategy and Structure: Chapters in the History of American Enterprise* (Boston: MIT Press, 1962).

3. Aaron De Smet et al., "Ready, Set, Go: Reinventing the Organization for Speed in the Post-COVID-19 Era," McKinsey, June 25, 2020.

4. This sidebar draws from an article I coauthored with Christopher G. Worley that addresses the role of agility in an AI-first organization and the role leaders can play in creating and building a change-fluent company. The article is tentatively titled "Building the Change Fluent Organization and Why It Matters."

5. Christopher G. Worley, Thomas Williams, and Edward E. Lawler III, *The Agility Factor* (San Francisco: Jossey-Bass, 2014).

6. Gast et al., "Purpose: Shifting from Why to How."

7. Peter Weill, MIT CIO Summit, MIT Sloan School of Management's Center for Information Systems Research, 2006; Peter Weill, "IT Portfolio Management and IT

Savvy—Rethinking IT Investments as a Portfolio," MIT Sloan School of Management, Center for Information Systems Research, Summer Session, June 14, 2007. Research was conducted by MIT via the SeeIT/CISR survey of firms, which were listed on U.S. stock exchanges.

8. Fabrice Roghé et al., "Boosting Performance through Org Design," BCG, July 17, 2017, https://www.bcg.com/publications/2017/people-boosting-performance-through-organization-design.

9. Stephen Heidari-Robinson and Suzanne Heywood, "Getting Reorgs Right: A Practical Guide to a Misunderstood—and Often Mismanaged—Process," *Harvard Business Review* (November 2016).

10. Leslie Carroll and John Hazan, "If Not Now, When?" Bain, September 21, 2020; Will Gosling, Michela Coppola, and Kate McCarthy, "May the Workforce Be with You," Deloitte, 2020.

11. Alan Murray and David Meyer, "The Pandemic Widens Rifts; Businesses Need to Help Heal Them," *Fortune*, May 11, 2020.

12. Christopher G. Worley and Claudy Jules, "COVID-19's Uncomfortable Revelations about Agile and Sustainable Organizations in a VUCA World," *Journal of Applied Behavioral Science* 56, no. 3 (2020): 279–283.

13. Sidney G. Winter, "Understanding Dynamic Capabilities," *Strategic Management Journal* 24, no. 10 (2003): 991–995.

14. David J. Teece, Gary Pisano, and Amy Shuen, "Dynamic Capabilities and Strategic Management," *Strategic Management Journal* 18 (1997): 509–533.

15. Constance Helfat, "How Apple and IBM Learned to Change with the Times," *U.S. News and World Report*, July 2, 2013, https://www.usnews.com/opinion/blogs/economic-intelligence/2013/07/02/apple-and-ibm-show-the-power-of-dynamic-capabilities.

16. Zach St. Louis, "Thomas Friedman on Human Interaction in the Digital Age," Aspen Institute, January 10, 2017.

17. Dani Johnson, "Responsive Orgs: Designing for Volatility and Change," Red Thread Research, June 2, 2020.

18. Ravin Jesuthasan, Tracey Malcolm, and Susan Cantrell, "How the Coronavirus Crisis Is Redefining Jobs," *Harvard Business Review*, April 22, 2020.

19. John D. Stoll, "Crisis Has Jump-Started America's Innovation Engine: What Took So Long?" *Wall Street Journal*, April 10, 2020, https://www.wsj.com/articles/crisis-has-jumpstarted-americas-innovation-engine-what-took-so-long-11586527243.

20. Aaron De Smet et al., "The Need for Speed in the Post-Covid-19 Era—and How to Achieve It," McKinsey, September 9, 2020.

21. Johnson, "Responsive Orgs."

22. "Organizational Performance Is a Team Sport," Deloitte Human Capital Trends, 2019.

23. Omar Abbosh, Paul Nunes, and Dr. Vedrana Savic, "Make Your Wise Pivot to the New," Accenture, June 14, 2018. See also Omar Abbosh, Paul Nunes, and Larry Downes, *Pivot to the Future: Discovering Value and Creating Growth in a Disrupted World* (New York: PublicAffairs, 2019).

24. James Allen and Dunigan O'Keeffe, "The Engine 2 Imperative: New Business Innovation and Profitable Growth under Turbulence," Bain, December 17, 2020; Benjamin Finzi, Vincent Firth, and Mark Lipton, "Ambidextrous Leadership," Deloitte Insights, October 18, 2018; Charles O'Reilly and Michael Tushman, *Lead and Disrupt: How to Solve the Innovator's Dilemma* (Stanford, CA: Stanford Business Books, 2016).

25. John P. Kotter, *Accelerate: Building Strategic Agility for a Faster-Moving World* (Boston: Harvard Business School Press, 2014).

26. Gary Hamel and Michele Zanini, "The End of Bureaucracy: How a Chinese Appliance Maker Is Reinventing Management for the Digital Age," *Harvard Business Review* (November–December 2018).

27. David Weinberger, *Everyday Chaos: Technology, Complexity, and How We're Thriving in a New World of Possibility* (Boston: Harvard Business Review Press, 2019).

28. Source: "Governing Workforce Strategies: New Questions for Better Results," Deloitte Human Capital Trends, 2020, https://www2.deloitte.com/us/en/insights/focus /human-capital-trends/2020/workforce-metrics.html; and "Leading Forward: Leading the Shift from Survive to Thrive," Deloitte Insights, 2021, https://www2.deloitte.com/us /en/insights/focus/human-capital-trends/2021/human-capital-workforce-disruption.html.

29. Malone, *Superminds*.

30. ESR, Warburg Pincus case study, https://warburgpincus.com/case-studies/esr/.

31. Christopher G. Worley and Edward E. Lawler III, *Management Reset* (San Francisco: Jossey-Bass, 2011).

32. Kim Bhasin, "Patagonia's New CEO Plots a Post-Trump Future for the Activist Brand," Bloomberg Green, December 16, 2020, https://www.bloomberg.com/news /features/2020-12-16/patagonia-s-new-ceo-plans-to-keeping-up-climate-fight-at-clothing -brand.

33. "Retail Growth by Not Growing," PYMNTS, December 2, 2015, http://www .pymnts.com.

34. See, for example, Susan Lund et al., "The Future of Remote Work: An Analysis of 2,000 Tasks, 800 Jobs, and Nine Countries," McKinsey Global Institute, November 23, 2020; and "Nine Future of Work Trends Post-Covid-19." In these studies, few executives said they are planning on remaining fully remote after the pandemic, but many were planning a hybrid future where employees could work remotely part of the time. More than 20 percent of the workforce could work remotely three to five days a week as effectively as they could if working from an office. Meanwhile, the Gartner poll showed that 48 percent of employees will likely work remotely at least part-time when the pandemic ends, versus 30 percent before the start of the pandemic.

35. John Macomber and Joseph Allen, *Healthy Buildings: How Indoor Spaces Drive Performance and Productivity* (Boston: Harvard Business Press, 2020).

36. "Building the Intelligent Enterprise," Execution in Perpetual Motion Research Study, Accenture Strategy, 2020.

37. Michael S. Malone, "DEC's Final Demise," *Forbes*, September 14, 2000, https://www.forbes.com/2001/01/19/0915malone.html.

38. David Kesmodel and Annie Gasparro, "Inside Kellogg's Effort to Cash In on the Health-Food Craze," *Wall Street Journal*, August 31, 2015.

39. Susan Lund et al., "What 800 Executives Envision for the Postpandemic Workforce," McKinsey Global Institute, September 23, 2020.

40. Jacques Bughin et al., "Skill Shift: Automation and the Future of the Workforce," McKinsey Global Institute, May 23, 2018.

41. Thomas W. Malone, "What AI Will Do to Corporate Hierarchies," *Wall Street Journal*, April 1, 2019.

42. Jing Zeng and Keith Glaister, "Value Creation from Big Data: Looking Inside the Black Box," *Strategic Organization* 16, no. 2 (2018): 105–140.

43. Alessandro Di Fiore, "Why AI Will Shift Decision Making from the C-Suite to the Front Line," *Harvard Business Review* blog, August 3, 2018.

44. "How Artificial Intelligence Is Changing the Workplace," BBC, 2017, http://www.bbc.com/storyworks/specials/how-artificial-intelligence-is-changing-the-workplace/.

45. Allan Schweyer, "The Impact and Potential of Artificial Intelligence in Incentives, Rewards, and Recognition," Incentive Research Foundation, September 24, 2018, http://theirf.org/research/the-impact-and-potential-of-artificial-intelligence-in-incentives-rewards-and-recognition/2558/.

46. Richard Felon, "The World's Largest Hedge Fund Is Developing an Automated 'Coach' That Acts Like a Personal GPS for Decision-Making," *Business Insider*, September 25, 2017, https://www.businessinsider.com/ray-dalio-bridgewater-automated-management-system-2017-9.

47. Tom DiChristopher, "Ray Dalio Sets Out to Clarify Bridgewater Capital's 'Unusual' Management Culture," CNBC, January 8, 2017, https://www.cnbc.com/2017/01/08/ray-dalio-sets-out-to-clarify-bridgewater-capitals-unusual-management-culture.html.

Chapter 6

1. Juliette Bourke and Bernadette Dillon, "The Diversity and Inclusion Revolution," *Deloitte Review* 22 (January 2018).

2. Vivian Hunt et al., "Delivering through Diversity," McKinsey, January 2018.

3. Anna Irrera, Jessica DiNapoli, and Imani Moise, "Take a Stance or Tiptoe Away? Corporate America's Battle with Social Activism," Reuters, October 27, 2020.

4. Salesforce Racial Equality and Justice Taskforce, July 1, 2020, https://www.salesforce.com/news/stories/progress-so-far-on-racial-equality-and-justice/.

5. Jagdeep Singh Bachher and Richard Sherman, "Intentionally Embracing Diversity Enhances Investment Returns," June 25, 2020, https://regents.universityofcalifornia.edu/regmeet/july20/i4attach.pdf.

6. Kate Rooney, "Coinbase CEO Discourages Politics at Work, Offers Generous Severance to Employees Who Want to Quit," CNBC, September 30, 2020, https://www.cnbc.com/2020/09/30/coinbase-ceo-offers-severance-to-employees-leaving-over-politics.html; Cleve Mesidor, "Coinbase's War on Inclusion in the Workplace," *Haitian Times*, May 25, 2021, https://haitiantimes.com/2021/05/25/coinbases-war-on-inclusion-in-the-workplace/.

7. Scanlon, Zupsansky, and Sawicki, "Achieving Diversity in Private Equity."

8. "Private Equity Recruiting: The Widening War for Leadership," Hunt Scanlon Media, 2019, https://arris.partners/wp-content/uploads/2019/05/2019_HS_PEreport-2-highlighted.pdf.

9. Constanze Eib, Claudia Bernhard-Oettel, and Constanze Leineweber, "Fairness in the Workplace Relates to Health over Time," *HR Magazine*, October 19, 2016.

10. Hunt et al., "Delivering through Diversity."

11. Alan Murray, "CEO Daily," *Fortune*, February 8, 2021.

12. Evan W. Carr et al., "The Value of Belonging at Work," *Harvard Business Review*, December 16, 2019.

13. Jennifer Orechwa, "Are Workplace Inclusion and Belonging Different?" A Better Leader, https://projectionsinc.com/abetterleader/are-workplace-inclusion-and-belonging-different/ (accessed December 2021).

14. Anita Sands, "Diversity and Inclusion Aren't What Matter: Belonging Is What Counts," *Medium*, March 26, 2019, https://anitasands.medium.com/diversity-and-inclusion-arent-what-matter-belonging-is-what-counts-4a75bf6565b5.

15. Pat Wadors, "Diversity Efforts Fall Short Unless Employees Feel That They Belong," *Harvard Business Review*, August 10, 2016.

16. Amy C. Edmondson, *The Fearless Organization: Creating Psychological Safety in the Workplace for Learning, Innovation, and Growth* (Hoboken, NJ: Wiley, 2018).

17. Paayal Zaveria and Joe Williams, "Four Years Ago, Salesforce Hired a Rock Star Executive," *Insider*, November 14, 2020, https://www.businessinsider.com/salesforce-office-of-equality-tony-prophet-struggled-get-results-2020-11.

18. Shaibya Dalal, "Grace, Allyship, and Leadership: A Conversation with Tony Prophet, Salesforce's Chief Equality Officer," Center for Equity, Gender, and Leadership (EGAL), November 18, 2019, https://berkeleyequity.medium.com/grace-allyship-and-leadership-a-conversation-with-tony-prophet-salesforces-chief-equality-c9462 66033d4.

19. "Salesforce Announces Tony Prophet as Chief Equality and Recruiting Officer," Salesforce, May 22, 2020, https://www.salesforce.com/news/stories/salesforce-announces-tony-prophet-as-chief-equality-and-recruiting-officer/.

20. Adrienne Day, "Driving Social Change with Data," *Stanford Social Innovation Review*, Summer 2020.

21. James Baldwin, "As Much Truth as One Can Bear," *New York Times Book Review*, January 14, 1962.

22. Ben Horowitz, "Taking the Mystery Out of Scaling a Company," Andreessen Horowitz, August 2, 2010, https://a16z.com/2010/08/02/taking-the-mystery-out-of -scaling-a-company/.

23. Alber Lin, "What Makes a Good Diversity Scorecard/Dashboard?" Diversity-Inc., https://www.diversityincbestpractices.com/what-makes-a-good-diversity-scorecard -dashboard/.

24. Laurence Bradford, "How These 4 Tech Companies Are Tackling Unconscious Bias," *Forbes*, September 19, 2018.

25. O. C. Richard, "Racial Diversity, Business Strategy, and Firm Performance: A Resource-Based View," *Academy of Management Journal* 43 (2000): 164–177.

26. Nahia Orduña, "AI-Driven Companies Need to Be More Diverse," World Economic Forum, July 16, 2019, https://www.weforum.org/agenda/2019/07/ai-driven -companies-need-to-be-more-diverse-here-s-why/.

27. S. E. Jackson, "Consequences of Group Composition for the Interpersonal Dynamics of Strategic Issue Processing," in *Advances in Strategic Management*, Vol. 8, ed. Paul Shrivastava, Anne Huff, and Jane Dutton (Greenwich, CT: Jai Press, 1992), 345–382.

28. Jeffrey Dastin, "Amazon Scraps Secret AI Recruiting Tool That Showed Bias against Women," Reuters, October 10, 2018, https://www.reuters.com/article/us -amazon-com-jobs-automation-insight/amazon-scraps-secret-ai-recruiting-tool-that -showed-bias-against-women-idUSKCN1MK08G.

29. McKinsey's Private Markets Annual Review, April 21, 2021, https://www .mckinsey.com/industries/private-equity-and-principal-investors/our-insights/mckinseys -private-markets-annual-review.

30. "Private Equity Recruiting: The Widening War for Leadership," *Hunt Scanlon Media*, 2016.

31. Courtney Connley, "Black and Latinx Founders Have Received Just 2.6% of VC Funding So Far in 2020, According to New Report," CNBC, October 8, 2020.

32. Michael Ewens and Richard R. Townsend, "Are Early Stage Investors Biased against Women?" *Journal of Financial Economics* 135, no. 3 (2020): 653–677, https:// www.sciencedirect.com/science/article/abs/pii/S0304405X19301758.

33. William Louch, "Carlyle Group Steps Up Bid to Improve Diversity," *Wall Street Journal*, July 31, 2020, https://www.wsj.com/articles/carlyle-group-steps-up-bid-to -improve-diversity-11596144482.

34. Basak, "Carlyle Group CEO Lee on Creating Inclusive Culture."

35. "Q&A with Joe Baratta and Marcus Felder on Blackstone's New Diversity Initiatives," Blackstone, Firm News, October 27, 2020, https://www.blackstone.com /insights/article/q-and-a-with-joe-baratta-and-marcus-felder-on-blackstones-new-diver sity-initiatives/.

36. Anne Sraders, "Private Equity Wields a Lot of Power to Promote Diversity: Here's How Carlyle Is Upping Its Efforts," *Fortune*, August 3, 2020, https://fortune.com/2020/08/03/private-equity-wields-a-lot-of-power-to-promote-diversity-heres-how-carlyle-is-upping-its-efforts/.

37. Don Tapscott and David Ticoll, *The Naked Corporation: How the Age of Transparency Will Revolutionize Business* (New York: Free Press, 2012); Lisa Hope Pelled, Kathleen M. Eisenhardt, and Katherine R. Xin, "Exploring the Black Box: An Analysis of Work Group Diversity, Conflict, and Performance," *Administrative Science Quarterly* 44 (1999): 1–28.

38. Ray Dalio, *Principles: Life and Work* (New York: Simon & Schuster, 2017).

39. Zaveria and Williams, "Four Years Ago, Salesforce Hired a Rock Star Executive."

40. Maria Eloisa Capurro, "Boardrooms Need Diversity, Yet Latinos Are Fighting for Seats," *Bloomberg Businessweek*, January 7, 2021.

41. Stacia Garr and Priyanka Mehrotra, "DEIB Tech 2021 Overview," January 19, 2021, https://redthreadresearch.com/deib-tech-2021-overview/.

42. "Managing Human Resources Is about to Become Easier," *Economist*, March 28, 2018, https://www.economist.com/special-report/2018/03/31/managing-human-resources-is-about-to-become-easier.

43. Cyrus Sanati, "How Big Data Can Take the Pain out of Performance Reviews," *Fortune*, October 9, 2015, http://fortune.com/2015/10/09/big-data-performance-review/.

44. "(1) If its number of directors is six or more, the corporation shall have a minimum of three female directors. (2) If its number of directors is five, the corporation shall have a minimum of two female directors. (3) If its number of directors is four or fewer, the corporation shall have a minimum of one female director." California Senate Bill No. 826. See also Jennifer Kristen Lee, Andrew D. Ledbetter, and Rachel M. Paris, "California Mandates Female Board Directors for Publicly Held Companies," DLA Piper, October 1, 2018.

45. Hunt et al., "Delivering through Diversity."

46. Rocío Lorenzo et al., "How Diverse Leadership Teams Boost Innovation," BCG, January 23, 2018.

47. Ty Kiisel, "Improving a Leading Indicator of Financial Performance: Employee Engagement," *Forbes*, December 14, 2011.

48. Sylvia Ann Hewlett, Melinda Marshall, and Laura Sherbin, "How Diversity Can Drive Innovation," *Harvard Business Review* (December 2013).

49. Irrera, DiNapoli, and Moise, "Take a Stance or Tiptoe Away?"

Chapter 7

1. Abraham Maslow, *Motivation and Personality* (New York: Harper, 1954). Maslow's hierarchy of needs is a theory based on the premise that people's basic needs for long-term survival and development are hierarchically ranked. In other words, as people's basic needs (for example, physiological needs appear at the bottom of the pyramid) are

met, those needs no longer serve as motivators and people begin to satisfy higher-order needs (with self-actualization, at the top of the pyramid, being the ultimate satisfied need).

2. Ellyn Shook and David Rodriguez, "Care to Do Better," Accenture, 2020.

3. "The Social Enterprise at Work: Paradox as a Path Forward," Deloitte Insights, Deloitte Global Human Capital Trends report, 2020, https://www2.deloitte.com /content/dam/Deloitte/cn/Documents/human-capital/deloitte-cn-hc-trend-2020-en -200519.pdf.

4. "'Unprecedented Times,' Meet the Un-carrier: T-Mobile Unveils Big Moves for Businesses," T-Mobile, March 4, 2021, https://www.t-mobile.com/news/business /unprecedented-times-meet-the-un-carrier-t-mobile-unveils-big-moves-for -businesses.

5. Bryan Robinson, "Future of Work: What the Post-Pandemic Workplace Holds for Remote Workers' Careers," *Forbes*, May 2, 2021, https://www.forbes.com /sites/bryanrobinson/2021/05/02/future-of-work-what-the-post-pandemic-workplace -holds-for-remote-workers-careers/.

6. Robert Booth, "Four-Day Week: Trial Finds Lower Stress and Increased Productivity," *Guardian*, February 19, 2019, https://www.theguardian.com/money /2019/feb/19/four-day-week-trial-study-finds-lower-stress-but-no-cut-in-output; Sarah Berger, "4-Day Work Week Is a Success, New Zealand Experiment Finds," CNBC, July 19, 2018, https://www.cnbc.com/2018/07/19/new-zealand-experiment-finds-4-day -work-week-a-success.html.

7. Nicole Lyn Pesce, "Microsoft's 4-Day Work Week Test in Japan Boosts Productivity by 40%—Other Studies Show It Can Also Make You Happier," *MarketWatch*, November 5, 2019.

8. Megan Huth, "Segmentors vs. Integrators: Google's Work-Life-Balance Research," re:Work, December 14, 2016.

9. Jeffrey Pfeffer, *Dying for a Paycheck: How Modern Management Harms Employee Health and Company Performance—and What We Can Do about It* (New York: HarperCollins, 2018).

10. Pfeffer, *Dying for a Paycheck*.

11. Ben Wigert and Jennifer Robison, "Remote Workers Facing High Burnout: How to Turn It Around," Gallup, October 30, 2020.

12. "The Employee Burnout Crisis," Kronos, 2016, https://www.kronos.com /resources/employee-burnout-crisis.

13. Ben Wigert and Sangeeta Agrawal, "Employee Burnout, Part 1: The 5 Main Causes," Gallup, July 12, 2018, https://www.gallup.com/workplace/237059/employee -burnout-part-main-causes.aspx.

14. Scott Foster and Anna Foster, "The Impact of Workplace Spirituality on Work-Based Learners: Individual and Organisational Level Perspectives," *Journal of Work-Applied Management* 11, no. 1 (2019): 63–75.

15. Spencer Feingold, "Former Aetna CEO Proposes Corporate Leadership That 'Upends the Capitalist Model,'" Cheddar News, March 20, 2019, https://cheddar.com/media /former-aetna-ceo-proposes-corporate-leadership-that-upends-the-capitalist-model.

16. Mark T. Bertolini, "Forget ROI: Aetna CEO's Perspective on Wellness and Functionality," *Corporate Wellness*, https://www.corporatewellnessmagazine.com /article/aetna-ceo-perspective-on-wellness-functionality (accessed December 2021); "How Aetna CEO Brings Health and Healing to Workplace," CBS News, March 26, 2015, https://www.cbsnews.com/news/aetna-ceo-mark-bertolini-healthy-workplace -healing-meditation-yoga/; Heather Caspi, "Aetna Pays Employees up to $500 per Year to Sleep," Healthcare Dive, April 7, 2016, https://www.healthcaredive.com/news/aetna -pays-employees-up-to-500-per-year-to-sleep/416991/.

17. Colleen Reilly, "Wellbeing Positively Impacts Firm Performance," *Forbes*, June 9, 2020, https://www.forbes.com/sites/colleenreilly/2020/06/09/wellbeing-positively -impacts-firm-performance/.

18. Tom Rath and Jim Harter, *The Economics of Wellbeing* (San Francisco: Gallup Press, 2014).

19. S. Lyubomirsky, L. King, and E. Diener, "The Benefits of Frequent Positive Affect: Does Happiness Lead to Success?" *Psychological Bulletin* 131, no. 6 (2005): 803–855.

20. "How Technology and Data Can Improve Access to Mental Health Resources," IBM, https://www.ibm.com/thought-leadership/institute-business-value/report/mental -health-tech.

21. Bertolini, "Forget ROI"; "How Aetna CEO Brings Health and Healing to Workplace"; Caspi, "Aetna Pays Employees up to $500 per Year to Sleep."

22. Jen Fisher and Anjali Shaikh, "Integrating Tech and Well-Being," Deloitte, September 8, 2020, https://www2.deloitte.com/us/en/insights/topics/value-of-diversity -and-inclusion/diversity-and-inclusion-in-tech/virtual-workplace-well-being.html.

23. "Go Beyond Burnout: Well-Being Index," Mayo Clinic, 2020, https://www .mywellbeingindex.org/.

24. The International Classification of Disease, Eleventh Revision (ICD-11) is a system of medical coding created by the World Health Organization (WHO) for documenting diagnoses, diseases, signs and symptoms, and social circumstances.

25. Michael Blanding, "National Health Costs Could Decrease If Managers Reduce Work Stress," *Harvard Business School, Working Knowledge*, January 26, 2015, https://hbswk.hbs.edu/item/national-health-costs-could-decrease-if-managers -reduce-work-stress.

26. American Psychological Association, "Paying with Our Health," February 4, 2015, https://www.apa.org/news/press/releases/stress/2014/stress-report.pdf.

27. "Healthy Leaders Plus Healthy Teams Equal a Healthy Organization," Firstbeat, October 27, 2017, https://www.firstbeat.com/en/user-stories/bmw-pacesetter-automotive -industry/.

28. American Psychological Association, "Paying with Our Health."

29. Ashley Stahl, "The Compensation Package Gen-Z and Millennials Want," *Forbes*, September 15, 2020, https://www.forbes.com/sites/ashleystahl/2020/09/15/the-compensation-package-gen-z-and-millennials-want/.

30. Giles Turnbull, "The Story behind the 'It's OK to . . .' Poster," SmartCompany, August 27, 2021, https://www.smartcompany.com.au/people-human-resources/its-okay-yellow-poster-google-wellbeing/.

31. Bertolini, "Forget ROI"; "How Aetna CEO Brings Health and Healing to Workplace"; Caspi, "Aetna Pays Employees up to $500 per Year to Sleep."

32. Jen Fisher, Nicole Nodi, and Brenna Sniderman, "Bridge across Uncertainty," Deloitte, August 18, 2020, https://www2.deloitte.com/us/en/insights/topics/talent/building-a-resilient-workforce-in-times-of-uncertainty.html.

33. Adam Grant, "How Jobs, Bosses and Firms May Improve after the Crisis," *Economist*, June 1, 2020.

34. From/To, "Special COVID-19 Edition: Everything You Wanted to Know but Were Afraid to Ask," https://www.cognizant.com/whitepapers/from-to-special-covid-19-edition-everything-you-wanted-to-know-about-the-future-of-your-work-codex5730.pdf.

35. Michael Levine et al., *WIN: Future-Proofing Your Workforce in the Age of Disengagement* (Independently published, 2020).

36. Erica Volini et al., "Designing Work for Well-Being: Living and Performing at Your Best," 2020 Human Capital Trends, Deloitte, https://www2.deloitte.com/us/en/insights/focus/human-capital-trends/2020/designing-work-employee-well-being.html.

37. Erin L. Kelly and Phyllis Moen, *Overload: How Good Jobs Went Bad and What We Can Do about It* (Princeton, NJ: Princeton University Press, 2020).

38. Global Happiness Council, *Global Happiness and Well-Being Policy Report*, 2019.

Chapter 8

1. "Is Performance Management Performing?" Accenture, 2016.

2. Ellyn Shook, Eva Sage-Gavin, and Mark Knickerham, "Putting Trust to Work: Decoding Organizational DNA," Accenture, 2019.

3. De Smet, Schaninger, and Smith, "The Hidden Value of Organizational Health."

4. Society for Personality and Social Psychology, "Cultures of Genius at Work: Organizational Mindsets Predict Cultural Norms, Trust, and Commitment," *Personality and Social Psychology Bulletin*, June 2019.

5. John R. Graham et al., "Corporate Culture: Evidence from the Field," National Bureau of Economic Research, March 2017, https://www.nber.org/papers/w23255.

6. Weill, MIT CIO Summit; Weill, "IT Portfolio Management and IT Savvy."

7. Worley, Williams, and Lawler, *The Agility Factor*.

8. Matthew Corritore, Amir Goldberg, and Sameer B. Srivastava, "The New Analytics of Culture," *Harvard Business Review* (January–February 2020), https://hbr.org /2020/01/the-new-analytics-of-culture.

9. Evans et al., "Is Artificial Intelligence Set to Transform Private Equity Dealmaking?"

10. Chahat Jain, "Artificial Intelligence in Venture Capital Industry: Opportunities and Risks" (master's thesis, Massachusetts Institute of Technology, February 2018).

11. Institute for Ethical AI and Machine Learning, "The Responsible Machine Learning Principles," https://ethical.institute/principles.html.

12. Alina Tugend, "The Bias Embedded in Tech," *New York Times*, June 17, 2019, F10.

13. Julianne Photopoulos, "Fighting Algorithmic Bias in Artificial Intelligence," *Physics World*, May 4, 2021, https://physicsworld.com/a/fighting-algorithmic-bias-in-artificial -intelligence/.

14. IBM, "Crystal: Delivering Loyalty-Driving Customer Services with Trust-Sphere Relationship Analytics on IBM Domino," https://www.trustsphere.com/wp -content/uploads/2016/08/Crystal-Case-Study_IBM.pdf.

15. Intertrust Group, "Over 90% of Private Equity Firms Believe AI Will Disrupt Their Sector by 2024," February 4, 2019.

16. C. C. Miller. "Google Ventures Stresses Science of Deal, Not Art of the Deal," *New York Times*, June 23, 2013.

17. Bartosz Trocha, "Data-Driven VCs: How 83 Venture Capital Firms Use Data, AI & Proprietary Software to Drive Alpha Returns," *Medium*, July 1, 2019.

18. Andrew Li, "Machine Learning and Big Data in Private Equity: Is Networking Still Needed?" *Medium*, December 20, 2018, https://medium.com/iveyfintechclub /machine-learning-and-big-data-in-private-equity-is-networking-still-needed -9f8912a61ee9.

19. Chris O'Brien, "How EQT Ventures' Motherbrain Uses AI to Find Promising Start-Ups," VentureBeat, July 26, 2020, https://venturebeat.com/2020/07/26/how-eqt -ventures-motherbrain-uses-ai-to-find-promising-startups/.

20. Jain, "Artificial Intelligence in Venture Capital Industry"; "A Machine-Learning Approach to Venture Capital," McKinsey & Company, June 26, 2017, https:// www.mckinsey.com/industries/high-tech/our-insights/a-machinelearning-approach -to-venture-capital.

21. Bartosz Trocha, "Data-Driven VCs: How 83 Venture Capital Firms Use Data, AI & Proprietary Software to Drive Alpha Returns," *Medium*, July 1, 2019, https:// medium.com/hackernoon/winning-by-eating-their-own-dogs-food-83-venture -capital-firms-using-data-ai-proprietary-da92b81b85ef.

22. Erin Griffin, "Can You Find Founders before They Know They Are Founders?" *Fortune*, August 1, 2014, http://fortune.com/2014/08/01/data-startup-founders-bloomberg -mattermark/; Lara O'Reilly, "The Head of Bloomberg's $150 Million VC Fund

Explains the Formula for Finding a Top AI Startup," August 7, 2016, https://www
.businessinsider.com/bloomberg-beta-head-roy-bahat-on-the-formula-for-ai-2016-8.

23. Priska Neely, "Fortune-Tellers, Step Aside: Big Data Looks for Future Entrepreneurs," *All Things Considered*, NPR, October 5, 2014, https://www.npr.org
/sections/alltechconsidered/2014/10/05/351851015/fortune-tellers-step-aside-big-data
-looks-for-future-entrepreneurs.

24. Trocha, "Data-Driven VCs."

25. Patrick Thibodeau, "New HR Tools Probe Employee Sentiment, Feelings,"
TechTarget, April 11, 2018, https://searchhrsoftware.techtarget.com/feature/New-HR
-tools-probe-employee-sentiment-feelings.

26. Steven Prokesch, "Reinventing Talent Management: How GE Uses Analytics to
Guide a More Digital, Far-Flung Workforce," *Harvard Business Review* (September–
October 2017), https://hbr.org/2017/09/inside-ges-transformation#reinventing-talent
-management.

27. Sarah Kimmel, "Microsoft Workplace Analytics for Office 365," Channel e2e,
July 10, 2017, https://www.channele2e.com/news/microsoft-workplace-analytics-office
-365-making-saas-productive/.

28. Agile Leader Potential (ALP), Heidrick & Struggles, https://www.heidrick
.com/en/services/leadership/agile-leader-potential.

29. Sandy Ogg, https://sandyogg.com/2019/03/28/identify-the-critical-roles-part-2/.

30. Allan Schweyer, "The Impact and Potential of Artificial Intelligence in Incentives, Rewards, and Recognition," Incentive Research Foundation, September 24,
2018, http://theirf.org/research/the-impact-and-potential-of-artificial-intelligence-in
-incentives-rewards-and-recognition/2558/.

31. "Maven7 Launches ONA Technology Product: OrgMapper in Asia Pacific
Region," *The Economic Times*, HRWorld, July 31, 2020, https://hr.economictimes
.indiatimes.com/news/hrtech/maven7-launches-ona-technology-product-orgmapper
-in-asia-pacific-region/77282370.

32. Shellie Karabell, "Instead of Amplifying Human Biases, Can Algorithms Help Fix
Them?" *Christian Science Monitor*, November 21, 2018, https://www.csmonitor.com
/Business/2018/1121/Instead-of-amplifying-human-biases-can-algorithms-help-fix-them.

33. PepsiCo and L'Oréal are clients of AI recruiter Mya (http://hiremya.com). Mya
can be used to identify biases in past hiring decisions. See Paul R. Daugherty, H. James
Wilson, and Rumman Chowdhury, "Using Artificial Intelligence to Promote Diversity," *MIT Sloan Management Review*, November 21, 2018.

34. Bryan Yurcan, "How AI Can Help Banks Keep Their Best Workers," EBN,
July 11, 2018, https://www.benefitnews.com/news/how-ai-can-help-banks-keep-their
-best-workers.

35. "Hitachi Develops Technology to Automatically Create Effective Advice to
Increase Worker Happiness Using Artificial Intelligence," Hitachi, June 27, 2016,
http://www.hitachi.com/rd/news/2016/0627.html; "Workstyle Advice from AI Help-

ing to Raise Workplace Happiness," Hitachi, June 26, 2017, http://www.hitachi.com/New/cnews/month/2017/06/170626.pdf; "Raising Organizational Happiness by Changing Work Styles: Demonstration Experiment on the Enhancement of Organizational Activation Levels Using an AI Application Program," Hitachi, September 2017, http://social-innovation.hitachi/ph/case_studies/ai_happiness/; Motonobu Kawai, "Hitachi AI Wants You to Be Fitter, Happier, More Productive," *Nikkei Asian Review*, July 27, 2017, https://asia.nikkei.com/Business/Hitachi-AI-wants-you-to-be-fitter-happier-moreproductive.

36. Evans et al., "Is Artificial Intelligence Set to Transform Private Equity Dealmaking?"

37. Jain, "Artificial Intelligence in Venture Capital Industry."

Chapter 9

1. Ketan Awalegaonkar, "Scaling AI: How to Make It Work for Your Company," Accenture, February 5, 2020.

2. Fountaine, McCarthy, and Saleh, "Building the AI-Powered Organization."

3. Patrick Hunger, Rudolf Bergstrom, and Gilles Ermont, "Implications of Robotics and AI on Organizational Design," Capco Institute, May 30, 2018, https://www.capco.com/Capco-Institute/Journal-47-Digitization/Implications-of-robotics-and-AI-on-organizational-design.

4. Gerd Leonhard, *Technology vs. Humanity: The Coming Clash between Man and Machine* (Zurich: Futures Agency, 2016).

5. "AI, Robotics, and Automation: Put Humans in the Loop," Deloitte Human Capital Trends, 2018.

6. Ajay Agrawal, Joshua Gans, and Avi Goldfarb, *Prediction Machines: The Simple Economics of Artificial Intelligence* (Boston: Harvard Business Review Press, 2018).

7. Awalegaonkar, "Scaling AI"; Fountaine, McCarthy, and Saleh, "Building the AI-Powered Organization."

8. "AI: Built to Scale," Accenture, November 2019, https://www.accenture.com/us-en/insights/artificial-intelligence/ai-investments.

9. Sam Ranbotham et al., "Reshaping Business with Artificial Intelligence," *MIT Sloan Management Review*, September 2017.

10. Michael Chui and Bryce Hall, "How High-Performing Companies Develop and Scale AI," *Harvard Business Review*, March 19, 2020, https://hbr.org/2020/03/how-high-performing-companies-develop-and-scale-ai.

11. Fountaine, McCarthy, and Saleh, "Building the AI-Powered Organization."

12. "Getting to Scale with Artificial Intelligence," McKinsey podcast with Simon London speaking with McKinsey senior partners Tim Fountaine and Tamim Saleh, November 13, 2019, https://www.mckinsey.com/business-functions/mckinsey-digital/our-insights/getting-to-scale-with-artificial-intelligence.

13. "Getting to Scale with Artificial Intelligence."

14. Gerald C. Kane et al., *The Technology Fallacy: How People Are the Real Key to Digital Transformation* (Cambridge, MA: MIT Press, 2019).

15. Sam Ransbotham et al., "Artificial Intelligence in Business Gets Real," *MIT Sloan Management Review* in collaboration with BCG Henderson Institute, September 17, 2018, https://sloanreview.mit.edu/projects/artificial-intelligence-in-business-gets-real/.

16. "Learn How Leading Companies Balance Cost and Care to Win in an Evolving and Unpredictable World," Mercer, Global Trends Study, 2020, https://www.marshmclennan .com/insights/publications/2020/march/2020-global-talent-trends-study.html.

17. Chui and Hall, "How High-Performing Companies Develop and Scale AI."

18. Martin Reeves and Daichi Ueda, "Designing the Machines That Will Design Strategy," *Harvard Business Review*, April 18, 2016, https://hbr.org/2016/04/welcoming -the-chief-strategy-robot.

19. Reeves and Ueda, "Designing the Machines That Will Design Strategy."

20. Ransbotham et al., "Artificial Intelligence in Business Gets Real."

21. Fountaine, McCarthy, and Saleh, "Building the AI-Powered Organization."

22. Chui and Hall, "How High-Performing Companies Develop and Scale AI."

23. Fountaine, McCarthy, and Saleh, "Building the AI-Powered Organization."

24. Khari Johnson, "Building AI-First Companies Requires More Than Hiring Data Scientists," VentureBeat, October 26, 2018, https://venturebeat.com/2018/10/26 /ai-weekly-building-ai-first-companies-requires-more-than-hiring-data-scientists/.

25. Chui and Hall, "How High-Performing Companies Develop and Scale AI."

26. Clockwise website use cases: https://www.getclockwise.com/customers.

27. Paul Daugherty and H. James Wilson, *Human + Machine: Reimagining Work in the Age of AI* (Boston: Harvard Business Press, 2018).

28. Rajeev Ronanki, "Building an AI-First Organization," *Forbes*, February 25, 2019, https://www.forbes.com/sites/cognitiveworld/2019/02/25/building-an-ai-first -organization/.

29. "Talent Intelligence and Management Report 2019–2020," Harris Interactive and Eightfold, 2020, https://pages.eightfold.ai/Report_Talent_Intelligence_and _Management_Report_2019-2020.html.

30. Louis Columbus, "Predicting How AI Will Improve Talent Management in 2020," *Forbes*, December 24, 2019, https://www.forbes.com/sites/louiscolumbus/2019 /12/24/predicting-how-ai-will-improve-talent-management-in-2020/#68adbdaadb60.

31. Fountaine, McCarthy, and Saleh, "Building the AI-Powered Organization."

32. Ellyn Shook, Mark Knickrehm, and Eva Sage-Gavin, "Putting Trust to Work: Decoding Organizational DNA," Accenture Research Report, https://www.accenture .com/_acnmedia/Thought-Leadership-Assets/PDF/Accenture-WF-Decoding -Organizational-DNA.pdf.

33. Chui and Hall, "How High-Performing Companies Develop and Scale AI."

34. Shook, Knickrehm, and Sage-Gavin, "Putting Trust to Work."

35. Chui and Hall, "How High-Performing Companies Develop and Scale AI."

36. Fountaine, McCarthy, and Saleh, "Building the AI-Powered Organization."

37. Chamorro-Premuzic, Wade, and Jordan, "As AI Makes More Decisions."

38. James Guszcza and Jeff Schwartz, "Superminds, Not Substitutes: Designing Human-Machine Collaboration for a Better Future of Work," *Deloitte Review* 27 (July 2020).

39. Stuart R. Levine and Thought Leaders, "Diversity Confirmed to Boost Innovation and Financial Results," *Forbes*, January 15, 2020; Rocío Lorenzo et al., "How Diverse Leadership Teams Boost Innovation," BCG Henderson Institute, January 23, 2018.

40. Guszcza and Schwartz, "Superminds, Not Substitutes."

41. Chamorro-Premuzic, Wade, and Jordan, "As AI Makes More Decisions."

Chapter 10

1. Steve Klemash, Bridget M. Neill, and Jamie C. Smith, "How and Why Human Capital Disclosures Are Evolving," EY Center for Board Matters, Harvard Law School Forum on Corporate Governance, November 15, 2019.

2. John Carreyrou, "Hot Startup Theranos Has Struggled with Its Blood-Test Technology," *Wall Street Journal*, October 16, 2015, https://www.wsj.com/articles /theranos-has-struggled-with-blood-tests-1444881901.

3. Joy Howell and Stephen Hibbard, "Navigating the Changed Landscape of Corporate Governance," *Harvard Management Update* 712 (2002): 7–8.

4. Organisation for Economic Co-operation and Development (OECD), "OECD Principles of Corporate Governance," Meeting of the OECD Council at Ministerial Level, 1999SG/CG995, https://www.oecd.org/officialdocuments/public displaydocumentpdf/?cote=C/MIN(99)6&docLanguage=En.

5. Andreas Beroutsos, Andrew Freeman, and Conor F. Kehoe, "What Public Companies Can Learn from Private Equity," McKinsey on Finance, January 1, 2007.

6. Eva Sage-Gavin, Yaarit Silverstone, and Barbara Spitzer, "Modern Boards," Accenture, 2020.

7. Francesca Cornelli and Öguzhan Karakas, "Private Equity and Corporate Governance: Do LBOs Have More Effective Boards?" in *Globalization of Alternative Investments Working Papers Volume 1: The Global Economic Impact of Private Equity Report 2008* (Cologny, Switzerland: World Economic Forum, 2008), 65, 72.

8. Steven N. Kaplan and Per Strömberg, "Leveraged Buyouts and Private Equity," *Journal of Economic Perspectives* 23 (2009): 121–129; Steven Kaplan, "The Effects of Management Buyouts on Operating Performance and Value," *Journal of Financial Economics* 24, no. 2 (1989): 217–218; EY, "Private Equity CFOs Rank Operational Efficiency as Top Priority, but Take Varied Approaches to Technology, Talent Management and Outsourcing to Achieve It," *Cision*, January 24, 2018, https://www.prnewswire .com/news-releases/private-equity-cfos-rank-operational-efficiency-as-top-priority -but-take-varied-approaches-to-technology-talent-management-and-outsourcing-to -achieve-it-300587198.html.

9. "Global Intangible Finance Tracker (GIFT) 2018. An Annual Review of the World's Intangible Value," *Brand Finance*, October 2018, https://brandfinance.com/wp-content/uploads/1/gift_1.pdf.

10. Elisabeth de Fontenay, "Private Equity's Governance Advantage: A Requiem," *Boston University Law Review* 99 (2019): 1095–1122.

11. Dave Ulrich and Justin Allen, "Private Equity's New Phase," *Harvard Business Review* (August 2016).

12. Eugene F. Fama and Michael C. Jensen, "Separation of Ownership and Control," *Journal of Law & Economics* 26, no. 2 (1983): 301–325.

13. Annalisa Barrett, "Sharpening the Board's Oversight of Human Capital Management," *NACD Directorship* (March/April 2020).

14. Dominic Barton, Dennis Carey, and Ram Charan, *Talent Wins: The New Playbook for Putting People First* (Boston: Harvard Business Review Press, 2018).

15. "Board Oversight of Human Capital Management," KPMG, 2020, https://boardleadership.kpmg.us/relevant-topics/articles/2020/board-oversight-human-capital-management.html.

16. "What Directors Think: Speed Kills," Corporate Board Member/Spencer Stuart, 2018, https://www.spencerstuart.com/-/media/2018/april/what-directors-think-2018.pdf.

17. Laela Sturdy, CapitalG, https://www.capitalg.com/team/laela-sturdy/.

18. Joern Block et al., "Private Equity Investment Criteria: An Experimental Conjoint Analysis of Venture Capital, Business Angels, and Family Offices," *Journal of Corporate Finance* 58 (2019): 329–352.

19. Joyce Guevarra, "COVID-19 Accelerating Purpose and Responsibility Trend in Private Equity," S&P Global Market Intelligence, October 9, 2020.

20. Dieter Holger and Emese Bartha, "U.K. Requires Companies to Report on Climate Change by 2025," *Wall Street Journal*, November 9, 2020, https://www.wsj.com/articles/u-k-requires-companies-to-report-on-climate-change-by-2025-11604964183.

21. U.S. Securities and Exchange Commission, "Sustainability, Equality, and Philanthropy at Salesforce—Fostering Employee Success," 2019 Proxy Statement, salesforce.com, inc., April 25, 2019, https://www.sec.gov/Archives/edgar/data/1108524/000119312519119702/d664082ddef14a.htm.

22. U.S. Securities and Exchange Commission, "CEO Pay Ratio," 2019 Proxy Statement, CVS Health Corporation, April 5, 2019, https://www.sec.gov/Archives/edgar/data/64803/000120677419001240/cvs3508731-def14a.htm.

23. "Ensuring Equal Pay for Equal Work," Boston Scientific, 2019, https://www.bostonscientific.com/en-US/careers/working-here/diversity-and-inclusion/equal-pay.html.

24. Letter from Larry Fink to Chief Executive Officers, "Purpose & Profit," BlackRock (January 2019), https://www.blackrock.com/americas-offshore/2019-larry-fink-ceo-letter. See also Letter from Larry Fink to Chief Executive Officers, "A Fundamental Reshaping of Finance," BlackRock (January 2020), https://www.blackrock.com/us/individual/larry-fink-ceo-letter.

25. Viral V. Acharya and Conor Kehoe, "Board Directors and Experience: A Lesson from Private Equity," McKinsey on Finance, 2010.

26. Bob Zider, "How Venture Capital Works," *Harvard Business Review* (November–December 1998): 131–139.

27. Malcolm Salter, "Learning from Private-Equity Boards," *Harvard Business School, Working Knowledge*, January 17, 2007, https://hbswk.hbs.edu/item/learning-from-private-equity-boards.

Chapter 11

1. Ogg, *Move: The CEO's Playbook for Capturing Value*; Dave Ulrich and Justin Allen, "PE Firms Are Creating a New Role: Leadership Capital Partner," *Harvard Business Review*, August 11, 2017.

2. Ulrich and Allen, "Private Equity's New Phase."

3. Two of the fastest-growing specialist roles are CFO of portfolio operations and head of talent, said Heidrick & Struggles in "Talent Chiefs Emerge among Fastest-Growing Roles in Private Equity," Hunt & Scanlon, 2019, https://huntscanlon.com/talent-chiefs-emerge-among-fastest-growing-roles-in-private-equity/.

4. "How Carlyle Creates Value, Case Study," https://www.carlyle.com/sites/default/files/case-studies/Dunkin_case_study.pdf.

Chapter 12

1. Jasmine Aguilera, "'An Epidemic of Misinformation': New Report Finds Trust in Social Institutions Diminished Further in 2020," *Time*, January 13, 2021, https://time.com/5929252/edelman-trust-barometer-2021/; 2021 Edelman Trust Barometer, global report published annually by global communications firm Edelman, https://www.edelman.com/trust/2021-trust-barometer.

2. Nikki Ekstein, "Airbnb's Future Is about 'Living,' Not Just Travel," Bloomberg, May 26, 2021, https://www.bloomberg.com/news/articles/2021-05-26/airbnb-s-future-according-to-ceo-brian-chesky-living-not-just-travel.

3. David Gelles, "A CEO Who Advises Other CEOs," *New York Times*, September 26, 2021.

4. David Gelles, "How to Lead in the Eye of a Storm," *New York Times*, May 3, 2020.

5. "What It Takes to Shift a Company's Culture: Chip Bergh of Levi Strauss & Co. Discusses Brand Transformation and CEO Activism," Fuqua Insights, March 2, 2020, https://www.fuqua.duke.edu/duke-fuqua-insights/dss-chip-bergh-how-ceos-can-shift-company%E2%80%99s-culture.

6. Worley and Jules, "COVID-19's Uncomfortable Revelations about Agile and Sustainable Organizations in a VUCA World."

7. John Whiteclay Chambers II, *The Tyranny of Change: America in the Progressive Era, 1890–1920* (New York: St. Martin's, 1992).

8. Robert Johansen, *Leaders Make the Future* (San Francisco: Berrett-Koehler, 2012).

9. Gelles, "How to Lead in the Eye of a Storm."

10. David Gelles, "At the Crossroads of Global Business," *New York Times,* October 10, 2021.

11. The concept of change fluency and other elements of this chapter were developed in full collaboration with my friend and colleague Christopher G. Worley and with meaningful contributions from colleagues in Google's Change and Design Forum.

12. See Argyris and Schön's theory on congruence and learning, which asserts that people hold maps in their heads about how to plan, implement, and review their actions. Chris Argyris and Donald A. Schön, *Theory in Practice: Increasing Professional Effectiveness* (San Francisco, CA: Jossey-Bass, 1974).

Acknowledgments

I owe special thanks to the leaders I've had the benefit of interviewing, who were gracious with their time and perspectives and from whom I learned so much. I also owe a special thanks to the people who read the manuscript in its various iterations. Among them, I include my friend and former colleague Sue Cantrell, who helped me clarify who I was writing for and why, and who worked with me on the research and cases described in this book. My thanks also to Lorraine Damerau for her dedication in helping me make sense of research data across the life cycle of an organization's maturity as it scales.

My friends and colleagues Marty Goldberg, Chris Worley, Ghazala Ovaice, Carmen Mayali, Seema Patel, Stephen Brown, David Reimer, Joe Bonito, Ellen Van Oosten, Darren Good, and Jessica DiVento, along with the blind manuscript reviewers, were relentless in their challenge to make me go deeper in my introspection and make it relevant and practical to leaders and boards across multiple contexts, not just tech or private markets. Lesley Iura managed the publishing process with keen insight and unflappable grace through every step, and Lucy McCauley was tireless in her editorial efforts, taking my words in a near-final manuscript and turning them up a notch to make it readable and engaging, urging me to inject more examples and connect threads from one chapter to another.

This book is dedicated to the leaders who spurred me on my journey toward building better organizations. I am grateful to the late

Arthur Freedman for his mentorship and guidance and for inspiring my passion for organization development as a graduate student at the American University and later in our joint work. I would also like to acknowledge Bob Thomas for his friendship, mentorship, and above all, his role-modeling as a scientist-practitioner. Thanks also to Ana Dutra, Roselinde Torres, Deb Brecher, David Smith, Yaarit Silverstone, Janice Simmons, Veronica Hopper Carter, John Carter, Johnnie Smith, Carl Jennings, Herb Stevenson . . . and to two future leaders who already inspire me to continue the work of building better organizations for an AI-first world, Sophie Jules and Ian Jules.

Thank you.

About the Author

Dr. Claudy Jules is a partner in McKinsey & Company's Washington, D.C., office. He is a leader in the Organization practice and a core member of the Technology, Media & Telecommunications and Private Equity & Principal Investors practices. Prior to joining McKinsey, Dr. Jules was at Google, leading its Center of Excellence on Organizational Health and Change. He also served as an advisor to the portfolio com-panies of CapitalG, Alphabet's growth equity investment fund. As a thought leader, he has written and spoken widely on leadership and organizational issues and has contributed to several business publications.

Berrett–Koehler
BK Publishers

Berrett-Koehler is an independent publisher dedicated to an ambitious mission: *Connecting people and ideas to create a world that works for all.*

Our publications span many formats, including print, digital, audio, and video. We also offer online resources, training, and gatherings. And we will continue expanding our products and services to advance our mission.

We believe that the solutions to the world's problems will come from all of us, working at all levels: in our society, in our organizations, and in our own lives. Our publications and resources offer pathways to creating a more just, equitable, and sustainable society. They help people make their organizations more humane, democratic, diverse, and effective (and we don't think there's any contradiction there). And they guide people in creating positive change in their own lives and aligning their personal practices with their aspirations for a better world.

And we strive to practice what we preach through what we call "The BK Way." At the core of this approach is *stewardship,* a deep sense of responsibility to administer the company for the benefit of all of our stakeholder groups, including authors, customers, employees, investors, service providers, sales partners, and the communities and environment around us. Everything we do is built around stewardship and our other core values of *quality, partnership, inclusion,* and *sustainability.*

This is why Berrett-Koehler is the first book publishing company to be both a B Corporation (a rigorous certification) and a benefit corporation (a for-profit legal status), which together require us to adhere to the highest standards for corporate, social, and environmental performance. And it is why we have instituted many pioneering practices (which you can learn about at www.bkconnection.com), including the Berrett-Koehler Constitution, the Bill of Rights and Responsibilities for BK Authors, and our unique Author Days.

We are grateful to our readers, authors, and other friends who are supporting our mission. We ask you to share with us examples of how BK publications and resources are making a difference in your lives, organizations, and communities at www.bkconnection.com/impact.

Dear reader,

Thank you for picking up this book and welcome to the worldwide BK community! You're joining a special group of people who have come together to create positive change in their lives, organizations, and communities.

What's BK all about?

Our mission is to connect people and ideas to create a world that works for all.

Why? Our communities, organizations, and lives get bogged down by old paradigms of self-interest, exclusion, hierarchy, and privilege. But we believe that can change. That's why we seek the leading experts on these challenges—and share their actionable ideas with you.

A welcome gift

To help you get started, we'd like to offer you a **free copy** of one of our bestselling ebooks:

www.bkconnection.com/welcome

When you claim your **free ebook**, you'll also be subscribed to our blog.

Our freshest insights

Access the best new tools and ideas for leaders at all levels on our blog at ideas.bkconnection.com.

Sincerely,

Your friends at Berrett-Koehler

Certified

Corporation